THE FUTURE OF QUALITATIVE RESEARCH IN HEALTHCARE

Digital methods in healthcare research have been steadily gaining ground but, until recently, were superseded by conventional face-to-face approaches wherever possible. However, the Covid-19 pandemic rendered in-person forms of data collection largely impossible, propelling digital approaches to the forefront. This book offers a digital lens on the participatory perspective of ethnography, a qualitative methodology. A series of chapters from internationally distinguished and rising authors presents digital platforms and techniques and applies these to a wide range of healthcare studies. The authors highlight the different aspects of digital research approaches as well as reflecting on and proffering digital approaches to qualitative research for the future. Will these new digital health techniques be embraced, or will researchers be keen to revert to the traditional methods? With its unique approach, this is an invaluable resource for both prospective and experienced qualitative researchers in a broad array of medical and health disciplines.

PROFESSOR PAUL M. W. HACKETT is the originator of the declarative mapping approach to social science and humanities research. He currently holds professorial positions at universities in the United States, United Kingdom, United States, and Nigeria. He has around 300 publications, including more than 25 books, and has held appointments at institutions including Cambridge, Oxford, Harvard, Tufts, Durham and Birmingham universities.

CHRISTOPHER M. HAYRE is an Associate Professor in Medical Imaging at the University of Canberra, Australia. He has published both qualitative and quantitative refereed papers and brought together several books in the field of medical imaging, health research, technology, and ethnography.

DAVE J. MULLER is Visiting Professor of Rehabilitation Psychology at the University of Suffolk.

MARCIA SCHERER is Professor of Physical Medicine and Rehabilitation at the University of Rochester Medical Center and President of the Institute for Matching Person & Technology.

AVA GORDLEY-SMITH is a PhD research student at the University of Wales Trinity Saint David.

THE FUTURE OF QUALITATIVE RESEARCH IN HEALTHCARE

The Role and Management of Digital Methods

EDITED BY

PAUL M. W. HACKETT
Emerson College

CHRISTOPHER M. HAYRE
University of Canberra

DAVE J. MULLER
University of Suffolk

MARCIA SCHERER
University of Rochester Medical Center

AVA GORDLEY-SMITH
University of Wales Trinity Saint David

CAMBRIDGE
UNIVERSITY PRESS

Shaftesbury Road, Cambridge CB2 8EA, United Kingdom

One Liberty Plaza, 20th Floor, New York, NY 10006, USA

477 Williamstown Road, Port Melbourne, VIC 3207, Australia

314–321, 3rd Floor, Plot 3, Splendor Forum, Jasola District Centre, New Delhi – 110025, India

103 Penang Road, #05–06/07, Visioncrest Commercial, Singapore 238467

Cambridge University Press is part of Cambridge University Press & Assessment, a department of the University of Cambridge.

We share the University's mission to contribute to society through the pursuit of education, learning and research at the highest international levels of excellence.

www.cambridge.org
Information on this title: www.cambridge.org/9781316513170

DOI: 10.1017/9781009072021

First published 2024

A catalogue record for this publication is available from the British Library.

Library of Congress Cataloging-in-Publication Data
NAMES: Hackett, Paul, 1960– editor. | Hayre, Christopher M., editor. | Muller, Dave J., editor. | Scherer, Marcia J. (Marcia Joslyn), 1948– editor. | Gordley-Smith, Ava, editor.
TITLE: The future of qualitative research in healthcare : the role and management of digital methods / edited by Paul M.W. Hackett, Emerson College, Christopher M. Hayre, University of Canberra, Dave Muller, University of Suffolk, Marcia Scherer, University of Rochester Medical Center, Ava Gordley-Smith, University of Wales Trinity Saint David.
DESCRIPTION: Cambridge, United Kingdom ; New York, NY : Cambridge University Press, 2024. | Includes bibliographical references and index.
IDENTIFIERS: LCCN 2024002825 | ISBN 9781316513170 (hardback) | ISBN 9781009073226 (paperback) | ISBN 9781009072021 (ebook)
SUBJECTS: LCSH: Medical care – Research – Methodology. | Qualitative research.
CLASSIFICATION: LCC RA440.85 F88 2024 | DDC 362.1072/1–dc23/eng/20240307
LC record available at https://lccn.loc.gov/2024002825

ISBN 978-1-316-51317-0 Hardback
ISBN 978-1-009-07322-6 Paperback

Dr Christopher M. Hayre dedicates this book to Evelynn Hayre, with eternal love.

Contents

Figures

Tables

Contributors

HIBA AHMED, Bloorview Research Institute

GLORIA ALBERTI, Lega F. D'Oro Research Center

SHANE BLACKMAN, Canterbury Christ Church University

TING CHUONG HOCK, University of Malaysia Sarawak

GEORGINA CLUTTERBUCK, University of Queensland

CHARLES EDMUND DEGENEFFE, San Diego State University

CHARLENE DOWNING, University of Johannesburg

SHARIFA EZAT, Universiti Kebangsaan Malaysia

DANYA FAST, University of British Columbia

GILLIE GABAY, Achva Academic College

JEFF GAVIN, University of Bath

AVA GORDLEY-SMITH, University of Wales Trinity Saint David

PAUL M. W. HACKETT, University of Suffolk

HOLLIE HADWEN, University of Suffolk

STEVE HAGELMAN, Ethnographic Research, Inc.

CHRISTOPHER M. HAYRE, University of Canberra

ROD KNIGHT, University of British Columbia

GIULIO E. LANCIONI, University of Bari

SHANTEL LEWIS, University of Johannesburg

SALLY LINDSAY, Bloorview Research Institute

DAVE J. MULLER, University of Suffolk

MARK F. O'REILLY, University of Texas in Austin

ADELE PHILLIPS, Canterbury Christ Church University

MD MIZANUR RAHMAN, University of Malaysia Sarawak

MELINA REA-HOLLOWAY, Ethnographic Research, Inc.

KAREN RODHAM, University of Chichester

RAZITASHAM SAFII, University of Malaysia Sarawak

ABG SAFUAN, Universiti Kebangsaan Malaysia

ROSALIA SAIMON, University of Malaysia Sarawak

MARCIA SCHERER, University of Rochester

GARY SENECAL, Albany State University

JEFF SIGAFOOS, Victoria University of Wellington

NIRBHAY N. SINGH, Augusta University

RODNEY STEHR, British Columbia Centre on Substance Use

RUTH STRUDWICK, University of Suffolk

VANESSA TOMAS, University of Toronto

ABIRAMI VIJAYKAUMAR, University of Toronto

PATRICK M. WHITEHEAD, Albany State University

REBECCA WISE, University of Bath

CHEN YOKE YONG, University of Malaysia Sarawak

Acknowledgements

The editorial team would like to acknowledge and thank each other for the mutual support, comradeship and, indeed, humour that was present as we brought the project together. This support was particularly appreciated in the trying times of Covid-19 during which the book was assembled. We would all like to thank Rowan Groat, Dave Repetto and Laura Simmons from Cambridge University Press for their support and help.

CHAPTER I

Introduction to Digital Platforms and Digital Research Approaches, Encryption, Cybersecurity and Bandwidth
Considerations for Qualitative Researchers

Christopher M. Hayre, Paul M. W. Hackett, Ava Gordley-Smith, Marcia Scherer, and Dave J. Muller

The introduction of digital approaches is perhaps the most significant change to the way that healthcare research is conducted that has been seen since computers first came into use. This introductory chapter will set the tone for the rest of the book. The book is divided into two parts: 1. digital platforms, and 2. approaches to healthcare research that are either uniquely digital or are adaptations of existing approaches to the online context. Within each of these parts, a collection of chapters by distinguished and rising authors present digital platforms and techniques and consider these as applied to a wide range of healthcare studies. This introduction will consider the broad area that the book addresses and will similarly be divided into the same two sections. The unique aspects of digital research approaches will be highlighted and emphasised, and the reader will be prepared for the chapters that follow.

Chapter 2: 'Doing Digital Qualitative Research: Key Ethical Considerations', by Rebecca Wise, Jeff Gavin and Karen Rodham, focuses on ethical challenges for researchers who are engaged in qualitative digital research. The authors argue that while the digital world has opened up significant opportunities for researchers, it has also presented complicated and multifaceted ethical challenges. The authors offer examples of these ethical issues by drawing from a range of research from diverse disciplines.

Chapter 3: 'Using Video Diaries for Remote Observational Research', by Steve Hagelman and Melinda Rea-Holloway, considers the essential benefits of using video diaries in corporate ethnography as a tool to collect observational data in health care and consumer research. Drawing on the authors' experiences, the chapter explores the strengths and limitations of video diaries, and serves as a guide for how to engage video diaries in ethnographic and qualitative research.

Chapter 4: '(In)Equitable Shifts: Mapping a Pivot to Digital Diary and Remote Research Methods with Queer Youth in the Times of Covid-19', by Rodney Stehr, Danya Fast, and Rod Knight, presents the authors' experiences of evolving research regarding sexual and gender-identity minority young people (ages 15–29) towards an online protocol using digital methods. The authors discuss their use of and experience with using digital diaries to conduct virtual longitudinal qualitative research, and present both the strengths and weaknesses of this method.

Chapter 5: '"To Be or Not to Be?" Qualitative Research upon and during a Pandemic Outbreak', by Gillie Gabay, aims to disentangle the problems qualitative researchers may experience when planning and implementing rigorous research upon and during a crisis. The chapter address practical and necessary concerns for the qualitative researcher and works as a guide for how best to conduct research during challenging times.

Chapter 6: 'Adopting Digital Methods: Conducting Qualitative Interviews and Focus Groups in the Midst of a Pandemic', by Ruth Strudwick and Hollie Hadwen, explores the foundational theory of qualitative research methods, specifically semi-structured interviews and focus groups, and the issues that arise when adopting a digital approach. The authors explore the practical considerations, challenges and benefits of utilising digital methods.

Chapter 7: 'Lessons Learned Conducting Online Qualitative Interviews during Covid-19', by Sally Lindsay, Hiba Ahmed, Vanessa Tomas, and Abirami Vijaykaumar, discusses the barriers to, advantages of and crucial lessons learned by the authors while conducting online interviews during the pandemic. The chapter engages a qualitative study focusing on the employment experiences of youth with and without disabilities throughout Covid-19.

Chapter 8: 'Virtual Interviewing in the Age of Covid-19: Considerations for Qualitative Research', by Charles Edmund Degeneffe, focuses on the use of virtual approaches to data collection in qualitative research during the Covid-19 pandemic. The chapter provides background information on virtual interviewing, investigating researcher and participant perspectives, and offers best-practice considerations qualitative researchers should be aware of when managing the technical aspects, participant engagement, and ethical issues of virtual interviewing.

Chapter 9: 'Minimizing the Impact Technology Has on Interviewer–Interviewee Rapport: An Existential-Phenomenological Analysis', by

Patrick M. Whitehead and Gary Senecal, discusses post-phenomenology as a form of conducting qualititative research. The chapter examines whether something of importance is concealed when qualitative researchers depend on the use of technology. A three-year international qualitative study on PTSD with active-duty military, which relied heavily on technology, is used to examine the strengths and weaknesses of combining technology with phenomenological healthcare research.

Chapter 10: 'Participatory and Invasive Online Worlds: Exploring the Research Method of Qualitative Digital Ethnography', by Adele Philips and Shane Blackman, argues that there is great value in utilising online ethnographic approaches. Whilst the chapter notes the caveats to these approaches, the authors position the strengths as outweighing the potential negatives.

Chapter 11: 'Using Online Survey Tools to Improve Access to International Experts: The 'E-Delphi'', by Georgina Clutterbuck, presents the E-Delphi method as a modern, flexible research approach with the potential to produce quality data in a time- and cost-effective manner. The chapter discusses the challenges and advantages of the method and suggests best practices for employment.

Chapter 12: 'Refining Interview Protocols for Online Interviews on the Employment of Persons with Down Syndrome: Insights from a Pilot Test', by Md Mizanur Rahman, Abg Safuan, Sharifa Ezat, Razitasham Safii, Chen Yoke Yong, Rosalia Saimon, and Ting Chuong Hock, notes the increased necessity for adopting online interviews in qualitative research during the Covid-19 pandemic. The chapter discusses the challenges related to ensuring the validity of the interview protocol, especially when involving people with intellectual disabilities. The authors conducted a pilot test in an attempt to validate the interview protocol and to solidify the trustworthiness of the data. The authors discuss the experience and their findings.

Chapter 13: 'Technology-Aided Programs to Support Leisure, Communication, and Daily Activities in People with Intellectual and Multiple Disabilities', by Giulio E. Lancioni, Nirbhay N. Singh, Mark F. O'Reilly, Jeff Sigafoos, and Gloria Alberti, provides an overview of studies assessing technology-aided programs to promote independent leisure and communication or combinations of independent leisure, communication and daily activities in people with mild to moderate intellectual disability often associated with sensory and/or motor impairments. The chapter presents the studies' programs and their outcomes and discusses three key challenges found within the studies.

Chapter 14: 'Virtual Qualitative Data Collection: A South African Autoethnographic Perspective', by Shantel Lewis, Charlene Downing, and Christopher M. Hayre, presents an account of virtual qualitative data collection using autoethnographic approaches. The chapter illustrates a PhD candidate's experience whilst conducting individual and focus group interviews virtually in a developing nation. The authors discuss the narrative and offer recommendations for conducting virtual qualitative data collection.

Chapter 15: 'Afterword', by Paul M. W. Hackett, Christopher M. Hayre, Ava Gordley-Smith, Marcia Scherer and Dave J. Muller, briefly discusses the authors' projections for the future of digital research tools in healthcare research. The authors share qualitative survey results to support their claims and present a forward-looking perspective to conclude the exchange of diverse views within this book.

CHAPTER 2

Doing Digital Qualitative Research
Key Ethical Considerations

Rebecca Wise, Jeff Gavin, and Karen Rodham

Introduction

As we write this chapter in June 2021, researchers are conducting and designing studies whilst navigating the ever-changing Covid-related restrictions. The Covid-19 pandemic has forced some researchers to rethink their approach to recruitment and data collection, and many have turned to the digital world to continue their research (see Nind, Meckin and Coverdale, 2020 for an overview). Indeed, as Howlett (2021, p. 1) has noted:

> The methods many of us came to employ, or will be employing, were not part of our original research plans, nor ones with which we have had much training or experience, or even gave much thought to, prior to the pandemic.

With this in mind, it is important to consider the ethical challenges for researchers who are, or who will be, employing qualitative digital research. However, it is important first to explain what we mean by 'digital research'. Put very simply, we define digital research as that which is conducted on or by the Internet or on or by digital social media. Similarly, the British Psychological Society (2021, p. 6) uses the term 'Internet-mediated research' (IMR), and broadly defines it as 'any research involving the remote acquisition of data from or about human participants using the Internet and its associated technologies'.

Digital research offers the qualitative researcher new opportunities to conduct their research. Perhaps they will conduct their interviews via video technology or through online messaging. Maybe they will choose to run online focus groups, which then allows people from all over the world to join in. Alternatively, perhaps they will collect pre-existing online qualitative data: for example, Instagram posts, Tweets, Snapchats and so forth. Or they could collect such data prospectively. Indeed, digital research presents researchers with myriad opportunities to collect data in ways that are often cheaper than traditional methods (e.g., no travel costs, no postage costs). It also provides access to a diverse participant pool (see, e.g., Gavin and Rodham, 2020; Lobe, Morgan and Hoffman, 2021; Rahman et al. 2021; Roberts, 2015). The digital environment also allows researchers to observe behaviour and communication. For example, Keim-Malpass et al. (2013) analysed online blogs written by young women living with cancer to better understand their experiences, whilst Talbot et al. (2017) wanted to understand whether and how photographs might be used in social media to encourage and inspire emulation of those depicted. Neither of these studies prompted the production of the data (blogs and photographs); the researchers simply analysed data which was freely available in the digital world. They were therefore able to observe their participants without influencing the communication or behaviour of interest.

Having defined what we mean by 'digital research' and highlighting some of the opportunities it presents researchers, it is important to remember that the digital world is fast paced and ever changing. For example, when Kosinski et al. (2015) were writing their article on the opportunities, challenges, ethical considerations and practical guidelines for using Facebook as a research tool, they noted that the American Psychological Association's website only listed three documents containing guidelines relating to research on the Internet, all of which had been written before Facebook came into being.

A couple of years later, the British Sociological Association (2017) stated that it was not possible to create guidelines that could address all current and future forms of digital research. This inability to keep up with the fast-changing online world and the impossibility of creating a set of all-encompassing rules that account for all eventualities means that the onus is on all of us to take collective responsibility. Similarly, the British Psychological Society's (2021) comprehensive internet-mediated research guidelines bring to researchers' attention issues with which they should familiarise themselves. At the same time, the guidelines raise awareness that as technology advances, changes and grows, it both extends opportunities for research and introduces extra complexities and challenges to interpreting and applying ethical principles in ways that might not at first be obvious.

In short, it is not possible to have a set of ethical rules that can deal with all situations. Indeed, if we consider our own personal lives for a moment, we can neither control nor plan for all eventualities. Yet we (mostly) find that we can apply our existing skills, experience and 'rules-of-thumb' to cope with (to steal a phrase from Donald Rumsfeld; see Seely, 2003) the 'unknown unknowns' that occasionally crop up unexpectedly in our lives. It is the same for researchers venturing into the ever-changing digital world. Here we need to think about how the multilayered digital world impacts on our approach to doing, managing and disseminating digital research – in other words, the basic ethical principles underpinning research remain universal (see The Belmont Report, written by the Department of Health, Education and Welfare (1979), for more detail):

> ***Respect for persons***: ensuring that individuals are treated as autonomous agents, and that anyone with diminished autonomy is protected.
> ***Beneficence:*** maximising possible benefits whilst minimising possible harms.
> ***Justice:*** ensuring participants are recruited and treated, and research outcomes are disseminated: fairly, equitably, and appropriately.

However, what is different now is how these principles might be applied in a fast-changing, multilayered context which brings a high risk of unintended consequences. Therefore, how the principles are applied *and* how unexpected happenings are dealt with will rely on researchers' and ethics committees' ability to act carefully, with due diligence, with the information they have at that time. Indeed, we have argued elsewhere (Gavin and Rodham, 2017) that researchers would do well to accept that ethics for our digital age requires the development of a different mindset: one that maintains the central ethical mantra of 'do no harm' but no longer relies on traditional, clear-cut 'If–Then' rules and regulations. Instead, the application of ethical principles has become more a process of solving puzzles.

In this chapter we focus on the key ethical challenges (puzzles) facing researchers engaged in qualitative digital studies and highlight questions we believe researchers should be asking themselves. We conclude with some important messages for supervisors, researchers and members of ethics committees.

Recruitment of Participants

In terms of the principle of justice outlined in the introduction to this chapter, researchers should consider who is likely to participate in the proposed research. Researchers should consider accessibility when designing their studies, whether they be analogue or digital. Work requiring face-to-face, in-person participation can be difficult for those with, for example, mobility or speech problems. Transport to and from the research location, or difficulty with communication, may exclude people from taking part. The digital world could allow members of previously excluded groups to participate by removing the need to travel or to communicate verbally. However, conducting interviews and focus groups online may also inadvertently exclude groups of people whose voices ought to be included. For example, this type of research could exclude those who cannot access the Internet, as well as those who do not have a private space where their participation in our research will not be disturbed or their contributions will not be overheard (if spoken) or seen (if written). For example, Howlett (2021, p. 9) noted that some of her participants were not alone during the data collection:

> One participant, for instance, introduced me to his two young daughters when they entered the room he was sitting in, and near the end of the conversation, he presented his cat to the camera. Similarly, the participant who sat in his family's backyard during the focus group introduced his mother to everyone on the call.

Confidentiality of participants' contributions cannot therefore be protected by researchers. As researchers we may not know whether anyone else is sharing the space with our participants and we have no power to ensure that participants' contributions are not overheard or seen. These issues have come to the fore in recent years as many of us moved our lives online to cope with the restrictions imposed upon us by the various Covid-related lockdowns. Many people have had to share computers, Internet connections and rooms, whilst others lacked the connection, equipment or finances to purchase data to enable them to access the Internet.

Similarly, observational research drawing on social media, such as X (formerly Twitter), Facebook or Instagram, may also inadvertently silence particular voices. This is particularly problematic in research that claims to be exploring 'public discourse' (e.g., Lachmar et al., 2017; McHugh, Superstein and Gold, 2019), public opinion (or 'collective sentiment' as it is often referred to when expressed on X; e.g., Cody et al., 2015) or public understandings of health and/or risk (e.g., Hou et al., 2021). Often, much of the public is excluded from such research. For example, software enabling the collection of social media data can only access publicly available posts; that is, it cannot collect posts from accounts that are set to private. On social media platforms such as Facebook or Instagram, this excludes almost half (45 per cent) of users (Tankovzka, 2021).

One way around this is to include 'participants' in data collection – for example, researchers can ask users for access to their pages; however, the compromise with this is that such an approach undermines the benefits of naturally occurring data. In other words, we know that if a participant knows they are being observed, they may alter the way they behave (see Cambridge, Witton and Elbourne, 2014 for an explanation of how the Hawthorne Effect has come to be interpreted). Furthermore, accessing someone's private Facebook, X or Instagram involves requesting and being accepted as a 'friend' or 'follower' of that person. This raises ethical questions with respect to boundaries between the researcher and the researched and the notion of a 'friend'.

Researchers will need to show that they have a clear rationale for their choice of desired participants/sample and would be well advised to explore the inclusion of strategies to help overcome some of the barriers in order to widen participation. For example, in a recent funding application (unpublished and awaiting outcome), one of the authors of this chapter (Rodham) was part of a team that built in the purchase of mobile phones and tablets to loan to those without access to equipment so that they could participate in their proposed study.

Consent

Consent is a cornerstone of conducting research ethically. Whilst some researchers have reportedly moved their research online as a means of circumventing the ethical approval process (see the example detailed by Roberts, 2015), the key issue is that the level of 'publicness' of social media data is not always clear cut (e.g., Gavin and Rodham, 2020; Lange, 2008; Roberts, 2015):

> In an IMR context, the distinction between public and private space becomes increasingly blurred. For one thing, much Internet communication can take place in both a private (e.g., the home) and public (e.g., open discussion forum) locations simultaneously. (BPS, 2021b, p. 8)

A post can be public in the sense that it reveals identifying information, but private in the sense that it is only accessible to approved 'friends' or 'followers' of the poster's private account (i.e., it is 'publicly private'). On the other hand, posts can contain no identifying information but be accessible to anyone with Internet access (i.e., 'privately public'). Such distinctions make basic ethical guidelines from our professional bodies difficult to interpret and put into practice in the context of the ways that social media use is understood by users. The UK Economic and Social Research Council (ESRC), for example, states that:

> Information provided in forums, social media or spaces on the internet that are intentionally public would be considered 'in the public domain', but the public nature of any communication or information on the internet or through social media should always be critically examined. (ESRC, 2021)

But this intentionality is at the core of this ethical dilemma with regards to collecting social media data. As we ask in a previous study on ethics (Gavin and Rodham, 2020, pp. 3–4), 'How can we be sure that someone posting information online knows or expects it to be public? Does it matter if information is posted (and collected for research) on discussion forums, Twitter, YouTube or Facebook?' The BPS recommendation is that on occasions where there is ambiguity about whether IMR data is in the public realm, as researchers we ought to consider the potential harm our research could cause:

> When there is a level of ambiguity concerning whether data are 'in the public domain' or not, researchers should particularly consider likely user perceptions and attitudes, and the extent to which undisclosed observation may have potentially damaging effects for participants, before making decisions on whether to use such data and whether gaining valid consent is necessary. (BPS, 2021a: p. 9)

Furthermore:

> Valid consent should be obtained where it cannot be reasonably argued that online data can be considered 'in the public domain', or that undisclosed usage is justified on scientific value grounds. (BPS, 2021a: p. 10)

Choice of Digital Platform

During the pandemic, familiarity with digital platforms increased hugely, and engagement with such platforms has thus become more normal amongst the Western general population. For example, in April 2020, Kate Murphy, writing for *The New York Times*, said: 'Last month, global downloads of the apps Zoom, Houseparty and Skype increased more than 100 percent as video conferencing and chats replaced the face-to-face encounters we are all so sorely missing.'

In the same way that the general population have been familiarising themselves with this technology, so too have researchers, and the choice of digital platforms is vast. When making decisions about which platform to use for their research, researchers should choose a platform that is intuitive or can be easily explained to ensure that those who may be less digitally competent can also participate. However, even with a platform which is common (e.g., Facebook, Instagram, WhatsApp) or that has become common since the start of the pandemic (e.g., Zoom or Teams), care must still be taken over our duty of care to our participants' confidentiality, anonymity and safety (see 'Duty of Care' section later in the chapter).

We must also be mindful that not all potential participants will have access to specific platforms. A solution, therefore, may be to include a range of platforms from which to collect data. However, as with every decision, there are potential consequences, so it is important to consider whether the decision to use different platforms could impact on the way in which data is collected. If so, will this reduce standardisation of the data collection process? And, consequently, will this impact on the quality or comparability of data collected?

Digital Platform Etiquette

If using video platforms such as Zoom or Teams, researchers will need to consider whether there should be guidance with respect to cameras being on or off. Part of conducting or participating in an interview or focus group involves reading body language and picking up on cues from the other person or people in the group. What might be the impact on a focus group if some members have their cameras off? How can people judge when to contribute to the conversation if they cannot see the cues that someone wants to speak? Of course, there are systems where an electronic hand can be raised, but this can make for a disjointed conversation, and one which requires the researcher to take on the role of active facilitator rather than occasional prompter.

The cameras on or off question brings to mind arguments that were once levelled against telephone interviews (e.g., Novick, 2008). At the start of their review of evidence for and against telephone interviews, Farooq and De Villiers (2017) note that qualitative interviews have traditionally been conducted on a face-to-face basis with the understanding that this provides the best environment to build and maintain rapport with interviewees to enable the gathering of rich in-depth data. However, Nandi and Platt (2017) explored how participants answered questions about identity via phone and face-to-face and found little evidence to suggest that the mode of interview impacted on the data collected. Whether data quality is better or worse when collected from participants whose cameras are off remains to be seen and may well depend more on the researcher's facilitation skills to keep interactions running smoothly that whether the data collection is online or in-person.

This last point about the researcher's facilitation skills is important if we consider the ethics of managing participant behaviour in online focus groups. In the United Kingdom, Jackie Weaver became an Internet sensation when recordings of a council meeting went viral. She was the meeting clerk and became so frustrated with the behaviour of the committee members as they traded insults that she eventually removed the Chairman and sent him to a virtual waiting room. Undoubtedly the meeting required a firm hand, but would that behaviour have happened in a 'real' (rather than a virtual) meeting? And what right did Weaver have to remove the Chair? What rights did the Chair have not to be removed? All these questions are pertinent when we think about the ethics of online participant interviews. In other words, do online interviews have the potential to change participants' behaviour, possibly making them feel able to say things they would not say in person? And who decides whose behaviour is intolerable? And, if you are conducting a focus group, do you simply 'remove' someone from the group? Should you make it clear in your participant information sheet that certain behaviours will not be tolerated, and participants might be 'removed'? Is it ethical to remove someone virtually when it would not be possible in person? You then need to consider the implications of that behaviour on the other participants, but also have plans in place to debrief the 'removed' participant. To a lesser extent, the same follows when the interview organiser has the ability to use the mute button to control who is speaking. What right does the researcher have to silence a participant?

Duty of Care

Although the research may be conducted via the digital world, the research participant will obviously be in a physical location – a location over which we as researchers have no control. This location could impact on their ability to contribute or to maintain anonymity or confidentiality. What could/should we do as researchers to minimise the risk that participants' identities and contributions are not compromised? Is it sufficient to ensure that the need for privacy is emphasised in the information we share with participants? Arguably, they alone know whether they can connect from a place that enables them to do so safely, securely and with privacy. If we outline the potential concerns, can we trust participants to make their own risk assessments? Turning back to the key ethical principles, the first (respect for persons) makes it clear that potential participants should be treated as autonomous agents. Therefore, we argue that if sufficient information is provided to enable participants to give their informed consent, they should be trusted to make a decision about the suitability of their physical environment.

With respect to maintaining participant anonymity, at the time of writing the quirks of both Zoom and MS Teams means that it is not possible to audio record without simultaneously video recording. Video recordings are rightly classified as including more sensitive personal data than audio recordings and therefore need careful handling, not least because users' names are often visible on screen and so will also be visible in the video recording. Similarly, if making a group on WhatsApp, users' names and contact numbers will appear in the group. Account names are visible to other members of Facebook groups. How could we address this? Is it practical or reasonable to ask participants to change names or perhaps create new accounts just for our research?

In terms of confidentiality, the ESRC states that information which is intentionally public (e.g., information posted on forums, in social media etc.) is considered in the public domain. However, this includes a caveat that 'the public nature of any communication or information on the internet or through social media should always be critically examined'. This nuanced approach is also recognised by the British Psychological Society (2021a: p. 11), who highlight this issue as one especially pertinent to the collection of online data:

> Researchers need to be aware that it is in many cases impossible to maintain absolute confidentiality of participants' personal information gathered online because the networks or systems are not in the full control of the researcher.

In addition to privacy, anonymity and confidentiality, researchers must consider the possibility that a participant may become distressed as a consequence of participating in the research. Having support systems in place is arguably not so straightforward when researcher and participant are not present 'in-person'. Questions researchers will need to think about include: what is our responsibility if a participant logs off during data collection? How will we know if there is simply an Internet connection problem? Might it be a sign that the participant is distressed or perhaps no longer interested in participating? What is our duty of care to someone who is talking to us over video if we become concerned about them? What happens if a participant appears to be at risk of harm, or of committing harm whilst they are online with us?

Managing Digital Qualitative Data

When considering the management of digital data, researchers must think about who owns the data: the researcher or the platform? Where are the platform's servers? Who can access the data? How do we keep digital data safe? How do we anonymise our digital data? What data is collected unless we opt out? For example, IP addresses are a means of identifying the device someone is using. If we were conducting an online survey using Qualtrics to collect the data, there is a box which can be ticked to prevent IP addresses being collected. But, for this to be effective, the researcher first needs to know about IP addresses, and then needs to know how to prevent them from being collected.

We can't help but wonder how many researchers are aware of the aforementioned issues. Linked to this, many researchers also supervise students. Students are increasingly completing their dissertations and postgraduate studies using digital data. What responsibility should higher education establishments have to ensure that students and supervisors are sufficiently trained and supported to navigate this process? Has this increasingly heavy reliance on digital data collection come too quickly for higher education establishments and supervisors to keep abreast of the implications of digital data collection? If so, we should all be mindful of the phrase commonly used in the United Kingdom and elsewhere that 'ignorance is no defence in the eyes of the law'.

Disseminating Qualitative Digital Data

When we write up our work so that we can share it, our responsibility to our participants remains at the fore. We are hoping that our work will be widely read and used by other researchers, practitioners and policy-makers. We must therefore do all we can to ensure that we protect the identity of our participants. For example, if we quote text that we have collected from digital resources we must be mindful of the ease by which identity can be uncovered. A person reading our work may decide to place the quotes we have used into a search engine; this could then bring up the original interaction or post. If this happens it is possible that the person who posted the text could have their identity revealed and so our promise of their anonymity is broken. This not only breaches trust but could also breach what in the United Kingdom is currently known as the UK General Data Protection Regulations (UK GDPR). If a person finds out that something they have posted digitally has been collected, analysed, stored and reported as part of a research project they are likely to have rights under UK GDPR.

How, then, might we prevent the identification of quotes we wish to use to illustrate our findings? If verbatim quotes can easily be traced using search engines, should we paraphrase the quotes before we publish them? The British Psychological Society (BPS, 2021a: p. 14) suggests that researchers should employ what they describe as 'maximal anonymization procedures', which could include paraphrasing of the quotes. In other words, if data is paraphrased post analysis, the paraphrasing would not impact on the researcher's ability to interpret the data they have collected. So, one problem is solved: paraphrasing the data post analysis preserves the integrity of the analysis *and* the anonymity of the participant.

However, the BPS recognises that the principle of proportionality should also be applied where consideration of the level or risk or harm of the participant being identified should be compared to the impact of paraphrasing on the scientific value, integrity and authenticity of the data collected. Proportionality here should be considered in the context of the drive towards ensuring research is both open and transparent.

It is becoming more common for researchers to be expected to deposit their data in an open science repository. With respect to qualitative data, how do we navigate the need to protect identity by paraphrasing the quotes versus the need for transparency and the concomitant requirement of sharing the original data with other researchers? Should we deposit the paraphrased text or the original text? If we do the latter, we are in effect accepting the risk that our participants' anonymity could be compromised. If we do the former, the data available for other researchers to analyse is not the actual data that we ourselves collected and analysed, which therefore defeats the purpose of open science.

Moving from text to audio recordings: we usually transcribe audio recordings and as part of the transcription process we anonymise any identifying information. In the spirit of transparency, should we then also share the audio recordings? The UK Data Service (ukdataservice.ac.uk) offer the following advice:

> Bleeping out real names or place names is acceptable, but disguising voices by altering the pitch in a recording, or obscuring faces by pixelating sections

of a video image significantly reduces the usefulness of data. These processes are also highly labour intensive and expensive.

If confidentiality of audio-visual data is an issue, it is better to obtain the participant's consent to use and share the data unaltered. Where anonymisation would result in too much loss of data content, regulating access to data can be considered as a better strategy.

In addition to these concerns, different platforms have different rules about what you can and cannot repeat. If you quote a tweet, for instance, X (June 2021) insists that it must be quoted in full, never paraphrased, and that the original poster must be named. It is therefore vital that researchers are up to date (or ensure they find accurate guidance) with the current regulations for whichever platform they are using.

Key Messages for Supervisors, Researchers and Members of Ethics Committees

Having highlighted several ethical challenges facing researchers engaged in qualitative digital studies, we pull together what we see as three key issues for supervisors, researchers and members of ethics committees to consider.

Digital competence: Researchers should make sure that they are confident and competent with the choice of technology they plan to use and that, if necessary, they are able to train participants to use the technology. Supervisors of student projects and members of ethical committees should take the time to familiarise themselves with the technology being proposed for use. Supervisors could turn to IT support staff and/or online learning technologists employed by their university. Ethics committee chairs should ensure that proposals are reviewed by members who have competence in and comprehension of qualitative research *and* the proposed digital methodology.

Digital rationale: Researchers and supervisors of student projects must first ensure that digital qualitative research is the most appropriate means of collecting data that will answer the research question. Second, they must ensure that the rationale is clearly articulated in any proposals/reports to help maximise the understanding of those reviewing the work. Doing so in a clear and auditable way is never more important than when working at the edges of something new. Those who audit, or who wish to replicate, what we do will need to understand the rationale, justification and thought processes that led us to take the steps we chose to take to complete our studies.

Digital inclusivity: It is important to consider the three key ethical principles and be aware of the groups you are including as well as those you may inadvertently be excluding by choosing to go digital. Be clear about your rationale and how your chosen approach gains you access to the participants you require in order to answer your question. Also take time to think about IT inclusivity; for example, Gray et al. (2020: p. 1294) note that: 'researchers utilizing video conferencing software will consider possible technical difficulties and determine if they possess the appropriate skills to conduct interviews on a virtual platform.' Researchers also need to consider potential participants' familiarity and competence with, as well as their ability to access, the proposed digital technology.

Conclusion

We return to the position we outlined in the introduction: in this fast-paced, ever-changing digital world, we as researchers, supervisors and ethics committee members need to become more comfortable moving away from clear-cut 'If–Then' ethical practices and towards the more amorphous position of becoming puzzle solvers who can apply the core ethical principles as well as methodological know-how from other areas to these complex and multilayered digital environments. Gray et al. (2020, p. 1294) note:

> Researchers seeking best practice recommendations and comparisons across video conferencing platforms will be limited because the research has focused on Skype . . . To date, we found no peer-reviewed published studies examining other video conferencing platforms, such as Zoom, in the qualitative literature.

This chapter has focused on exploring how we as researchers do the right thing without inadvertently doing the wrong thing. We might do well to consider the words of Noel, the narrator in Niall Williams' (2019) novel *This Is Happiness*:

> You understand nothing in the time when it's happening. I've decided that's a fair creed to live by. Most of the time you don't estimate the good or the bad you do, and you have to operate on a small and labouring engine of hope with a blind windscreen and pray you're going in a direction that's not too far off good intention.

This is a good analogy for navigating all aspects of qualitative research in the digital world, for as Goodyear and Bundon (2021) noted, 'even as you write about a social media platform, an online community, a new device or application, it is moving around you'. We cannot always see where we are going. We do not know all the possible impacts of the work we are engaging in. The trick, as far as we are concerned, is that when engaged in digital qualitative research it should be approached with good intentions (ethical integrity) and the ability to respond, to adapt and to act ethically when unknown unknowns suddenly become known.

References

British Psychological Society (2021a) Ethics Guidelines for Internet-Mediated Research. www.bps.org.uk/news-and-policy/ethics-guidelines-internet-medi ated-research.

British Psychological Society (2021b) Code of Human Research Ethics. www.bps .org.uk/sites/www.bps.org.uk/files/Policy/Policy%20-%20Files/BPS%20Code %20of%20Human%20Research%20Ethics.pdf.

British Sociological Association (2017) Guidelines on Ethical Research. www .britsoc.co.uk/ethics.

Cambridge, J., Witton, J., and Elbourne, D. R. (2014) Systematic Review of the Hawthorne Effect: New Concepts are Needed to Study Research Participation Effects. *Journal of Clinical Epidemiology*, *67*, 267–77.

Cody, E. M., Reagan, A. J., Mitchell, L., Dodds, P. S., and Danforth, C. M. (2015) Climate Change Sentiment on Twitter: An Unsolicited Public Opinion Poll. *PloS One*, *10*(8), e0136092.

Department of Health, Education and Welfare (1979) *The Belmont Report: Ethical Principles and Guidelines for the Protection of Human Subjects of Research.*

Economic and Social Research Council (n.d.) Internet-Mediated Research. www .ukri.org/councils/esrc/guidance-for-applicants/research-ethics-guidance/ internet-mediated-research/.

Farooq, M. B. and De Villiers, C. D. (2017) Telephonic Qualitative Research Interviews: When to Consider Them and How to Do Them. *Meditari Accountancy Research*, *25*(2), 291–316.

Gavin, J. and Rodham, K. (2017) Ethical Research in the Digital Age. *Psychology Review*, *23*(1), 2–5.

Gavin, J. and Rodham, K. (2020) Ethics of Online Research with Human Participants. In Hayre, C. and Hackett, P. (Eds.), *Handbook in Ethnographic Research in Health and Well-Being*. London: Routledge, pp. 23–32.

Goodyear, V. and Bundon, A. (2021) Contemporary Digital Qualitative Research in Sport, Exercise and Health: Introduction. *Qualitative Research in Sport, Exercise and Health*, *13*(1), 1–10.

Gray, L. M., Wong-Wylie, G., Rempel, G. R., and Cook, K. (2020) Expanding Qualitative Research Interviewing Strategies: Zoom Video Communications. *The Qualitative Report*, *25*(5), 1292–301.

Hou, Z., Tong, Y., Du, F., et al. (2021) Assessing COVID-19 Vaccine Hesitancy, Confidence, and Public Engagement: A Global Social Listening Study. *Journal of Medical Internet Research*, *23*(6), e27632.

Howlett, M. (2021) Looking at the 'Field' through a Zoom Lens: Methodological Reflections on Conducting Online Research During a Global Pandemic. *Qualitative Research*, *22*(3), 387–402. https://doi.org/10.1177/1468794120985691.

Irvine, A. (2011) Duration, Dominance and Depth in Telephone and Face-to-Face Interviews: A Comparative Exploration. *International Journal of Qualitative Methods*, *10*(3), 202–20.

Keim-Malpass, J., Albrecht, T. A., Steeves, R. H., and Danhauer, S. C. (2013) Young Women's Experiences with Complementary Therapies during Cancer Described through Illness Blogs. *Western Journal of Nursing Research*, *35*(10), 1309–324.

Kosinski, M., Matz, S. C., Gosling, S. D., Popov, V., and Stillwell, D. (2015) Facebook as a Research Tool for the Social Sciences: Opportunities, Challenges, Ethical Considerations, and Practical Guidelines. *American Psychologist*, *70*(6), 543–56.

Lachmar, E. M., Wittenborn, A. K., Bogen, K. W., and McCauley, H. L. (2017) #MyDepressionLooksLike: Examining Public Discourse about Depression on Twitter. *JMIR Mental Health*, *4*(4), e43.

Lange, P. G. (2008) Publicly Private and Privately Public: Social Networking on YouTube. *Journal of Computer-Mediated Communication*, *13*(1), 361–80.

Lobe, B., Morgan, D., and Hoffman, K. A. (2021) Qualitative Data Collection in an Era of Social Distancing. *International Journal of Qualitative Methods*, *19*, 1–8. https://doi.org/10.1177/1609406920937875.

McHugh, M. C., Saperstein, S. L., and Gold, R. S. (2019) OMG U# Cyberbully! An Exploration of Public Discourse about Cyberbullying on Twitter. *Health Education and Behavior*, *46*(1), 97–105.

Murphy, K. (2020) Why Zoom is Terrible. *New York Times*.

Nandi, A. and Platt, L. (2017) Are There Differences in Responses to Social Identity Questions in Face-to-Face versus Telephone Interviews? Results of an Experiment on a Longitudinal Survey. *International Journal of Social Research Methodology*, *20*(2), 151–66.

Nind, M., Meckin, R., and Coverdale, A. (2020) *Changing Research Practices: Undertaking Social Research in the Context of Covid-19*. Southampton: National Centre for Research Methods.

Novick, G. (2008) Is there a Bias against Telephone Interviews in Qualitative Research? *Research in Nursing and Health*, *31*, 391–8.

Rahman, S. A., Tuckerman, L., Vorley, T., and Gherhes, C. (2021) Resilient Research in the Field: Insights and Lessons from Adapting Qualitative Research Projects during the Covid-19 Pandemic. *International Journal of Qualitative Methods*, *20*, 1–16. https://doi.org/10.1177/16094069211016106.

Roberts, L. (2015) Ethical Issues in Conducting Qualitative Research in Online Communities. *Qualitative Research in Psychology*, *12*(3), 314–25.

Seely, H. (2003) *Pieces of Intelligence: The Existential Poetry of Donald H. Rumsfeld. Slate.* https://slate.com/news-and-politics/2003/04/the-poetry-of-donald-rumsfeld.html.

Sturges, J. E. and Hanrahan, K. J. (2004) Comparing Telephone and Face-to-Face Qualitative Interviewing: A Research Note. *Qualitative Research,* 4(1), 107–18.

Talbot, C., Gavin, J., van Steen, T., and Morey, Y. (2017) A Content Analysis of Thinspiration, Fitspiration and Bonespiration on Social Media. *Journal of Eating Disorders,* 5, 40. https://doi.org/10.1186/s40337-017-0170-2.

Tankovzka, H. (2021) US Social Media User Account Privacy 2018. *Statista.*

UK Data Service (n.d.) Research Data Management.

Williams, N. (2019) *This Is Happiness.* London: Bloomsbury Publishing.

CHAPTER 3

Using Video Diaries for Remote Observational Research

Steve Hagelman and Melinda Rea-Holloway

Introduction

No matter how many years we have done ethnography, we never get over how fascinating it is to watch people "do" real life. Most of the time, we use video that we have collected during our fieldwork and video diaries that have been recorded by our participants to help us drop in and learn from real people. Recently, we had front row seats to watching families navigate the changes COVID-19 caused in their work routines, their school habits, and their technology use. Video diaries allowed us to immerse ourselves into their lives from afar and to see how the pandemic had changed the ways they moved through their days and through the world at large.

The marriage between ethnography and video diaries, then film diaries, dates back to at least 1966, when Sol Worth and John Adair gave cameras to a group of six Navajos. Before they started, none of the six had ever used a camera, or had even seen a film. Worth and Adair taught them the essentials of filmmaking and sent them off to make movies, resulting in a series of short films called *Navajo Film Themselves* and a subsequent book, *Through Navajo Eyes* (Worth and Adair, 1972). Seeking to understand the intersection between culture and filmmaking, their objectives were far different than for most contemporary video diary research, but the then novel approach would eventually evolve into an indispensable method for many qualitative researchers, ourselves included.

From an experiment in filmic communication to its common use today, at least in market research, the popularity of video diaries owes a debt of gratitude to the advancement of digital video technology. Prior to the 1990s, video was largely analog and your choices were large, fairly expensive film- or tape-based standards such as VHS. Over time, tapes got smaller and went digital, with 8mm and mini-DV becoming popular in the 1990s and 2000s, respectively. After Siemens and SanDisk released the first removable flash storage in 1998 (Gsmarena.com, 2018), it wasn't long before memory cards replaced tapes in camcorders, leading to smaller, easier-to-transport cameras, like the "Flip" video camera. These were also inexpensive enough that outfitting each research participant with their own camera became an acceptable expense in a market research budget. The advancement of cell phone cameras, phone storage, and data upload speeds have since made phone diaries a viable option too. Because of this ever-increasing accessibility, video diaries have become commonplace in consumer-focused, qualitative research projects.

The Strengths of Video Diaries

In our work in consumer/corporate ethnography, we use video diaries to tackle a wide range of research topics. The majority of our projects have a video diary component where we ask our participants to use their cameras to *show us* what they do (documenting actual actions or physical objects) and *tell us* about themselves and their lives (asynchronous interviewing). They do this in context, in the moment when whatever we are studying is happening. Here are a few instances where diaries really shine.

Repetitive Behavior

One of the most useful applications of video diaries is observing repetitive behaviors and routines. Observing someone's medication regimens, their snack times, or every time they use their phone for weeks at a time is too resource intensive for most researchers to do in person. Still, this type of data can be invaluable for our clients, and video diaries make its collection practical. It helps them see how intervening contextual factors impact how their products are used. How does being in a hurry impact breakfast? How does a family tragedy change how someone browses the internet? Can a blizzard impact how a cat's litter box is taken care of? Understanding variations in routines and these "what happens when?" questions help product designers and marketers get in touch with how their products are used in an array of real-life contexts.

The litter box example illustrates this well. Recently, we had forty research participants keep a video diary for around a month, recording every time they scooped or cleaned their litter boxes. If we just did a single, in-person visit with participants, we would have seen forty instances of litter box care, many of which would clock in at just a couple of minutes. Instead, thanks to the video diaries we had forty households recording their scooping and cleaning multiple times daily for a month, and we ended up with hundreds of data points to work with – a lot of clumps. Without these diaries we wouldn't have understood how variable litter-box care could be, what happens when litter-box care goes awry, and how life events, big and small, could make the litter box fall under the radar. And yes, it turns out that a blizzard can have an impact. One of our Colorado participants couldn't return home for days because of a blizzard. Once she did get home, she was greeted by an overstuffed litter box and a cat in a foul mood.

Similarly, we have done multiple diary studies where we have asked people with diabetes to record, on camera, every time they measure their glucose levels. While actual habits vary a lot, checking your numbers multiple times a day is generally recommended, depending on the type of diabetes you have, its severity, and how you're treating it. Like the litter-box study, having participants record their glucose monitoring for weeks at a time resulted in exponentially more data than an approach with an in-person visit or two. This repetitive, persistent data collection helped us develop insights into the wheres, whens, whys, and, tellingly, *the why nots* of glucose monitoring.

Behavior That Happens at Odd Hours or Spontaneously

Video diaries are also great at capturing life's more spontaneous moments and behaviors that can occur at odd hours. Once we worked on a project on what it was like to be a first-time parent. Caring for an infant doesn't happen on a strict, nine-to-five schedule, and the video diaries allowed us to be there for all of the joys and struggles of new parenthood, whether they occurred at 3 p.m. or 3 a.m. We did another project on a rare medical condition where some patients took a "cocktail" of medications with a dosing frequency that made getting a full night's sleep impossible. Our participants' middle of the night entries when waking up to take their pills resulted in much richer and more impactful data than had we just talked about their medication routines in an interview. The insights we gleaned from the video diaries helped our clients understand that living with the condition involved more than just dealing with its symptoms.

24/7 Access

In addition to allowing researchers to access specific, sometimes difficult to capture, moments in time, video diaries allow researchers to *be* "with" participants around the clock and to be poised to gather data morning, noon, and night. Video diaries give participants the flexibility to not only capture action as it naturally occurs, but to also make entries whenever something arises or as the mood strikes them. Our participants hop onto their cameras all the time to tell us about a thought that has occurred to them or to show us some piece of the action that did not make an earlier entry. During one study on household chores, our participants showed us each time they loaded or unloaded their dishwashers, but they also often turned on their cameras to show us how dirty dishes ended up in the sink between loads or to talk about how they were frustrated by the amount of last-minute cleaning they had to do right before bedtime.

Private Contexts and Backstage Spaces

Video diaries also allow us to observe behaviors and settings where a researcher might not be welcomed or might otherwise disrupt the context. We did a study of theme parks where we wanted to follow our participants for their entire vacations. Although we did spend a lot of time with each family in person, the video diaries made it possible for them to document most of their trip themselves. They allowed our participants to be on their own for the majority of the time while still helping us to develop a comprehensive understanding of their experiences. Other researchers have used video diaries to unobtrusively study life's more private moments, such as Christmas rituals (Muir and Mason, 2012) and breastfeeding practices (Taylor, 2015). Surprisingly enough, there are a lot of situations where people would rather not have an ethnographer by their side.

Intimate Data

The very mention of a "diary" conjures up images of hitherto withheld, private revelations, but do our video diaries really inspire participants to be *more* open and intimate with us? Sort of. Ethnographers can develop closeness and intimacy with participants in person, but video diaries do have a knack of producing surprising candor. We have found that the sort of trust necessary to be open and forthright in their entries develops in a natural way over the days and weeks as diarists grow accustomed to the idea of sharing their lives on camera. Similarly, Jacelon and Imperio (2005) found in their diary study that although early entries tended to be simple, factual chronicles, the diarists became more personal and introspective as time passed. We also build trust with participants through our regular check-ins with them: we communicate with them throughout the diary period, helping them get to know the people that will be watching the videos they are creating.

Video diaries offer a rare opportunity for unencumbered self-expression, which can lead someone to put their heart and soul into their entries. With some of our studies, like the cat litter project, giving participants "a voice" might not be much of a factor, but for other projects it is. If we can give someone with a chronic health condition, for example, a platform to share their experience openly with an engaged audience, it might have a positive impact on their life and on their journey as a patient.

Finally, since our participants may be keeping their cameras for an extended period of time, we're much more likely to catch them in a sharing, emotional mood than if we were only to see them in a single visit. It is not uncommon for a rough day or a tiff with a spouse to prompt a very personal, emotionally charged diary entry. The camera can provide an ideal venue for people to vent and open up about their lives in general, which gives us a better understanding of the contexts surrounding their overall challenges and frustrations. So, although a video diary might not provide a cat owner with much of an emotional outlet regarding their litter tray, it can provide a sounding board for daily frustrations about things such as time crunches and division of domestic labor.

The emotional entries that diaries can inspire may at times make them seem more "authentic" than other types of data. Diary entries might seem unfettered by social mores, but this isn't necessarily the case. Interacting with a camera can be as performative as interacting with a person. Diarists are still managing impressions and they are still carrying around their social baggage (Pini, 2001). Recording diary entries may even be more performative than in-person data collection, given the prevailing exposure to online vlogs and reality shows where people often ramp up their personalities for entertainment effect (Faulkner and Zafiroglu, 2010). Although, in our experience, it is rare for people (or at least for adults) to overly "ham it up" for the camera, it would be a mistake to believe that the absence of a physical interviewer meant that the entries are not recorded with some "observing other" in mind. It is typical for people to talk *to us*, saying that they want to show things to *us*, or that *we* would find this or that interesting. We are still there, influencing in the interaction, just not physically.

The Drawbacks of Video Diaries

In-Clinic Data and Other Off-Limits Spaces

There are some instances where video diaries do not make sense. Workplace studies tend not to be ideal, nor are studies where filming might be prohibited or otherwise not welcomed. We spend a lot of time doing observational research in healthcare spaces, for example, and healthcare providers may find it difficult to record a video diary in their privacy-sensitive workplaces. Written diaries, however, have been used effectively to document patients' experiences of their time in clinics and hospitals (Webster et al., 2019), and we have asked participants to take their cameras when they visit their doctor. We always do so with some hesitancy, stressing that we only want them to do it if they feel completely comfortable with the idea. We also give clear instructions to only film in the exam room and, of course, to obtain their health care providers' permission before turning the camera on.

A Lack of Control Compared to In-Person Research

Data from video diaries also may not provide the same level of reach and control over data collected by a researcher in person. That is one reason why our video diary projects are typically paired with in-person interviews and observations, either before, during, or after the participants complete their diaries. The diary-interview method (Zimmerman and Weider, 1977) is an effective approach whereby after the researcher reviews all of the diary entries (whether they are video, audio, or text diaries), they follow up with an interview to collect further "color" and detail.

Projects that rely entirely on video diaries, without any in-person research, can be done, but they require caution. The absence of a face-to-face interview, for one, means that you are relying on participants to answer any direct questions from the video diary guide with sufficient detail and complexity. Participants will not necessarily know when or how much to elaborate upon, and what details to include when answering questions on a video diary, and this might leave the researcher wanting more information. Online platforms that let you follow up on participant uploads mid-project can be helpful with this, but they cannot replace the in-the-moment back and forth that in-person fieldwork can provide. Just the ability to look around freely and to be able to smell, hear, and touch the environment adds a lot to an ethnographer's understanding. Being there physically helps the researcher to make sense of the situation, read the participant's body language, and ask questions based on what they see and hear. All of this can make in-person fieldwork more dynamic than video diary data, where questions and tasks are typically formulated before much is known about the individual participants and their unique circumstances.

Similarly, an experienced ethnographer will have a better idea of the kinds of data that will be important to document. When a participant decides to start and stop the recording and what they focus on during the recording all determine how helpful a piece of observational data is. When a researcher is there making the observations and recording the action, the whole picture is more likely to be captured in the frame for later analysis. For example, participants might not always record what comes before and after the action the researcher is interested in, but such data is helpful in adding context and depth to a study. Participants may also fail to point the camera at the object of interest, and so the researcher is unable to see what just happened in the same way they would during in-person fieldwork.

Sarah Pink (2001) argues that leaving decisions on what to film up to the participants is actually an advantage of video diaries, in that it helps the researcher understand the participant's perspective on what is going on. This is an idea fundamental to the aforementioned Worth and Adair (1972) film project and scratches the Malinowskian (1922) itch to understand the "native point of view." With a lot of market research, however, we often ask our participants to record straight forward things (e.g., "Please record every time you eat breakfast."), so we are walking a fine line between giving our participants interpretative freedom and making sure they show and tell us exactly what we need to see and hear.

Video Diaries in Health Care Research

Pen-and-paper diaries have been used in healthcare research since the 1970s (Hall, 2020), and although video diaries are a comparatively recent addition to the healthcare research toolkit, we use them extensively to learn how people manage their health and illness in everyday life. Privacy concerns limit their use in clinical settings, but for patient-focused projects they are hard to beat in terms of their ability to provide deep insights into the patient experience. In fact, the sort of candor found in video diaries may be absent with in-clinic research that is focused on observing patient interactions with their healthcare providers. Patients are selective about what they report to their healthcare providers for a variety of reasons. These can include patients' assessments of what is important and unimportant to report, stigmas around "complaining" about health issues, power differentials impeding communication, and the simple challenge of recalling symptoms and episodes months after they occur (Elliott, 1997). Again, video diaries, in contrast, provide people with an always-available platform to talk about their experiences with health and illness to a nonjudgmental, interested audience.

Specific applications of video diaries in healthcare research include documenting:

- Treatment (and prevention) regimens, including medication, diet, and exercise routines
- Health information seeking
- Medical device use in context
- The daily lives and challenges of patients with specific illnesses and conditions.

We did a study on lupus that exemplified the value of video diaries in understanding the patient experience. Lupus is well known for causing "flares." Sometimes a person with lupus might feel fine, but at other times it can flare up and cause an array of symptoms such as severe fatigue, rashes, and joint pain. Video diaries allowed us to understand what flares looked and felt like for our participants and how they impacted their lives. We could not have achieved the same level of empathy and understanding without their diaries. Although lupus might be more unpredictable than some other conditions, many with chronic illnesses have good days and bad days, and video diaries offer us precious insights into the changing dynamics of their lives.

Incorporating Video Diaries Step-by-Step

The second half of this chapter presents the reader with a step-by-step guide on how to implement video diaries into their research projects. Other researchers may prefer alternative strategies, and every project will require a different approach (Janssens, 2018), but we have found that these general guidelines work well for us.

Choosing Cameras or Phones

This issue might be completely moot in the future but, as of this writing, the first decision to make when embarking on a video diary project is whether to send participants camcorders or set them up to record their entries with their phones.

Camcorder diaries and phone diaries each have advantages and disadvantages. The primary advantage of using a camcorder is the essentially unlimited amount of data you can capture. After the participant fills one memory card, they just need to put another one in. Mobile phones, on the other hand, have finite internal storage and uploading large amounts of video with a phone can be cumbersome and frustrating for the participant. This is not a problem in studies where you might want to observe a behavior that only takes a couple minutes at a time, or where you are asking questions that require only brief responses. However, other research subjects, such as preparing dinner, may require participants to record for long stretches, and having the freedom to record lengthy entries without consequence is a necessity for these types of projects.

Phones do have some advantages over camcorders. They can be a significantly faster route to collecting data. Data can start to come in the same day you begin the research, and you have access to the data as soon as it is recorded and uploaded. This allows you to start the analysis right away, and it helps you see how your participants are progressing. You can give them advice or direction if their recordings are missing the mark or if their entries are slow in coming to you. You can also ask them more timely follow-up questions.

In addition, participants are more likely to carry their phones wherever they go, and when a recording opportunity presents itself, especially whilst they're out and about, there is a greater chance they will have their phone on hand to document it.

If you opt for phone diaries, we would suggest using an online platform designed for research diaries, although we have, on occasion, had participants manually upload their videos to a cloud storage service. These video diary platforms are designed to make it easy for the user to record and upload their videos, the diary guides are built into the app, and the videos are automatically transcribed.

Developing a Video Diary Guide

Writing an effective video diary guide is a critical step in the process. This may be the participant's first experience of video diarying, and they will rely heavily on the guide to explain what to do and how to do it. We have found that guides that facilitate good video diaries share a few qualities:

1. They have focus but are also open-ended; 2. They are simple; 3. They proactively lay out the expectations and requirements of the process.

1. Good Guides Have Focus and Are Simultaneously Open-Ended

The objectives of the video diary need to be clear to the participant, which requires that they first must be clear to the researcher. Before writing the guide, it is important to decide exactly what you want to get from the diaries. Do you want participants to record specific behaviors? Do you want them to answer specific questions? Would it better suit your goals if you gave your diarists a more open invitation to document their lives and their thoughts, whatever those end up being? Jones et al. (2014) found that having very open-ended instructions led to participants being uncertain about what to record. The quality of their diaries suffered as a result, despite the researchers' hopes that the added freedom would lead to more empowered and spontaneous responses. Giving participants some direction is a good idea, but just how much will depend on your research goals. For our projects, we offer direction but also encourage our participants to show and tell us anything that might help us to better understand their lives and the project topic. We let them know that they have the freedom to make diary entries on anything they think is important or relevant.

How long participants will keep their diaries is another key decision and will vary based on what you need from the diaries. Two or three weeks is fairly standard for us, but this can be shorter if timelines and/or budgets necessitate it. It can be longer, too, if you are studying an event with an extended life cycle (e.g., going through chemotherapy), if you want to look at change before and after a specific event (e.g., having a baby), or if you are studying how people and their behaviors change over time. We have done longitudinal studies in the past where participants have kept their video diaries for a full year. At a certain point, participants will face diary fatigue, even with shorter diaries, and it is important to consider this in what you ask of your participants.

2. Good Guides Are Simple

Although it is tempting to include every question and activity you can think of, video diaries should not be tedious to complete, nor should they be a full-time job. There is no set-in-stone rule for what constitutes a diary that's too extensive, too time consuming, or too complex, but you do not want your research to inspire comparisons to Milgram (1974). In general, it is a bad sign if the guide is more than a few pages long, including the introduction and instructions. We always provide our participants with monetary incentives for doing the diaries, so if the guide *has* to be dense, with lots of tasks and questions, the incentive should reflect that, or you might consider including an incentive if you hadn't done so before.

A good video diary guide also uses clear and precise language and is void of academic and business jargon. Questions and requests should be direct and should only include ambiguity when you are open to and interested in participant interpretation. Like a lot of things in life, it is a good idea for a second set of eyes to make sure everything makes sense and is reasonable.

3. Good Guides Lay Out Expectations and Needs

In addition to listing specific questions and tasks that participants should record, diary guides should include any instructions and advice that will help set the participant up for success. Our guides have evolved over the years as we have identified certain patterns in subpar diaries. Some key instructions we include are:

a. *Start recording right away.* We have learned that people won't necessarily start their diaries immediately. Our studies are never the top priority in their lives, and unless we stress to them how important it is that they begin right away, they won't. If it takes a week or more for our participants to start recording, it can disrupt an entire project timeline.

b. *Record the action and themselves.* For the "show me" questions, where we want to observe actions or objects, we ask participants to focus their cameras on the action or object. To make this easier, when we send them camcorders we include a small tripod so they can record themselves hands-free. We also recommend that they recruit a family member or friend to record them if they're documenting behaviors that require moving around a lot (e.g., doing laundry). If there is anything specific we need to see, such as what's on their computer screen for a tech study, we ask them to focus on that.

    Sometimes when participants answer questions for the video diary, they might point the camera at a wall or the video diary guide instead of pointing it at themselves. If the guide has a lot of "tell me" questions (questions that require a verbal response), it can be helpful to ask participants to record themselves or whatever they are talking about, particularly if you are creating an edited video with their entries.

c. *They are the experts.* We always stress that the participants are the experts, and they'll know best what to show us. Our guides include a basic explanation of the research goals, paired with a request that they record *anything* that will help us reach those goals, even if it is not included in the guide. Although the research participants are not ethnographers, encouraging them to not be "boxed in" by the guide helps their diaries become more inductive and ethnographic.

d. *Get others involved.* For most projects, we want entire families involved in the process. We typically interact with a single, primary contact throughout, but we stress that keeping a video diary should not be a solo effort. How involved the rest of the family will be is ultimately determined by the salesmanship of our primary contact and their family's willingness. Still, we include questions to help facilitate their engagement. For one, nearly every guide we create asks family members to introduce themselves. Also, whenever it makes sense, we include the families in the language of our requests. For example, instead of "Show us every time you make dinner." We might write, "Show us every time you or a family member makes dinner." A lot of times diary entries will still be dominated by the primary participants, but including this sort of verbiage does help.

On a side note, having friends and family participate in a video diary can change the dynamic between the diarist and the camera. Holliday (2005) found that when a "known other" (e.g., a friend or a family member) is filming, the entries can become more guarded or more performative. The filmed person will present themselves in much in the same way they normally present themselves to that known other (Goffman, 1959). As a result, comparing solo entries to entries filmed with family members can produce a more complex understanding of who the participants are and the different roles they play in their lives.

e. *Emphasize the value of repetition.* Asking people to repeatedly record mundane, everyday things can defy logic for some (Pilcher, Martin and Williams, 2015). They might not be able to fathom why we would want to see them going about their ordinary routines even once, so asking them to record their routines repeatedly, day after day, it can be a hard sell. They assume that they do it the same way each time ("So what's the point?"), that we'll get bored watching it, and that they'll get bored recording it. In fact, in an audio diary study by Williamson et al. (2015), participants reported that the fear of being repetitive was the single worst part of participating in the study. As a result, we include a note in the guide to assure them that we will not be bored and actually want to see repeated instances of their behaviors – as many as they can stand to record.

One area we do not spend a lot of time instructing them on is their camera work. It is not that we do not care how their video looks; we just want their focus to be on documenting their lives, not on how well those lives are framed or lit. Depending on your goals and stakeholder expectations, however, you may want to include some essential videography tips in the guide.

Verbal Guidance

The video diary guide should be complemented by verbal guidance throughout the process. Alaszewski (2006) argues that face-to-face meetings are useful to initially orient diarists; however, because our participants usually do not live in the same area where we live, we typically communicate with them via phone and email. This communication should cover technical details on how to use the equipment or platform and should also give them a general sense of the kinds of things we want them to record. We start by explaining the work that we do (ethnography) and the specific project goals. Then we cover the nuts and bolts of the process. This includes our start and end dates, any consent forms we need them to sign, the process for shipping back memory cards (we include a FedEx envelope in the package to make it easy for them), and when they can expect to receive their incentive payments.

Let the Diaries Commence!

Once all of the participants are set up with their cameras and their instructions, the next step is to let life unfold. As they begin their recordings, it becomes our job to do what we can to make sure they are keeping up with their diaries and are not experiencing any confusion or stumbling blocks. We might send them reminders or request updates on how they are doing. We might need to send them new memory cards. We might field questions about what to record or how to work the equipment. It is good practice to reach out to participants at least weekly to check that everything is going smoothly. They have a lot of other things going on in their lives, and it is easy for people to put their diaries off or forget about them entirely.

We also try to provide as much positive feedback as we can in our interactions with participants. Diarists can experience self-doubt about their entries, and often worry that they are not providing what we need (Elliott, 1997). It is always helpful to offer words of encouragement and assure them that they are doing a good job and providing us with useful information. If their entries have room for improvement, gentle nudges with clear guidance can help get them back on track.

No matter how much you check in with and encourage participants, some people will be better diarists than others. Various factors can impact this. Some people are more accustomed to and comfortable with opening up about themselves, whether because of cultural factors or personal histories. A lot of it comes down to personality. Williamson et al. (2015) found that the people who were less prodigious with their diaries were also less talkative during their interviews, indicating that they might struggle no matter how much help and positive encouragement the researcher provides.

Analyzing and Reporting on Video Diary Data

When the data starts rolling in, the analysis begins. For us, analyzing video diary data is largely the same inductive, thematic coding process as analyzing data collected in person. Others might adopt unique approaches. In her diary study of men with Duchenne muscular dystrophy and their sense of identity, Barbara Gibson (2005) implements what she calls the "movie method" of analysis – an approach that examines the socially situated aspects of diary creation. This technique focuses on the roles and relationships of the diarist and other actors on the screen, the audience's influence on the narrative, and what is left on "the cutting room floor" (i.e., what is not included in the diary). Others have treated video diary analysis collaboratively, involving their participants in reviewing and commenting on the videos they have made (Brown et al., 2010).

Some online diary platforms include special tools for analysis, such as built-in coding systems or self-generated word clouds based on how frequently key words appear in the video transcripts. Some of these tools may be more useful than others, but most of the same tenets of ethnographic data analysis are as applicable to video diary data as to any other qualitative data.

When it comes to reporting findings, video diary data can produce a lot of lively footage for an edited video, whether your audience is a corporate client or fellow academics. Although the video may never be regarded as great cinematography, there is an intimacy and an energy inherent in video diary footage. They might be ordinary people doing ordinary things, but video diaries offer us glimpses into private spaces and moments we usually do not have the privilege of seeing. They help us get up close and personal with people that we can empathize with, and that can make for compelling viewing.

Summary

This chapter has outlined the pros and cons of video diaries and has offered some recommendations for how to execute a video diary project. Video diaries can produce dynamic, engrossing material and can help us capture types of observational data that would be difficult, if not impossible, to achieve with in-person methods. Diaries provide qualitative healthcare researchers with a powerful tool for developing context-rich insights into everyday habits, routines, and rituals around health and illness.

The future of video diary research looks bright. Phones are quickly becoming the go-to medium for implementing video diaries, and, as the technology advances, their drawbacks, primarily space and upload speed limitations, will likely dwindle. Everything points to video diaries becoming an increasingly accessible approach for qualitative researchers, and a user-friendly experience for the people who let us into their lives.

References

Alaszewski, A. (2006). *Using Diaries for Social Research*. London: Sage.

Brown, C., Costley, C., Friend, L. and Varey, R. (2010). Capturing their Dream: Video Diaries and Minority Consumers. *Consumption Markets & Culture*, 13(4), pp. 419–436.

Elliott, H. (1997). The Use of Diaries in Sociological Research on Health Experience. *Sociological Research Online, [online]* Volume 2(2). www.socreson line.org.uk/2/2/7.html (accessed Feb. 24, 2021).

Faulkner, S. and Zafiroglu, A. (2010). The Power of Participant-Made Videos: Intimacy and Engagement with Corporate Ethnographic Video. *Epic*. www .epicpeople.org/the-power-of-participant-made-videos-intimacy-and-engage ment-with-corporate-ethnographic-video/ (accessed Feb. 22, 2021).

Gibson, B. (2005). Co-Producing Video Diaries: The Presence of the "Absent" Researcher. *International Journal of Qualitative Methods*, 4(4), pp. 34–43.

Goffman, E. (1959). *The Presentation of Self in Everyday Life*. Garden City: Doubleday.

Gsmarena.com. (2018). Counterclockwise: Short History of the Memory Card. www.gsmarena.com/counterclockwise_short_history_of_the_memory_card-news-34263.php (accessed Nov. 30, 2020).

Hall, G. (2020). Ethnographic Diaries and Journals: Principles, Practices, and Dilemmas. In P. Hackett and C. Hayre, eds., *Handbook of Ethnography in Healthcare Research*, 1st ed. Abingdon: Routledge, pp. 277–288.

Holliday, R. (2005). Reflecting the Self: Video Diaries, Identity Performances and Queer Methodologies. In C. Knowles and P. Sweetman, eds., *Picturing the Social Landscape: Visual Methods and the Sociological Imagination*, 1st ed. London: Routledge, Taylor & Francis Group, pp. 49–64.

Jacelon, C. and Imperio, K. (2005). Participant Diaries as a Source of Data in Research With Older Adults. *Qualitative Health Research*, 15(7), pp. 991–997.

Janssens, K., Bos, E., Rosmalen, J., Wichers, M. and Riese, H. (2018). A Qualitative Approach to Guide Choices for Designing a Diary Study. *BMC Medical Research Methodology*, 18(140). https://bmcmedresmethodol.biomed central.com/articles/10.1186/s12874-018-0579-6 (accessed Feb. 22, 2021).

Jones, R., Fonseca, J., De Martin Silva, L., et al. (2014). The Promise and Problems of Video Diaries: Building on Current Research. *Qualitative Research in Sport, Exercise and Health*, 7(3), pp. 395–410.

Malinowski, B. (1922). *Argonauts of the Western Pacific: An Account of Native Enterprise and Adventure in the Archipalegoes of Melanesian New Guinea*. London: G. Routledge.

Milgram, S. (1974). *Obedience to Authority: An Experimental View*. London: Tavistock.

Muir, S. and Mason, J. (2012). Capturing Christmas: The Sensory Potential of Data from Participant Produced Video. *Sociological Research Online*, 17(1), pp. 1–19.

Pilcher, K., Martin, W. and Williams, V. (2015). Issues of Collaboration, Representation, Meaning and Emotions: Utilising Participant-led Visual Diaries to Capture the Everyday Lives of People in Mid to Later Life. *International Journal of Social Research Methodology*, 19(6), pp. 1–16.

Pini, M. (2001). Video Diaries: Questions of Authenticity and Fabrication. *Screening the Past*. www.screeningthepast.com/2014/12/video-diaries-questions-of-authenticity-and-fabrication/ (accessed Feb. 22, 2021).

Pink, S. (2001). *Doing Ethnography: Images, Media and Representation in Research*. London: Sage.

Taylor, A. (2015). "It's a Relief to Talk ... ": Mothers' Experiences of Breastfeeding Recorded in Video Diaries. PhD. Bournemouth University, School of Health and Social Care.

Webster, C. S., Jowsey, T., Lu, L. M., et al. (2019). Capturing the Experience of the Hospital-Stay Journey from Admission to Discharge using Diaries Completed by Patients in their Own Words: A Qualitative Study. *BMJ Open*, 9, e027258.

Williamson, I., Leeming, D., Lyttle, S. and Johnson, S. (2015). Evaluating the Audio-Diary Method in Qualitative Research. *Qualitative Research Journal*, 15(1), pp. 20–34.

Worth, S. and Adair, J. (1972). *Through Navajo Eyes: An Exploration in Film Communication and Anthropology*. Bloomington, IN: Indiana University Press.

Zimmerman, D. and Wieder, D. (1977). The Diary: Diary-Interview Method, *Urban Life*, 5(4), pp. 479–498.

CHAPTER 4

(In)Equitable Shifts
Mapping a Pivot to Digital Diary and Remote Research Methods with Queer Youth in the Times of Covid-19

Rodney Stehr, Danya Fast, and Rod Knight

Introduction

The Covid-19 pandemic and associated public health measures have introduced challenges to conducting in-person qualitative research. In this chapter, we examine a series of challenges and opportunities that have arisen in our qualitative research as we shifted our in-person research activities with sexual and gender minority youth (SGMY) to digital and remote methods. We discuss how digital diaries, combined before and after with remote interviewing, can generate insights into how SGMY's health-related experiences unfold across time. We also raise several technological issues and equity concerns that may complicate digital and remote approaches with SGMY. Our aim is to document and address some of the key practical and ethical implications that can arise when shifting to digital and remote methods.

A Pivot from In-Person to Remote and Digital Qualitative Approaches

Much has been written about how to optimize qualitative data collection activities, including via techniques to establish participant–researcher rapport and trust, maintain confidentiality, and ensure the conditions for participation are safe (Chabot et al., 2012; Fast, 2016; Kirk, 2007; Knight et al., 2017). In our research involving SGMY, for example, we use a variety of strategies, including taking the time to ensure participants are comfortable and that our body language is open, friendly, and professional. We have a safety protocol to ensure participants who disclose to us that they are at risk of experiencing immediate harms can be connected with support before we part ways. A critical component of our research is to create the conditions that allow participants to discuss potentially stigmatizing topics with us, including experiences with substance use-related harms and mental health challenges. It is fair to say, however, that most of our previous work has relied primarily on in-person interactions to establish rapport, trust, confidentiality, and safety.

With the onset of the Covid-19 pandemic in the spring of 2020, it became clear that using in-person methods to continue conducting our research was neither safe nor feasible for the foreseeable future. Contingency planning immediately focused on how our research involving SGMY could be conducted remotely while continuing to prioritize participant safety and well-being. This planning included considerations of equity, including whether and how a shift toward remote and digital approaches would allow us to identify and interrogate how inequities occur within and across intersecting positionalities, including with regards to Indigeneity, disability, gender, sexuality, class, and race.

After reviewing and considering various digital and remote methods, solicited digital diaries emerged as a data collection technique that appeared to meet many of our needs. Diaries have been used in both qualitative and quantitative health research for more than ninety years (Milligan and Bartlett, 2019). Solicited digital diaries go beyond traditional, handwritten forms and have been described as being more inclusive because they can be "creatively adapted to meet the skills of those for whom written diaries may prove exclusionary" (Milligan and Bartlett, 2019). Digital adaptations of solicited diaries can feature a variety of different techniques to expand accessibility, including via the incorporation of video, audio, and photography to reach populations that may face barriers to participating in traditional written diaries (Cooley et al., 2014, Milligan and Bartlett, 2019, Jacelon and Imperio, 2005, Thomas et al., 2015). An important strength associated with solicited diaries, whether completed digitally or in written form, is the emphasis on repeat points of contact with research participants – an approach that can provide opportunities to capture patterns, trends, and key events in "real time" as well as over time (Bolger et al., 2003, Bijker et al., 2015).

As we reviewed the literature in this area, we found that others have used digital diaries to understand the factors and contexts that influence various health outcomes, including with regards to substance use- and mental health-related experiences among adolescents and SGMY (Koning et al., 2010, Heron et al., 2019, Ferraz et al., 2021). Digital diaries have also been used across a variety of other substantive areas, including with regards to adolescents and food environments (Staiano et al., 2012), religious mobile apps and how they are used by evangelical Christians (Bellar, 2017), and the experiences of midlife women with daily hot flashes (Miller et al., 2009). Promisingly, these and other studies have reported high levels of retention and completion rates when using digital diary-based methods (Cherenack et al., 2016). And while opportunities to establish rapport can be disrupted or complicated when using remote and digital approaches (Oliffe et al., 2021), researchers have also described how these approaches may create conditions in which participants are less concerned about a researcher's social judgments (Cleary and Walter, 2011).

Based on our review of digital diary methods, we began developing a protocol intended to capture, over periods as long as three months, how substance use and mental health featured within the evolving experiences of SGMY during the Covid-19 pandemic. We divided the diary entries into two sections. One section featured a set of repeating optional prompts that participants could use to help them get started writing their diaries; these included questions that asked how they had been for the last few days, to describe their recent daily routines and changes in these, things that had made them laugh, and things that they missed. The second section included a set of guiding questions that changed for each entry, including topics such as social media use, substance use, mental health, and sexual health, as well as asking about the participant's knowledge and reaction to these. The choice to have prompts rather than an open-ended format was to help focus responses on specific areas of interest to the researchers (Filep et al., 2018), and to offer support to participants who may not normally engage with diaries and thus would benefit from guidance. However, similar to others who have used digital diaries (Milligan and Bartlett, 2019), we let participants know that they could write about any issues of importance to them, and that they could go "off topic" from the prompts provided.

We also decided to employ a hybrid approach to data collection that, in addition to digital diaries, would feature two remote semistructured interviews that could take place by phone or via Zoom video conferencing software. Both before and since the onset of Covid-19, researchers have documented several challenges and concessions associated with using video conferencing and phones for interviews, including a lack of control over the participant's interview environment and reduced ability to pick up on body language and facial expressions (Oliffe et al., 2021, Jenner and Myers, 2019, Archibald et al., 2019). Conversely, video interviews can allow for greater flexibility (e.g., in terms of scheduling) and overall cost savings (Oliffe et al., 2021, Jenner and Myers, 2019, Archibald et al., 2019). Video and remote interviewing also provides opportunities for participants to join from their own private or personal settings – an important consideration when discussing highly personal issues, but which can also be complicated if those settings are not private (Jenner and Myers, 2019). Others have described how the technical aspects of using video conferencing software for qualitative interviewing incurs key considerations around having a backup plan in the face of an unstable Internet connection and the need for the researcher to optimize their own Internet connection (e.g., hardwiring to the Internet rather than relying on WIFI) (Gray et al., 2020).

A Digital Diary and Remote Interviewing Protocol

With all of this in mind, we designed our digital diary and remote interviewing protocol to include an intake interview of approximately 30 minutes and a follow-up interview of approximately 60 minutes. We gave participants the option to participate in interviews via Zoom or phone call. We carried out a total of seven intake and follow-up interviews over the phone and twenty intake and follow-up interviews over Zoom. During the intake interviews, participants were introduced to the digital diary process, and were asked a series of general questions regarding their experiences regarding substance use and mental health in the context of Covid-19.

Following the completion of the first interview, participants received a semiweekly (every 3–4 days) email invitation to fill out a total of six diary entries over a period of three weeks (or more, as needed). We hosted the solicited digital diaries on a secure survey interface named REDCap – one of only a few interfaces that was free for us to use through our institutional affiliations and fully compliant with provincial and federal research regulations and privacy laws. Participants were given up to a week to complete each entry but were always provided with the opportunity to ask for an extension (participants could take as long as they needed to complete the six entries). Upon completion of the diaries, participants were invited to participate in the one-hour follow-up interview. During the follow-up interviews, the diary entries were discussed and questions were asked based on information that was shared in the diaries. We also took this opportunity to evaluate participants' overall experiences with the digital diary process by asking them questions about their experiences with the diaries.

Data collection began at the end of November 2020. Over a period of seven months, we recruited fifteen participants (ages 15–25). Each participant took 1–2 months to complete the study. Participants identified across a variety of sexual and gender identities, could speak and understand

---

Demographics

Age range (18–25); average age: 22;

60% of the sample identified as white, and the remaining 40% identified as Chinese, Korean, South Asian, or Latinx;

46.7% of the sample identified as non-binary, and the remaining participants identified as cis or a variety of different overlapping gender identities (e.g., "female" and "genderqueer");

60% of the participants identified as bisexual, 53.3% as queer, 33.3% as gay, and 26.7% as pansexual;

66.7% indicated that they do not have the option to work remotely for their job, 33.3% no longer had a job due to covid;

Substance use

Lifetime

100% of participants recorded experiences with alcohol, 93.3% with cannabis, 53.3% with psychedelics, 26.7% with cocaine/benzodiazepines;

Last 30 days

66.7% disclosed alcohol consumption, 73.3% disclosed cannabis use, 26.7% disclosed psychedelic use, 13.3% disclosed use of benzodiazepines;

ACCESS TO CELLPHONE OR COMPUTER

80% had access to a cellphone with data, and 73.3% had access to a cellphone with WIFI;

93.3% had access to a private computer or laptop where they live.

PROGRAMS AND SERVICES USED IN PAST YEAR

73.3% accessed a primary care provider, 80% accessed a counselor or psychologist, 26.7% indicated accessing drop-in programming, a psychiatrist, or a mental health team, respectively.

Figure 4.1 Summary of the demographics of the research participants.

English, and lived in Metro Vancouver. See for a summary of the sample sociodemographics.

We will further describe our experiences of pivoting toward the use of digital diaries and remote interviews with SGMY. We examine how these techniques allowed us to develop a longitudinal qualitative data set that provided important insights into health-related experiences over time, and to identify and explore unanticipated areas of inquiry. We interrogate some of the ethical and practical challenges and opportunities we faced, including with regards to barriers to participation and the accessibility of digital diary and remote methods, as well as our experiences of meeting privacy and safety needs.

Identifying Shifting Patterns and Unanticipated Areas of Inquiry

Multiple opportunities to share experiences over the course of two interviews, alongside the digital diary entries, enabled us to identify and explore unanticipated areas of inquiry that may not have been possible if we had only used one method or had not conducted this work longitudinally. Specifically, because most participants took upwards of 1–3 months to complete their participation in the study, multiple points of engagement over time meant that: (a) there were several opportunities for participants to meet the researcher and familiarize themselves with the study design; (b) participants were able to revisit and reflect on their experiences over a longer period and have more control over what they shared; and (c) we were able to ask individualized questions during the follow-up interview that would not have otherwise been possible. We were also able to ask participants about their experiences with the study more broadly, and with the digital diaries specifically.

As the study progressed, we learned that digital diaries could provide important insights into how the progression of the pandemic impacted participants' frequency of substance use and the types of substances they used. For example, we were able to identify how participants' patterns of substance use and calculations of risk were shaped by their experiences of the pandemic and to report these in anonymized form. For example, Chris Rose described in a diary entry how increased overdose deaths since Covid-19 had impacted his willingness to return to the "harder" substances that he had used prior to the arrival of the pandemic:

> Substance use during the pandemic has greatly shifted in my life. I was an occasional "hard drug" or "party drug" user prior to the pandemic. Now, with the increase of overdose and op[i]oid deaths since covid began, I am too concerned to revert back to using those drugs. Furthermore, with parties and clubs not happening, there isn't much incentive to do them anyway. I do consume more pot (which I had previously quit before the pandemic) and alcohol now than before covid. I drink a few nights a week and smoke likely those same nights. (Chris Rose, diary entry)

Chris Rose's shift away from the "occasional 'hard drug'" was accompanied by an increase in consumption of other substances – namely, alcohol and cannabis. The longitudinal study design featuring digital diary and remote interviews also provided opportunities to draw clearer lines between their own lives and the impacts of Covid-19 on their experiences with mental health and substance use. For example, during the intake interviews, participants generally described that Vancouver's overdose crisis did not directly affect them.

However, over the course of successive entries and interviews, participants began providing more detail about how the overdose crisis had impacted them, including deeply personal stories about their own experiences with overdose or the loss of individuals close to them (parents, partners, friends) due to overdose. This reflects previous findings on repeated points of contact providing researchers with deeper insights into participants' experiences with a phenomenon over time (Bolger et al., 2003, Bijker et al., 2015).

Our study design also provided the conditions to identify unanticipated areas of inquiry. For example, one of the earliest findings that emerged in the diaries was that the pandemic introduced and entrenched barriers to accessing mental health care among SGMY. This finding arose within Chris Rose's diary entries and their description of struggles to access the medications and support they needed:

> My ability to access health care hasn't changed too much in covid because of online clinics, but support services have been difficult to access. I stopped seeing a counselor because I didn't like the online format. I couldn't get access to PREP because the men's clinic wasn't taking on new patients during covid. Trying to change my medication during covid has been very difficult and uncertain. (Chris Rose, diary entry)

The combination of intake and follow-up interviews with longitudinal solicited digital diary entries allowed us to explore unanticipated areas of inquiry and pilot questions among multiple participants. In the follow-up interview with Chris Rose, we took the opportunity to ask them to expand on their challenges with medications. It became clear that their status as an "out-of-province" resident and a student complicated their ability to access the services they needed. It also became evident that differences in interprovincial pharmacare coverage meant that in British Columbia they could not afford the medication they needed to address their pandemic-related mental health challenges. Upon learning this, we extended this line of questioning to the other participants and found that the topic of insurance coverage and pandemic-related interruptions to care had wide-ranging relevance for several other participants.

As such, throughout our data collection and analysis, we were able to identify both shifting patterns over time, as well as unanticipated areas of inquiry. Our approach allowed us to visit and revisit emergent themes (e.g., with regards to insurance coverage and pandemic-related interruptions) over the course of several months through both interview and diary formats.

Limitations of Digital Diaries and Remote Interviewing: Whose Voices Are Missing?

An early concern with our sampling strategy was around the capacity of our online ads to encourage participation among a diverse sample of SGMY. Initially, we relied primarily on recruiting through social media. We then decided to supplement digital outreach with a mixture of circulating recruitment materials among our community partners, snowball sampling, and targeted recruitment of past research participants who met our sampling criteria. While we were able to recruit a gender-diverse sample, we were unable to recruit queer and Two-Spirit Indigenous youth or Black SGMY. Furthermore, while some of the youth participants in the study had experiences with emergency housing supports, none of the youth disclosed being street-involved.

Street-involved youth and Black and Indigenous SGMY have distinct and significant experiences of the overdose crisis and Covid-19 pandemic that are missing from our data. A lack of street-involved youth and Black and Indigenous SGMY in this study means that we do not have a sense of how these individuals would experience or react to the use of digital diary methods. Street-involved youth, for example, frequently navigate digital spaces via mobile phones and publicly accessible computers (Selfridge and Mitchell, 2021). It is likely that consistent access to public computers may have been temporarily interrupted because of the closure of public libraries and drop-in spaces at the beginning of the pandemic, thereby further restricting their ability to participate. While we were unable to generate data with and for street-involved youth and Black and Indigenous SGMY, it is our hope that we can identify other remote methods and strategies that are more inclusive, while also acknowledging that supplementing– or altogether replacing – remote methods with in-person activities (e.g., via the spaces and places where SGMY spend time) may be a more appropriate solution for some groups of youth.

Digital Diaries and Accessibility: Whose Voices Are Included?

Initially, we had anticipated that the extended duration of the study would be a barrier to participation. Two solicited diary entries a week, for a total of six entries, to be completed over the course of a month felt like it could be a lot to ask of participants. However, when consulted during the follow-up interviews, participants described digital diaries as being a low-barrier and accommodating approach, something that several participants with a disability described as being particularly novel and important. We came to realize that our use of digital diaries and remote interviewing had enabled the inclusion of individuals who might have otherwise not participated in our research. By shifting to digital methods, we had unintentionally moved toward an approach that was more broadly accessible for some than the in-person methods we had traditionally used. For example, one participant described how the digital, self-paced nature of the diaries was important for individuals who might not always be able to make in-person interviews due to physical and mental health challenges or other more important demands on their time:

> If I'm just having a low day, where I'm in a lot of pain or I'm too tired to really leave the house, an in-person thing is not going to really be accessible, and it's not going to be a priority for me. Whereas something like a diary entry I can do even when I'm not feeling super well. Um, yeah, and just recognizing that a lot of people are working, you know, nine to five jobs, or they're taking care of children, or they have school, and there's a lot of reasons why it's – it would just be really difficult I think to go and meet someone in the middle of the day. And I think it's a lot of – it's a bigger sacrifice that you're asking for in research participants if it's in person. (Big Mac, follow-up interview)

Among participants who were living with chronic pain, and/or disclosed having a disability, the diaries were described as a low-barrier way to engage with the study on their own terms that allowed for ongoing, continued participation in a longitudinal study design – something they described as not being possible for them via in-person approaches. Another participant talked about how the diary entry format was comfortable for them to engage with because it was a familiar mode of communication that was already a part of their online lives:

> I think it's important to mention the context, that I am – I'm autistic, and I've used social media and blogging forever, to communicate with people. So I feel like it felt more like blogging, or like, you know, making a sad tweet and people can – I find that generally kind of easier, because then people can approach that content at their pace, and I'm just kind of like throwing that communication out into the void, and be like, "Hey, I have these needs that aren't getting met." So, you know, throwing words out into the void. I'm kind of used to it. It feels pretty normal. (May, follow-up interview)

Our conversations with participants challenged us to reflect on how our traditional reliance on in-person research activities (e.g., semistructured interviewing, fieldwork) can exclude disabled and neurodiverse individuals. Our assumptions around what constitutes accessible methods of data collection can have ableist dimensions. At this juncture, in moving forward with our research we find ourselves strongly leaning toward a mix of digital and in-person approaches as a means of promoting equitable access to research participation.

Technical Issues

The hybrid approach of using both digital diaries and remote semistructured interviewing by phone call or video conferencing software also brought to light how the former method can mediate inconsistent or limited high-speed Internet access – an issue previously documented by others (Gray et al., 2020, Archibald et al., 2019, Oliffe et al., 2021). Throughout the course of the data collection, there were repeated instances when Zoom calls were cut off during the course of an interview, requiring participants to repeat what they had said multiple times. There were numerous other technical issues with Zoom which made it difficult to understand what was being said and complicated the transcription process. One participant also noted their inability to access high-speed Internet due to their location in Metro Vancouver:

> You'd think living in Metro Vancouver, we could access high-speed Internet here. But we live in a rural part of Metro Vancouver, apparently, which whoever knew [Vancouver borough] had a rural part to it? So no Internet company has got high-speed Internet out here ... So like, you know, my sister was trying to watch her show this morning, and I was trying to do a Zoom call this morning. It doesn't work. You can't stream and do a Zoom call at the same time. (Victor, follow-up interview)

In contrast to Zoom calls, diary entries could be filled out in a self-paced manner, and participants generally found this method to be less affected by poor or inconsistent WIFI access.

Of course, successful uptake of any digital and remote methods (e.g., Zoom calls, digital diaries) is shaped by access to information and communication technologies (e.g., mobile phone or computers) that in turn require robust WIFI infrastructure. This limitation is especially important to consider when undertaking research with those living in more rural, remote, and resource-limited settings. Despite the challenges with Internet speed and video conferencing (e.g., Zoom) when carrying out remote semistructured interviews, participants did not indicate that quality or consistency of Internet connection presented any barriers to filling out their diary entries online.

Privacy and Safety Concerns

In a diary entry, ZK reflected that, in the context of Covid-19, "Everything happens at home now, which means I have less privacy and less & space to myself in general." Most of the participants in the study lived with either a partner, family member(s), or roommates. In some cases, participants were students who were attending school remotely over the course of the study. Prior to the data collection, we sought to be clear with participants during eligibility screening and the informed consent process that we could not carry out a remote interview without them first guaranteeing that they had access to a private space. Living with people presented barriers to participation and complicated the guarantee of complete confidentiality. For example, one participant tried to schedule their remote interview during a time when their roommates were not home. WIFI issues throughout the conversation meant that the interview extended into the time period when their roommates returned, and the call had to be ended early. Because some participants opted to keep their cameras switched off during our Zoom calls, it was difficult to ascertain whether the space they were calling from was, in fact, private. We did not mandate that participants turn on their cameras because we acknowledged that many of them may have already spent a significant amount of their day engaged in video conferencing and we did not want to contribute to feelings of "Zoom fatigue" (Wiederhold, 2020); this did mean that for a portion of the interviews we were not privy to body language or facial expressions and had to rely on tone of voice.

For younger participants who lived with family, barriers to guaranteeing privacy took form such as an instance where the first author (RS) heard a parent come into their room and make a short inquiry (e.g., "Have you eaten yet?"). Despite the relatively minor nature of the interruptions, we worried about whether participants' privacy and confidentiality were being breached in these instances. While participants consistently reassured us that they did not have concerns, ZK's statement about how "everything was happening at home" during the pandemic complicated our ability to make the same kinds of promises to young people about confidentiality as we could have done if they were doing an in-person interview with us in our field office.

Conversely, concerns around privacy did not come up in conversations with participants about their experiences of using digital diary methods. Instead, participants talked about the comparative accessibility of digital diaries when compared to both in-person and remote interviews:

I can see how it would be easier if you're someone who can only access Internet in public spaces. It's probably easier to do a diary entry sitting in a mall or something than it is to do a whole Zoom interview in a mall. So I think probably this sort of diary entry is still more accessible than other traditional means of surveying populations. (Big Mac, follow-up interview)

In the context of our study, digital diaries seemed to allow participants to better participate across settings with variable levels of privacy, and this method was far less reliant on strong WIFI connections. The use of both digital diaries and interviews was a means of balancing out each method's shortcomings. Remote interviewing was useful for getting participants to expand on sometimes sparse diary entries. Diary entries allowed for longitudinal data collection that seemed to be largely unimpeded by Internet connectivity and access to a private space.

As we began implementing the digital diaries, we also found that this medium presented us with distinct challenges around ensuring participants' well-being and safety in comparison to both in-person and remote interviews. For example, the confessional nature of diary entries introduced new challenges with regards to keeping participants safe, including assessing whether they were at risk of experiencing immediate harms. For instance, at times, we found it challenging to interpret tone from the diary texts when participants were discussing mental health challenges – something we can address in "real time" via a team protocol when we are in-person. However, it quickly became clear that our in-person protocols for ensuring participants' safety were insufficient with regards to the digital diaries, so we quickly established procedures to review all text within 24 hours of receiving a diary submission and to determine if there were any disclosures of immediate harms that we would need to address. While we did not ultimately need to contact any of the participants due to concerns around disclosures of harm, our experiences underscored the importance of adapting and developing robust safety protocols when using digital diaries – particularly when dealing with issues such as substance use and mental health.

Conclusion

The application of digital diary methods alongside remote semistructured interview techniques can allow us to capture SGMY's evolving experiences during the overlapping Covid-19 pandemic and overdose crises. Our study design enabled us to revisit some of the details from participants' diary entries during interviews, which allowed us to gain deeper insights into what was shared and to explore unanticipated areas of inquiry and unexpected findings. Our use of digital and remote methods also provided opportunities for participants who may have been unable to access our in-person research activities, including those who disclosed living with chronic pain and/or living with a disability. We also faced a variety of challenges, including participants' inconsistent access to good-quality Internet connection and private spaces. However, because we relied on a phased approach that employed digital diary methods alongside remote semistructured interviews, we found the limitations of one method (e.g., remote interviewing interrupted by poor Internet) could be somewhat balanced by the strengths of another (e.g., the ability to submit entries at any time with digital diaries). Additional research is recommended to understand the appropriateness of these methods for studies with Black, Indigenous, and street-involved youth in both our setting and similar settings, as these were populations not accounted for in our study sample. Future work should also explore how digital diaries may be used as a complementary option for research engagement alongside other in-person methods in order to increase accessibility. Overall, we found digital diary methods to be an effective way to document the experiences of SGMY in the times of Covid-19, and participants perceived digital diaries as a low-barrier and accessible way to participate in qualitative health research.

Funding Acknowledgments

This study was funded by a grant from the Canadian Institutes of Health Research (CIHR). Coauthor RS's research was funded by the Canada Graduate Scholarship-Master's program (CGS-M). DF and RK are supported by scholar awards from Michael Smith Health Research BC.

References

Archibald, M. M., Ambagtsheer, R. C., Casey, M. G. & Lawless, M. 2019. Using Zoom Videoconferencing for Qualitative Data Collection: Perceptions and Experiences of Researchers and Participants. *International Journal of Qualitative Methods*, 18, 160940691987459.

Bellar, W. 2017. Private Practice: Using Digital Diaries and Interviews to Understand Evangelical Christians' Choice and Use of Religious Mobile Applications. *New Media & Society*, 19, 111–125.

Bijker, R. A., Haartsen, T. & Strijker, D. 2015. How People Move to Rural Areas: Insights in the Residential Search Process from a Diary Approach. *Journal of Rural Studies*, 38, 77–88.

Bolger, N., Davis, A. & Rafaeli, E. 2003. Diary Methods: Capturing Life as It Is Lived. *Annual Review of Psychology*, 54, 579–616.

Chabot, C., Shoveller, J. A., Spencer, G. & Johnson, J. L. 2012. Ethical and Epistemological Insights: A Case Study of Participatory Action Research with Young People. *Journal of Empirical Research on Human Research Ethics*, 7, 20–33.

Cherenack, E. M., Wilson, P. A., Kreuzman, A. M., et al. 2016. The Feasibility and Acceptability of Using Technology-Based Daily Diaries with HIV-Infected Young Men Who Have Sex with Men: A Comparison of Internet and Voice Modalities. *AIDS and Behavior*, 20, 1744–1753.

Cleary, M. & Walter, G. 2011. Is E-mail Communication a Feasible Method to Interview Young People with Mental Health Problems? *Journal of Child and Adolescent Psychiatric Nursing*, 24, 150–152.

Cooley, S. J., Holland, M. J., Cumming, J., Novakovic, E. G. & Burns, V. E. 2014. Introducing the Use of a Semi-Structured Video Diary Room to Investigate Students' Learning Experiences during an Outdoor Adventure Education Groupwork Skills Course. *Higher Education*, 67, 105–121.

Fast, D. 2016. My Friends Look Just Like You. *Medicine Anthropology Theory*, 3, 2.

Ferraz, D., Dourado, I., Zucchi, E. M., et al. 2021. Effects of the COVID-19 Pandemic on the Sexual and Mental Health of Adolescent and Adult Men Who Have Sex with Men and Transgender Women Participating in Two PrEP Cohort Studies in Brazil: COBra Study Protocol. *BMJ Open*, 11, e045258–e045258.

Filep, C. V., Turner, S., Eidse, N., Thompson-Fawcett, M. & Fitzsimons, S. 2018. Advancing Rigour in Solicited Diary Research. *Qualitative Research*, 18, 451–470.

Gibson, K. 2020. Bridging the Digital Divide: Reflections on Using WhatsApp Instant Messenger Interviews in Youth Research. Qualitative Research in Psychology, 1–21.

Gray, L. M., Wong-Wylie, G., Rempel, G. R. & Cook, K. 2020. Expanding Qualitative Research Interviewing Strategies: Zoom Video Communications. *Qualitative Report*, 25, 1292–1301.

Heron, K. E., Lewis, R. J., Shappie, A. T., et al. 2019. Rationale and Design of a Remote Web-Based Daily Diary Study Examining Sexual Minority Stress, Relationship Factors, and Alcohol Use in Same-Sex Female Couples Across the United States: Study Protocol of Project Relate. *JMIR Research Protocols*, 8, e11718–e11718.

Jacelon, C. S. & Imperio, K. 2005. Participant Diaries as a Source of Data in Research with Older Adults. *Qualitative Health Research*, 15, 991–997.

Jenner, B. M. & Myers, K. C. 2019. Intimacy, Rapport, and Exceptional Disclosure: A Comparison of In-Person and Mediated Interview Contexts. *International Journal of Social Research Methodology*, 22, 165–177.

Jowett, A., Peel, E. & Shaw, R. 2011. Online Interviewing in Psychology: Reflections on the Process. *Qualitative Research in Psychology*, 8, 354–369.

Kirk, S. 2007. Methodological and Ethical Issues in Conducting Qualitative Research with Children and Young People: A Literature Review. *International Journal of Nursing Studies*, 44, 1250–1260.

Knight, R., Chabot, C. & Shoveller, J. 2017. *Qualitative Research with Young Men about Sexual Health*. London: SAGE Publications Ltd.

Koning, I. M., Harakeh, Z., Engels, R. C. M. E. & Vollebergh, W. A. M. 2010. A Comparison of Self-Reported Alcohol Use Measures by Early Adolescents: Questionnaires Versus Diary. *Journal of Substance Use*, 15, 166–173.

Miller, C. L. M. D., Kerr, T. P. D., Fischer, B. P. D., Zhang, R. M. S. & Wood, E. P. D. 2009. Methamphetamine Injection Independently Predicts Hepatitis C Infection Among Street-Involved Youth in a Canadian Setting. *Journal of Adolescent Health*, 44, 302–304.

Milligan, C. & Bartlett, R. 2019. Solicited Diary Methods. In: Liamputtong, P. (ed.) *Handbook of Research Methods in Health Social Sciences*. Singapore: Springer Singapore, pp. 1–18.

Oliffe, J. L., Kelly, M. T., Gonzalez Montaner, G. & Yu Ko, W. F. 2021. Zoom Interviews: Benefits and Concessions. *International Journal of Qualitative Methods*, https://doi.org/10.1177/16094069211053522.

Selfridge, M. & Mitchell, L. M. 2021. Social Media as Moral Laboratory: Street Involved Youth, Death and Grief. *Journal of Youth Studies*, 24, 531–546.

Staiano, A. E., Baker, C. M. & Calvert, S. L. 2012. Dietary Digital Diaries: Documenting Adolescents' Obesogenic Environment. *Environment and Behavior*, 44, 695–712.

Thomas, R. J., Ramanujam, K., Velusamy, V., et al. 2015. Comparison of Fieldworker Interview and a Pictorial Diary Method for Recording Morbidity of Infants in Semi-Urban Slums. *BMC Public Health*, 15, 43.

Wiederhold, B. K. 2020. Connecting Through Technology During the Coronavirus Disease 2019 Pandemic: Avoiding "Zoom Fatigue". *Cyberpsychology, Behavior and Social Networking*, 23, 437–438.

CHAPTER 5

"To Be or Not to Be?" Qualitative Research upon and during a Pandemic Outbreak

Gillie Gabay

Qualitative Research in a Pandemic

The COVID-19 pandemic is still unfolding, with vast public global health challenges and unsettling long-term threats to social stability, economic prosperity, and human health (Unadkat & Farquhar, 2020). Qualitative research focuses on the multifaceted presentations of overt and covert circumstances, in this case, coping with COVID-19. Although qualitative research has much to contribute to the knowledge on coping with medical emergencies, most studies on pandemics are quantitative (Vindrola-Padros et al., 2020). The scant qualitative research on health crises is mainly retrospective (Buchanan & Denyer, 2013). Designing and implementing rigorous qualitative research with members of front-line professions or with members of religious minorities, who may be already struggling during a pandemic, is challenging (Vindrola-Padros et al., 2020).

Beyond the challenge of giving voice to professionals and members of religious minorities, it is also challenging to provide actionable insights from qualitative studies in a timely manner (Johnson & Vindrola-Padros, 2017; Vindrola-Padros et al., 2020). While rapid qualitative studies have explored causes of the outbreak, health needs, and the utilization of health facilities, qualitative studies can also complement epidemiological and clinical studies (Teti et al., 2020; Shah et al., 2020; Van Bavel et al., 2020; Johnson & Vindrola-Padros, 2017). But guidelines of physical distancing, quarantine, time constraints, and mask wearing inhibit the ability to fulfill our responsibility as qualitative researchers, to collect data through face-to-face interviews or through focus groups (Teti, Pichon, & Myroniuk, 2021). Researchers may be a potential vehicle for the spread of COVID-19, forcing researchers to stay away from study populations (Annelli, 2020). Will we qualitative researchers be left out of the research arena in a crisis? Will we leave the research to quantitative researchers? We will not. Rather, the contrary is true. These extraordinary challenges that qualitative researchers encounter call for actions that differ from those of traditional methods of qualitative research. These novel actions open up opportunities for new methods. It is, therefore, essential to revisit qualitative methods of research and explore nontraditional ways to facilitate quantitative research for the dissemination of knowledge regarding experiences upon and during the outbreak of a pandemic.

This chapter is based on experience gained while conducting three qualitative narrative studies at the outbreak of the COVID-19 pandemic in Israel from March 2020 throughout its three waves. One study explored the lived experiences of front-line clinicians of COVID-19 divisions, who were struggling with overflowing hospitals and with caring for infected patients with a deadly virus for which there is no clinical protocol, under constraints of shortages of staff and equipment. The second study explored the lived experiences of a hidden population, members of the Ultra-Orthodox community, who refused to be hospitalized, as the law requires, in public hospitals and established alternative culture-adaptive underground home hospitals. The third study explored perceptions regarding science among Jewish Ultra-Orthodox males, exploring themes underlying refusal or hesitancy toward the COVID-19 vaccine. Below, I elaborate on the methods: recruiting participants, obtaining informed consent, conducting interviews, analyzing data, and ensuring quality criteria.

Recruiting Front-Line Health Professional or Members of Religious Minorities

For clinical directors of COVID-19 divisions, information regarding who the division directors are was provided by colleagues who are physicians. After retrieving cellphone numbers for the twenty-one division directors through social networks, I sent messages to each director, presenting the goal of the study in one sentence and asking for a 45-minute interview at a time of their choice. To my surprise, two thirds of the group responded positively. With the Jewish Ultra-Orthodox participants in both studies, the challenge pertained mostly to data accessibility and reliability (Cohen & Arieli, 2011). Since using standard sampling methods with hidden populations yields a high rate of nonresponse, I needed to adopt an appropriate sampling technique (Gabay & Shafran-Tikva, 2020; Salganik & Heckathorn, 2004). I therefore used an adaptive-sampling design selection procedure (Thompson & Collins, 2002).

Based on my experiences of interviewing insular communities such as Jewish Orthodox and traditional Muslim societies, I paid attention to specific aspects of Jewish Orthodox culture such as modesty, speech codes, and the need for rabbinic endorsement (Rier, Schwartzbaum, & Heller, 2008). Such characteristics of the Jewish Orthodox population influenced the studies on underground COVID-19 home hospitals, and on themes underlying behavioral intentions toward the COVID-19 vaccine. The unique characteristics of the community shaped the design, sampling, data collection, and interviewing protocols. The endorsement of the Rabbi, the religious authority, was critical for conducting the study and for recruiting participants, which were males only. Without the Rabbi's endorsement we would have had no cooperation. The ultra-Orthodox community is one of several sub-groups within the Orthodox community that, overall, has a range of attitudes regarding the role of women (Ringel, 2007). Orthodox Jewish women who study or work outside the boundaries of their community, moving in and between the 'secular' and 'religious' spaces of work and home, face restrictions regarding their gender-role expectations (Longman, 2008). Moreover, research on sensitive topics such as those studied is off limits to women, and therefore they cannot cooperate with researchers (Zalcberg, 2015).

Since being a secular woman was a major barrier to approaching Ultra-Orthodox males, who were the samples target of the studies, a male colleague assisted me in making connections with the community. My colleague had performed previous studies with members of the target population, and through his contacts I gained the trust of a Lithuanian rabbi, who served as a moderator, with whom I collaborated to plan the study and encourage willingness of community members to participate in the study. Interviews were conducted through the Zoom platform (Spreen, 1992). The rabbi-moderator's role was to make the connection between me, my colleague, and the participants. It was important that the rabbi endorses the studies and blesses their participation.

Initial Contact with Interviewees

I held a short phone conversation with each participant to introduce myself, explain the study goals and its methodology, and request minimal disturbances during the interviews (Lobe & Morgan, 2021). I assured those who agreed to participate that their contribution would be anonymized and confidential, and that I would conceal any information that may identify them (Morse, 2007). I scheduled interviews per their requests.

I informed participants that they could stop the interview at any point they choose, and they confirmed their understanding that parts of their interview might be published (Morse, 2007).

Obtaining Informed Consent

Given the above challenges, I asked the institutional ethics committee for rapid processing of granting me ethical approval. Upon receiving the approval, I compiled a digital informed consent form using 'Google Forms' and sent it (via WhatsApp) to the clinicians who had agreed to participate. Informed consent forms were faxed to representatives of the community who agreed to take the form to community members who had agreed to participate in the study, following the rabbi's endorsement, so they could sign it.

It was important to assure participants that their contribution would be anonymous and confidential, and that any information potentially linking their interview with their personal identity or the identity of the community/hospital with which they are affiliated would be concealed (Morse, 2007). Interviews were scheduled for a time that was most convenient for each participant. The interviewees were informed that they could stop the interview at any point. Upon beginning the interview, interviewees acknowledged their understanding that parts of their interview will be published (Morse, 2007).

Planning Interviews as the Outbreak Occurred

I complied with the quarantine imposed in Israel from March 15, 2020, for 41 days, during the first wave of the COVID-19 pandemic. Patient overflow in hospitals was heavy and leaders of COVID-19 divisions and of religious minorities were immersed in clinical work, managerial work, and addressing needs that emerged in the community. I faced recognized challenges of data collection in qualitative research during a health crisis and was unable to conduct face-to-face interviews (Teti, Pichon, & Myroniuk, 2021). As a qualitative researcher, however, my responsibility was to study the lived experiences of front-line clinicians and of members of minority populations during the breakout and in real time, rather than retrospectively (Rahaman, Tuckerman, Vorley, & Ghehehes, 2021). Given the above constraints of the pandemic, I adopted a digital, internet-based method (Zoom videoconferencing platform) for data collection as a means of conducting research that enables flexibility in time and space (Mirick &

Wladkowski, 2019). Zoom supports real-time audio and video, including recording and full-motion video, and has been extensively used for research (Archibald et al., 2019).

Participatory Research as a Pilot

Since virtual methods of interaction may alter the relationship between the researcher and participants, I conducted preliminary research by conducting trial interviews with representatives of the samples, front-line clinicians who were not part of the sample, and Ultra-Orthodox moderators, to test whether Zoom could serve as an adequate form of interaction for the research (Hall et al., 2021; Vindrola-Padros, 2021). Since participants in the pilot reported that the Zoom platform conveyed a sense of intimacy and enabled them to build trust, I concluded that using Zoom does not compromise effective communication with interviewees, although paying heed to body language through the Zoom platform is difficult.

The Procedure

All participants were already using Zoom for work sessions or for Torah studies. To the division directors, I sent a link for the interview on Zoom a few days in advance. No personal data was entered into the invitation. I canceled the Zoom recording function to assure confidentiality and recorded the interviews using an external recorder for transcribing the data (Anderson & Corneli, 2018). There was no 'waiting room' set up and the participants could only enter the Zoom meeting using a password we had produced. Interviewees did their best to ensure an adequate private space for the interview. To facilitate natural interaction during the interview, I used the video facility, which was more empathetic for participants and allowed me to pick up on nonverbal cues (Rahman et al., 2021). A wide bandwidth, adequate lighting, and the quality of the participants' video cameras, including among Ultra-Orthodox participants who had borrowed tablets and I-Pads for their Torah studies, enabled smooth interviews. I maintained the anonymity of participants in storing the data (Andersen & Corneli, 2018). I explained the goals and the methodology of the study and asked participants to minimize disturbances during the interviews (Lobe & Morgan, 2021). To elicit participants lived experiences under the constraints of the pandemic, the narrative interviews were shorter than is typical for narrative interviews (Zhang & Wildemuth, 2009).

Interviews Upon the Breakout of a Pandemic

While the focus on quality in research is mainly on the interview planning, theory, and analysis, the interaction between the interviewees and the interviewer, which is critical in collecting rich data and is essential for high-quality qualitative research, receives less attention (Mason, 2017). Studies on interviews outlined the interview steps and developed interview guidelines, framing the question, content, style, and wording of questions (Charmaz, 2014; Josselson, 2013; Lune & Berg, 2016; Mason, 2017; Tjora, 2018). All of these are important structural elements. However, the interaction itself, particularly in a crisis, is crucial to establishing interview–interviewer trust (Gabay, 2019). I worded one general, open-ended question to encourage participants to share a deep, unstructured narrative (Josselson, 2013). Most participants, in all three studies, responded with silence to the question and commented that it was a complex question. However, once they started sharing their experience, there was no need to elicit further details nor to amplify their answers; the barriers fell, and additional questions were not necessary (Josselson, 2013). Participants shared their stories while introspecting. I made every effort to make them feel that I was not judging them, and that they were accepted no matter what they said, or how they acted (Gabay, 2019).

High-quality listening enables interviewees to clarity their thoughts, gain insights, and share their reflections (Nemec et al., 2017). Studies that stress the importance of the interviewer–interviewee interaction are scant (Flick, 2018; Morse, 2020; Lavee & Itzchakov, 2021). Lavee and Itzchakov (2021) discuss listening as part of calibrating the interviewer as a human research instrument. Although interpersonal listening is fundamental to the quality of qualitative studies, there are few studies relating to this (Charmaz, 2014; Lune & Berg, 2016; McClelland, 2017; Lavee & Itzchakov, 2021). Interpersonal listening entails attention, comprehension, and relational components (Itzchakov, 2020; Kluger et al., 2021). Attention refers to being fully present, avoiding internal and external distractions (Ames et al., 2012). Comprehension refers to the extent to which the interviewer signals that they are understanding the interviewees. The relational facet refers to the good intentions that the listener needs to have toward the interviewee (e.g., acceptance, empathy, a nonjudgmental approach) (Itzchakov et al., 2017; Rogers & Roethlisberger, 1991).

Interpersonal listening must be active and, at times, multidimensional (Lune & Berg, 2016; McClelland, 2017). The relational facets require not only interpersonal listening but also intralistening as the interviewer self-explores their attitudes by looking at their authenticity, speech fluency, trust, self-disclosure, liking, open-mindedness, and self-insight (Bavelas et al., 2000; Huang et al., 2017; Itzchakov & Kluger, 2017; Lavee & Itzchakov, 2021; Ramsey & Sohi, 1997; Shannon, 2011; Weber et al., 2004). When speakers perceive good listening, they experience numerous emotional, cognitive, and behavioral benefits (Bodie, 2012; Itzchakov et al., 2018; Pollak et al., 2011). When interviewees perceive the interviewer as a good listener, they report emotional, cognitive, and behavioral benefits (Itzchakov et al., 2018). In a crisis, the reality in which the interviewees live is uncertain, ambiguous, volatile, and therefore threatening, and reality is threatening. I needed to acknowledge the uncertainties and complexities in the interviewees' worlds.

High-quality listening creates a safe space for interviewees, facilitating the emergence of contradictions and paradoxes that are important to understanding the complex phenomena that are explored during a crisis. Upon the outbreak of the pandemic, the thoughts of the interviewees were less focused at times, with disturbances throughout the interviews. I found the interviews, especially in light of the outbreak of the Covid crisis, to differ from regular interviews, as they were shorter and the data that I obtained was very rich, heavily depending on the interaction between me and the interviewees (McClelland, 2017).

My interpersonal and intrapersonal listening skills were key to obtaining rich data through in-depth interviews enhancing trustworthiness, credibility, and rigor – highlighting, again, that as a researcher I am a "human instrument" (Denzin & Lincoln, 2008; Lavee & Itzchakov, 2021; Lune & Berg, 2016; Morrow, 2005; Morse, 2020). I was aware of the potential difficulty in understanding what the interviewees were saying; I made every effort to be empathetic and nonjudgmental toward them and to treat them with respect. My nonverbal cues entailed constant eye contact, head nodding, pleasant facial expressions, and leaning forward. Beyond the challenge of recruitment and cooperation, I was aware that the interview is a process of meaning-making, and that I may not understand the meaning of the content from the interviewee's perspective, whether clinical directors of COVID-19 divisions at hospitals, Ultra-Orthodox male participants hospitalized in underground home hospitals, or Ultra-Orthodox males rejecting vaccinations. I was aware that their reality, perspective, and terminolog, may be unclear to me, and I needed to actively listen to decide when to ask for clarifications and avoid interpreting what they said based on my experiences or on media reports. I was cautious that my interpretation of what they said did not differ from the meaning that the interviewees were trying to convey (Lavee, 2017).

I needed to be aware of my inner dialogues before listening to the interviewees (Egan, 2013), and to become aware of possible judgments and disagreements with interviewees and put them aside, remembering that each interviewee is entitled to their own perception of reality, so judgments may cause poor listening and biased interpretations. It was important that I asked for examples to validate my understanding of their intended meaning. If there were no examples in their narrative to clarify their meaning, I stopped to paraphrase unclear content, to assure my understanding of their perspective.

Creating trust through the interview was also challenging. Nonverbal language, such as dress codes, may unconsciously insinuate a different, and perhaps a disrespectful, meaning. To demonstrate active listening, I offered interviewees appropriate nonverbal responses. I made sure my nonverbal language was congruent with the content they raised; I sent a nonverbal message of comfort and was empathetic (Lune & Berg, 2016). If interviewees had sensed that I was not actively listening, they may have become less fluent, strongly impacting my ability to obtain many supportive quotes (Pasupathi & Billitteri, 2015). During the interviews, there were moments of silence, perhaps to enable the participants to process their thoughts and feelings (Kumar & Cavallaro, 2018). I made no attempt to comment, ask questions, or judge what the participants said. I thanked all participants for their contribution.

Since the interviewees were from a different culture than mine, listening was key to making them feel psychologically safe, enabling me to delve "beneath the surface" (Charmaz, 2014; Castro et al., 2016; Itzchakov et al., 2016; Itzchakov, 2020; Itzchakov et al., 2017). High-quality, active, deliberate listening encompassed both hearing and understanding the perspective of the interviewees and their meaning. Lack of clarity may be natural in a time of a crisis. Therefore, I used silence to enable the processing of the interviewee and enhance their psychological safety by meeting their immediate needs, rather than asking more questions, guiding the interviewees, or filling the silence with words.

After the Interviews

After audio-recording all interviews, I transcribed them. Following data analysis, I translated the findings from Hebrew to English. Data was generated in a short window of time, and was collected rapidly

(Lancaster et al., 2020). The data analysis, however, took as long as was required. After each interview, I recorded the logistics, methodologic decisions, and my personal values, reflections, and insights (Guba & Lincoln, 1994).

Framing the Study

In quantitative and qualitative methods, the theoretical framework structures the study, supports its rationale, sets the research questions, and guides the hypotheses' development and exploring or testing the research questions. The theory provides a lens through which the researcher supports their thinking and their analysis of the data. Determining the theoretical framework is one of the most important stages in the research process. In contrast to quantitative studies, in qualitative studies the theory emerges from the data analysis. In a qualitative study a less structured theoretical framework is essential to avoiding preconceptions regarding the findings. The theoretical framework emerges from the data analysis. It is a conceptual framework that provides a logical structure of linked concepts within the theoretical framework. It is a way to identify and construct an epistemological and ontological view regarding the phenomenon under consideration. The conceptual framework defines concepts within the problem.

Data Analysis

I performed a thematic analysis, a qualitative method that fits well with my epistemology, with the theoretical anchor of each study and with the research questions for identifying, analyzing, organizing, describing, and reporting themes within data sets (Nowell et al., 2017; Saldaña, 2021). Thematic analysis is effective for exploring the perspectives of the participants, for highlighting similarities among them, and for generating unanticipated insights (Nowell et al., 2017). I familiarized myself with the data, reading it again and again, and generated initial code descriptions using inductive coding (Saldaña, 2021). I searched for themes and reviewed them. The data analysis process was iterative, reflective, and developed over time, involving constantly moving back and forth between analysis phases.

The generated themes and categories conveyed the meaning that participants intended to make. I identified links between the themes, produced a list of primary themes which captured participants' main concerns, and presented evidence using quotations from the interview. Elements derived from patterns within utterances, such as recurring meanings and feelings, were also marked as themes (Saldaña, 2021). By bringing together elements of lived experiences, which are often meaningless when viewed alone, I was able to make sense for each specific context of the studies.

Themes and behavior patterns emerged from the data through six analytical steps: I read and re-read the interviews and listed patterns of experiences through direct quotes. I then identified all data that related to the patterns already classified. I sorted all data according to the corresponding patterns. I combined and categorized related patterns into sub-themes to obtain a comprehensive view of the emerging patterns. I pieced together themes in a meaningful way to form a comprehensive picture representing participants' interpretation of their coping experience. The interviews revealed unanticipated themes, facilitating an in-depth understanding of the participants' reality from their perspective at the initial outbreak of an extreme health crisis. The unstructured narrative interviews relied on the interviewee's subjective, spontaneous responses to the question, thereby enabling an understanding of their perceptions without imposing any prior categorization which might narrow the field of inquiry (Josselson, 2013).

Maintaining Quality Standards in Qualitative Research in a Crisis

To ensure that findings are relevant and actionable, I aimed at collecting data in real time rather than retrospectively. I was transparent and disclosed the purpose of each study and the rights of participants. I asked how they felt, to create a sense of connectedness (Morse, 2015). I attempted to make participants feel comfortable as they shared their narrative. To capture the nature of each phenomenon, I took no shortcuts and spent extended time in data analysis, as required by the conservative qualitative research standards (Vindrola-Padros et al., 2020). Qualitative research has been criticized, relative to quantitative research, for lacking scientific rigor (Cope, 2014). Seminal research has developed criteria to assess the quality of qualitative research (Attride-Stirling, 2001; Guba & Lincoln, 1994; Walby & Luscombe, 2017). Researchers proposed quality criteria for qualitative research, covering credibility, transferability (thick data description), dependability, rigor, credibility, and confirmability that parallel the quantitative criteria of internal validity, external validity, and objectivity (Geertz, 1973; Lincoln & Guba, 2011; Tracy, 2010; Tracy & Hinrichs, 2017). Asking the right questions and wording the questions correctly affects quality as it invites the interviewee to share a complex narrative while eliciting openness and creating space for thinking and reflection

(Charmaz, 2014; Josselson, 2013). High-quality qualitative research encompasses a rigorous research design, interview preparation, wording of questions, richness of data, and theory and analysis that fit the ontology and epistemology of the researchers (Charmaz, 2014; Forrester & Sullivan, 2018; Lune & Berg, 2016; Mason, 2017; Tjora, 2018).

In a crisis, more so than under regular circumstances, I needed to be aware of my values regarding the issues at question and put them aside (resilience, vaccinations, COVID-19 hospitalizations). To calibrate myself as a human research instrument, I paid full attention to the interviewee throughout the interaction; I was fully present, and I withheld my thoughts, questions, and comments. Despite my own concerns, I remembered to focus throughout the in-depth, unstructured interviews, actively listening to the interviewees without judgment. This is harder said (or written) than done, and therefore requires much awareness and practice. The interviews revealed unanticipated themes, facilitating an in-depth understanding of the reality of the interviewees. The unstructured interviews relied on the interviewee's subjective, spontaneous responses to the question, thereby enabling us to understand their perceptions without imposing any prior categorization which might narrow our field of inquiry (Josselson, 2013). To capture the nature of the phenomenon, I took no shortcuts and spent extended time in data analysis, as required by the conservative qualitative research standards (Vindrola-Padros et al., 2020; Saldaña, 2021).

Finally, from the perspective of the researcher as a human instrument judging coding, theming, decontextualizing, and recontextualizing the data, rather than objective reality, I ensured that the coding creates trustworthiness through credibility, transferability, dependability, and confirmability (Guba & Lincoln, 1994). I recorded the study logistics, my methodological decisions, my personal values, my reflections after each of the interviews, and my insights (Guba & Lincoln, 1994).

Conclusion

These qualitative studies, performed at the outbreak of COVID-19 and through its three waves in Israel, highlight the importance of qualitative research during times of crisis. Interviewees reflected upon the resources they developed, the actions they took, and the lessons they learned. They shared their personal and community voice, enhancing their reflections as they faced adversity in a complex new situation (Vindrola-Padros et al., 2020). The cultural attributes of the interviewees may have influenced the findings. Also, there may be a potential lack of picking up on nonverbal cues that were not discernible via the Zoom interviews (Weller, 2017). This chapter illustrates methods by which, despite various challenges, qualitative research can be performed rigorously at the outbreak of a pandemic and across its waves. Participants viewed the interviews as an important, rare, private time for reflection under the circumstances of the pandemic and its dynamics. I feel grateful for the privilege of being there, at the right time and place. I am very thankful for the attention, time, and contribution of all participants. "To be or not to be?" The answer is, indeed, to be.

Reference

Ames D, Maissen LB, & Brockner J (2012) The role of listening in interpersonal influence. *Journal of Research in Personality*, 46(3): 345–349.

Anderson E, & Corneli A (2018) 100 Questions (and answers) about research ethics (Vol. 5). SAGE Publications.

Annelli C (2020) Teachers, students and social margins on the Italian screen. *Italica*, 97(1).

Archibald MM, Ambagtsheer RC, Casey MG, & Lawless M (2019) Using Zoom videoconferencing for qualitative data collection: Perceptions and experiences of researchers and participants. *International Journal of Qualitative Methods*, 18: 1609406919874596.

Attride-Stirling J (2001) Thematic networks: An analytic tool for qualitative research. *Qualitative Research*, 1(3): 385–405.

Bavelas JB, Coates L, & Johnson T (2000) Listeners as co-narrators. *Journal of Personality and Social Psychology*, 79(6): 941.

Bodie GD (2012) Listening as positive communication. In Socha T & Pitts M (eds) *The Positive Side of Interpersonal Communication*. New York: Peter Lang Publishing Inc., 109–125.

Castro DR, Kluger AN, & Itzchakov G (2016) Does avoidance-attachment style attenuate the benefits of being listened to? *European Journal of Social Psychology*, 46(6): 762–775.

Charmaz K (2014) *Constructing Grounded Theory*. Thousand Oaks: Sage.

Cohen N, & Arieli T (2011) Field research in conflict environments: Methodological challenges and snowball sampling. *Journal of Peace Research*, 48(4): 423–435.

Cope DG (2014) Methods and meanings: Credibility and trustworthiness of qualitative research. *Oncology Nursing Forum*, 41(1): 89–91.

Denzin NK, & Lincoln YS (2008) Introduction: The Discipline and Practice of Qualitative Research. In Denzin NK & Lincoln YS (eds) *The Sage Handbook of Qualitative Research*. Thousand Oaks: Sage, 1–32.

Egan G (2013) *The Skilled Helper: A Problem-Management and Opportunity-Development Approach to Helping*. Chicago: Cengage Learning.

Flick U (2018) *Designing Qualitative Research*. Thousand Oaks: Sage.

64   GABAY

Forrester MA, & Sullivan C (2018) *Doing Qualitative Research in Psychology: A Practical Guide*. Thousand Oaks: Sage Publications Limited.

Gabay G (2019) Patient self-worth and communication barriers to trust of Israeli patients in acute-care physicians at public general hospitals. *Qualitative Health Research*, 29(13): 1954–1966.

Gabay G, & Shafran-Tikva S (2020) Sexual harassment of nurses by patients and missed nursing care: A hidden population study. *Journal of Nursing Management*, 28(8): 1881–1887.

Guba EG, & Lincoln YS (1994) Competing paradigms in qualitative research. *Handbook of Qualitative Research*, 2(163–194): 105.

Hall J, Gaved M, & Sargent J (2021) Participatory research approaches in times of Covid-19: A narrative literature review. *International Journal of Qualitative Methods*, 20: 16094069211010087.

Huang K, Yeomans M, Brooks AW, et al. (2017) It doesn't hurt to ask: Question-asking increases liking. *Journal of Personality and Social Psychology*, 113(3): 430.

Itzchakov G, & Kluger AN (2017) Can holding a stick improve listening at work? The effect of Listening Circles on employees' emotions and cognitions. *European Journal of Work and Organizational Psychology*, 26(5): 663–676.

Itzchakov G & Kluger AN (2019) Changing the other party's attitude with high quality listening. In Schneider A & Honeyman C (eds) *Negotiation Essentials for Lawyers*. American Bar Association, 129–134.

Itzchakov G, Castro DR, & Kluger A (2016) If you want people to listen to you, tell a story. *International Journal of Listening*, 30(3): 120–133.

Itzchakov G, DeMarree KG, Kluger AN, et al. (2018) The listener sets the tone: High-quality listening increases attitude clarity and behavior-intention consequences. *Personality and Social Psychology Bulletin*, 44(5): 762–778.

Itzchakov G, Kluger AN, & Castro DR (2017) I am aware of my inconsistencies but can tolerate them: The effect of high-quality listening on speakers' attitude ambivalence. *Personality and Social Psychology Bulletin*, 43(1): 105–120.

Itzchakov G, Kluger A, Emanuel-Tor M, et al. (2014) How do you like me to listen to you? *International Journal of Listening*, 28(3) 177–185.

Itzchakov G (2020) Can listening training empower service employees? The mediating roles of anxiety and perspective-taking. *European Journal of Work and Organizational Psychology*, 29(6): 938–952.

Johnson GA, & Vindrola-Padros C (2017) Rapid qualitative research methods during complex health emergencies: A systematic review of the literature. *Social Science & Medicine*, 189, 63–75. https://doi.org/10.1016/j.socscimed.2017.07.029

Josselson R (2013) *Interviewing for Qualitative Inquiry: A Relational Approach*. New York: Guilford Press.

Kluger A, Malloy TE, Pery S, et al. (2021) Dyadic listening in teams: Social relations model. *Applied Psychology: An International Review*, 70(3): 1045–1099.

Kumar S, & Cavallaro L (2018) Researcher self-care in emotionally demanding research: A proposed conceptual framework. *Qualitative Health Research*, 28(4): 648–658.

Lancaster K, Rhodes T, & Rosengarten M (2020) Making evidence and policy in public health emergencies: Lessons from COVID-19 for adaptive evidence-making and intervention. *Evidence and Policy*, 16(3): 477–490.

Lavee E (2017) Low-income women's encounters with social services: Negotiation over power, knowledge and respectability. *British Journal of Social Work*, 47(5): 1554–1571.

Lavee E, & Itzchakov G (2021) Good listening: A key element in establishing quality in qualitative research. *Qualitative Research*, 14687941211039402.

Lincoln YS, Lynham SA, & Guba EG (2011) Paradigmatic controversies, contradictions, and emerging confluences, revisited. *The Sage Handbook of Qualitative Research*, 4(2), 97–128.

Lobe B, & Morgan DL (2021) Assessing the effectiveness of video-based interviewing: A systematic comparison of video-conferencing based dyadic interviews and focus groups. *International Journal of Social Research Methodology*, 24(3): 301–312.

Longman C (2008) Sacrificing the career or the family?: Orthodox Jewish women between secular work and the sacred home. *The European Journal of Women's Studies*, 15(3), 223–239.

Lune H, & Berg BL (2016) *Qualitative Research Methods for the Social Sciences*. 8th ed. Long Beach: Pearson Education.

Mason J (2017) *Qualitative Researching*. Thousand Oaks: Sage.

Mays N, & Pope C (2020) Quality in qualitative research. In *Qualitative Research in Health Care*. 4th ed. New Jersey: Wiley, 211–233.

McClelland SI (2017) Vulnerable listening: Possibilities and challenges of doing qualitative research. *Qualitative Psychology*, 4(3): 338.

Mirick RG, & Wladkowski SP (2019) Skype in qualitative interviews: Participant and researcher perspectives. *The Qualitative Report*, 24(12): 3061–3072.

Morrow SL (2005) Quality and trustworthiness in qualitative research in counseling psychology. *Journal of Counseling Psychology*, 52(2): 250.

Morse J (2020) The changing face of qualitative inquiry. *International Journal of Qualitative Methods*, 19: 1–7.

Morse JM (2007) Ethics in action: Ethical principles for doing qualitative health research. *Qualitative Health Research*, 17(8): 1003–1005.

Morse JM (2015) Critical analysis of strategies for determining rigor in qualitative inquiry. *Qualitative Health Research*, 25(9): 1212–1222.

Nemec PB, Spagnolo AC, & Soydan AS (2017) Can you hear me now? Teaching listening skills. *Psychiatric Rehabilitation Journal*, 40(4): 415.

Nowell LS, Norris JM, White DE, & Moules NJ (2017) Thematic analysis: Striving to meet the trustworthiness criteria. *International Journal of Qualitative Methods*, 16(1): 1609406917733847.

Pasupathi M, & Billitteri J (2015) Being and becoming through being heard: Listener effects on stories and selves. *International Journal of Listening*, 29(2): 67–84.

Pollak KI, Alexander SC, Tulsky JA, et al. (2011) Physician empathy and listening: associations with patient satisfaction and autonomy. *The Journal of the American Board of Family Medicine*, 24(6): 665–672.

Rahman SA, Tuckerman L, Vorley T, & Gherhes C (2021) Resilient research in the field: Insights and lessons from adapting qualitative research projects during the COVID-19 pandemic. *International Journal of Qualitative Methods*, 20, 16094069211016106.

Ramsey RP, & Sohi RS (1997) Listening to your customers: The impact of perceived salesperson listening behavior on relationship outcomes. *Journal of the Academy of marketing Science*, 25(2): 127.

Rier DA, Schwartzbaum A, & Heller C (2008) Methodological issues in studying an insular, traditional population: A women's health survey among Israeli Haredi (ultra-Orthodox) Jews. *Women & Health*, 48(4): 363–381.

Ringel S (2007) Identity and gender roles of Orthodox Jewish women: Implications for social work practice. *Smith College Studies in Social Work*, 77 (2–3): 25–44.

Rogers CR, & Roethlisberger FJ (1991) HBR classic – barriers and gateways to communication (Reprinted from Harvard Business Review, 1952). *Harvard Business Review*, 69(6): 105–111.

Saldaña J (2021) *The Coding Manual for Qualitative Researchers*. Sage.

Salganik MJ, & Heckathorn DD (2004) Sampling and estimation in hidden populations using respondent-driven sampling. *Sociological Methodology*, 34(1): 193–240.

Shah K, Abdeljawad T, Mahariq I, & Jarad F (2020) Qualitative analysis of a mathematical model in the time of COVID-19. *BioMed Research International*, 2020. https://doi.org/10.1155/2020/5098598

Shannon MT (2011) Please hear what I'm not saying: The art of listening in the clinical encounter. *The Permanente Journal*, 15(2): 114–117.

Spreen M (1992) Rare populations, hidden populations, and link-tracing designs: What and why? *Bulletin of Sociological Methodology/Bulletin de Methodologie Sociologique*, 36(1): 34–58.

Sullivan W (2008) *Clean Language: Revealing Metaphors and Opening Minds*. New York: Crown House Publishing.

Teti M, Schatz E, & Liebenberg L (2020) Methods in the Time of COVID-19: The vital role of qualitative inquiries. *International Journal of Qualitative Research*, 19. https://doi.org/10.1177/1609406920920962.

Teti M, Pichon L & Myroniuk TW (2021) Community-engaged qualitative scholarship during a pandemic: Problems, perils and lessons learned. *International Journal of Qualitative Methods*, 20, 16094069211025455.

Thompson SK, & Collins LM (2002) Adaptive sampling in research on risk-related behaviors. *Drug and Alcohol Dependence*, 68, 57–67.

Tjora A (2018) *Qualitative Research as Stepwise-Deductive Induction*. Abingdon: Routledge.

Tracy SJ, & Hinrichs MM (2017) Big tent criteria for qualitative quality. *The International Encyclopedia of Communication Research Methods*, 1–10. http://dx .doi.org/10.1002/9781118901731.iecrm0016.

Tracy SJ (2010) Qualitative quality: Eight "big-tent" criteria for excellent qualitative research. *Qualitative Inquiry*, 16(10): 837–851.

Unadkat S, & Farquhar M (2020) Doctors' wellbeing: Self-care during the Covid-19 pandemic. *BMJ*, 368. https://doi.org/10.1136/bmj.m1150.

Van Bavel JJ, Baicker K, Boggio PS, et al. (2020) Using social and behavioral science to support COVID-19 pandemic response. *Nature Human Behavior*, 1–12. doi.org/10.1038/s41562-020-0884-z.

Vindrola-Padros C, Chisnall G, Cooper S, et al. (2020) Carrying out rapid qualitative research during a pandemic: Emerging lessons from COVID-19. *Qualitative Health Research*, 30(14): 2192–2204. https://doi.org/10.1177/1049732320951526.

Vindrola-Padros C, & Johnson GA (2020) Rapid techniques in qualitative research: A critical review of the literature. *Qualitative Health Research*, 30(10): 1596–1604. doi.org/10.1177/1049732320921835.

Walby K, & Luscombe A (2017) Criteria for quality in qualitative research and use of freedom of information requests in the social sciences. *Qualitative Research*, 17(5): 537–553.

Weber K, Johnson A, & Corrigan M (2004) Communicating emotional support and its relationship to feelings of being understood, trust, and self-disclosure. *Communication Research Reports*, 21(3): 316–323.

Weller S (2017) Using internet video calls in qualitative (longitudinal) interviews: Some implications for rapport. *International Journal of Social Research Methodology*, 20(6): 613–625

Zalcberg S (2015) "They won't speak to me, but they will talk to you": On the challenges facing a woman researcher doing fieldwork among male Ultra-Orthodox victims of sexual abuse. *Nashim: A Journal of Jewish Women's Studies & Gender Issues* (29): 108–132.

Zhang Y, & Wildemuth BM (2009) Unstructured interviews. In Wildemuth B. (ed.) *Applications of Social Research Methods to Questions in Information and Library Science* (pp. 222–231). Santa Barbara: Libraries Unlimited.

CHAPTER 6

Adopting Digital Methods
Conducting Qualitative Interviews and Focus Groups in the Midst of a Pandemic

Ruth Strudwick and Hollie Hadwen

This chapter will explore the theory underpinning qualitative methods, namely semi-structured interviews and focus groups, and issues of methodological coherence in adopting a digital approach.

Punctuated by reference to contemporary literature, we will offer an in-depth exploration of the practical considerations of adopting digital methods. This will include the challenges of building a rapport with the participant (particularly given the potential for discussion of sensitive issues), familiarity with technology for both researcher and participant, scheduling (in terms of time and location), and data protection issues (including the potential for video recording, the legalities of data storage, and the impact this has upon the choice of videoconferencing platform). We will go on to explore pertinent ethical considerations, including institutional approval, informed consent, confidentiality, and the ongoing ethical responsibilities of the researcher engaged in qualitative research.

We will draw upon our experiences of using synchronous online video-conferencing platforms to conduct semi-structured interviews and focus groups, integrating our reflections throughout. Whilst necessitated by the Covid-19 pandemic, the associated need for social distancing, and the potential for further regional restrictions being imposed, we argue that our experiences of adopting digital methods transcend the current global situation, offering opportunities to facilitate qualitative research that may extend beyond geographical borders, attenuate fiscal limitations, and enable greater collaboration between researchers.

Theoretical and Methodological Considerations

The qualitative researcher is interested in and enquires into the meaning that individuals or groups ascribe to a social or human problem; qualitative research allows for the exploration of people's thoughts, feelings, and ideas (Creswell, 2007). Qualitative methods provide further insight into and rich data about complex issues, exploring meanings rather than the 'hard facts' that quantitative research seeks. Qualitative researchers use different data collection methods to understand and extract data about the topic they are studying. These data sources include participant observation, semi-structured interviews, focus groups, questionnaires, and the study of artefacts such as books or works of art. This chapter will focus on the use of semi-structured interviews and focus groups as qualitative data collection methods.

Interviews are used as a data collection method to gain insights into a person's subjective experiences, opinions, and motivations rather than facts or behaviours. They are used to describe and understand meanings (Kvale, 1996), providing rich and detailed data (Bowling, 2004). It could be argued that interviews are largely subjective and that the interviewer can influence the participants to answer in a certain way, such as by using leading questions and through probing. Therefore, qualitative researchers need to be reflexive in their data collection and be aware that there could be a tendency towards bias both in the selection of the participants that are interviewed and the way in which the interviews are carried out. No two interviews in a research study will be the same, as each of the participants will answer the question in a different way, and so the researcher needs to have an awareness of how they could 'lead' the participant and take steps to reduce bias.

Interviews can take several different forms. They may be distinguished by the degree to which they are structured; for example, a structured interview would follow set questions in a predetermined order, almost like reading a questionnaire, whereas an unstructured interview may have one or two questions or areas for discussion but allow the participant to speak freely about a topic, and a semi-structured interview, which is the most commonly used format, has open questions which follow an interview guide but still allow the participant to speak freely about their own opinions and experiences. Qualitative interviews are interactive and the researcher can adapt to the participant's responses, allowing for unexpected responses or topics to also be considered. Interviews are usually audio recorded to facilitate verbatim transcription, and may be video recorded, to enable subsequent analysis of non-verbal communication (Coolican, 2019).

Focus groups are group interviews which explore participants' expertise and experiences and seek to find out how and why people behave in certain ways. Participants interact with one another and with the facilitator during a focus group and group dynamics are used to stimulate discussion. The interaction between participants is key and can generate ideas and rich data. Participants can explore and clarify their views during the focus group discussion (Kitzinger, 1996). Focus groups usually consist of between four and eight people and are led by a moderator. The moderator might be the researcher, or they may be someone independent from the research. An independent moderator may be used if the researcher knows the participants and does not want this to influence the discussion. There is usually an interview guide or series of questions to pose to the group. As for a qualitative interview, the focus group can be audio or video recorded. Focus groups are useful for bringing together homogeneous groups of participants who have expertise in and experience of the topic, and about which they can share detailed information and discuss their thoughts and feelings. Focus groups allow for sharing and comparison of experiences amongst the participants and can be used to gain consensus. In focus groups the moderator will need to be aware that participants may seek approval from other participants and be influenced by the group; therefore, they may not express their opinions because they may not wish to show disagreement with other participants. Focus groups can be dominated by highly vocal participants, and thus the moderator should encourage all participants to speak and to moderate contributions from more dominant participants. Like individual interviews, focus groups can also be prone to bias and subjectivity. The researcher needs to be aware of this, and the use of an independent moderator may go some way to reducing bias and subjectivity.

As acknowledged earlier, the qualitative researcher must adopt a reflexive approach throughout: from the initial idea and formulation of the research question through to the data analysis and write up. In her current research exploring educator experiences of supporting students with pastoral needs, author HH occupies the dual role of practitioner (educator) and researcher (doctoral student), and thus may be considered an 'insider' as she has chosen to study a group to which she belongs (Breen, 2007). Whilst this may offer some advantages in terms of access to and familiarity with the social setting, politics, and complexity of pre-registration professional healthcare education in British universities, along with a level of acceptance from participants that may serve to promote openness (Dwyer and Buckle, 2009), it also presents challenges for conducting effective interviews. As an educator with pastoral responsibilities, there is a risk of making assumptions about the meaning of events for participants, or, conversely, the participant assuming the researcher's understanding (Unluer, 2012). This closeness underlines the importance of identifying and reflecting upon one's own experiences, assumptions, and preconceptions, to engage with the experiences of participants on their own terms (Larkin and Thompson, 2012).

There are different approaches to reflexivity, with many researchers maintaining a reflexive journal. Author HH found a bracketing interview of value in preparing for qualitative interviews, in which her primary supervisor interviewed her using the draft semi-structured interview schedule. Bracketing interviews have been used by other researchers to increase researcher self-awareness (Boddy et al., 2016; Walker et al., 2017). Author HH found that this enabled her to gain a better appreciation of her assumptions and feelings about providing pastoral support and led to a rewording of the prompts and probes to avoid leading the participant.

Whichever approach to reflexivity is adopted, this should be meaningful and encourage the researcher to consider the impact of the self on the interview or focus group. The researcher should reflect upon the impact of using online means to collect data, our thoughts upon which are explored in the practical considerations section of the chapter.

In summary, it is not advisable to simply perform a 'direct swap' from interviews or focus groups conducted in-person to online, as there are some key differences which need to be considered and accounted for, which we discuss in the next section ('Practical Considerations'). The researcher needs to be assured that a change to digital methods will not change the focus and coherence of their methodology. The online interviews or focus groups still need to enable the collection of data in the way that was originally intended in order to answer the research question.

Practical Considerations

In this section, we discuss some of the practical considerations associated with using digital methods to collect qualitative data. It should be noted at this point that there is a plethora of online approaches to data collection, ranging from asynchronous, text-based methods, such as email, to synchronous, audio-visual methods, such as those afforded by the videoconferencing platforms Microsoft Teams, Skype, and Zoom.

Practical considerations include, but are not limited to, building a rapport with the participant (particularly given the potential for the discussion of sensitive issues), familiarity with technology for both researcher and participant, scheduling in terms of time and location, and data protection issues, including the potential for video recording, the legalities of data storage, and the impact this has upon the choice of videoconferencing platform.

Our most recent research has employed the videoconferencing platform Microsoft Teams, and thus the ensuing discussion focusses upon our experiences of using synchronous, audio-visual methods.

Building a Rapport With the Participant

There are challenges in building a rapport with participants via an online platform, particularly if you are planning to discuss sensitive issues. Eye contact is more problematic as you are not always able to make direct eye contact with one another as it is difficult to look at the camera and be able to see the person or people on the screen too. This makes non-verbal communication more difficult to perceive and interpret, particularly if there are several people on screen at the same time in a focus group. This could mean that the words used by a participant, or the researcher, are misinterpreted by those listening as they are not reinforced by non-verbal cues. Participants may choose to turn their camera off, which makes establishing rapport even more challenging. We would advocate encouraging participants to keep their cameras on wherever possible; however, this does raise a further issue of privacy, as is discussed later in the chapter.

Having the preferred names of those taking part on the screen underneath or alongside people's image can be helpful; this is particularly useful in a focus group when participants have not met one another before and therefore do not know each other's names. Having names on the screen serves as a reminder and can also help the researcher to remember names and assist everyone in referring to one another by name. This is not always possible in an in-person focus group or interview, unless name labels are used. Clearly names will need to be removed from the transcript, but knowing people's names during a focus group does help the conversation to flow and allows for better interaction between and rapport with participants.

Qualitative research requires the interviewer to listen attentively and to avoid interrupting the participant (Hinton and Ryan, 2020). When utilising digital methods, there can be issues with brief time delays and subtle non-verbal cues being missed, which mean that participants and researchers may unintentionally interrupt one another. This is because it is often difficult to gauge when someone has finished speaking or when someone wants to start speaking. The interviewer may therefore not be able to be so attentive to the participant in this situation. This can also make it more challenging to moderate a focus group, as non-verbal cues are not always perceived, and it can prove difficult to stop people talking if they are dominating the group. Author RS found the absence of direct eye contact to be one of the biggest challenges when conducting online focus groups in comparison to doing so in person.

Supporting the Participant Experiencing Distress

The emergent and sometimes unpredictable nature of qualitative research interviews and focus groups can lead to participants becoming upset or distressed (Jolley, 2020). If a participant does become upset, this is not easy to manage online. As researchers, we have a duty of care to our participants and need to consider how we will deal with distressed participants and what we can do to support them when we are geographically remote. As identified later in the chapter, some safeguards need to be put in place beforehand that participants are aware of (e.g. counselling), should they need support after the interview/focus group. One of author HH's participants became distressed during an online interview when recalling a specific experience. As a researcher, a health care professional and an individual, she found it difficult to support the participant remotely. She felt uncomfortable and somewhat powerless in that situation, as she was less able to convey compassion through non-verbal communication over Microsoft Teams. She allowed the participant time to compose herself and offered her the opportunity to take a break, but the participant was happy to continue. At the end of the interview, the audio recording was paused, and the participant debriefed. The debrief, which was not included within the data analysis, provided HH with an opportunity to ensure the participant had recovered and to direct them towards more formal support (e.g. the participant's employer's occupational health service) should this be required.

Access to and Familiarity With Technology

Access to technology and the internet is often cited as a barrier to adopting digital methods in qualitative research (Cohen, Mannion, and Morrison, 2018); however, we would argue that the onus should be on the researcher to consider the characteristics of the population of interest when planning their approach. The Office for National Statistics (ONS) states that, as of February 2020, 96 per cent of households in Great Britain have access to the internet, up from only 57 per cent in 2006 (ONS, 2021a). This suggests that it is becoming more feasible to conduct interviews and focus groups using videoconferencing platforms within England, Scotland, and Wales. For example, in seeking to explore the lived experience of diagnostic radiography educators employed by higher education institutions in the United Kingdom during the autumn of 2020, author HH conducted semi-structured interviews over Microsoft Teams. The decision to employ digital methods was thought to be achievable, given that all educators had been working remotely since March 2020 when the first national lockdown began. In drafting the research proposal for submission to the local Research Ethics Committee (REC), it was noted that the majority of educators would have access to suitable technology and the internet, both at home and at their place of work.

Whilst 99 per cent of 16- to 44-year-olds in the United Kingdom are recent users of the internet, this drops to only 54 per cent in adults over the age of 75 (ONS, 2021b). This may pose challenges to researchers contemplating using digital methods to explore the experiences, perspectives, and opinions of older people. Similarly, only 81 per cent of adults living with a disability are recent internet users (ONS, 2021b), meaning that almost one-fifth of the population of interest may be unintentionally excluded from participating, thereby affecting the credibility and transferability of the study. Age and disability are not the only factors affecting internet access. The UK Consumer Digital Index (Lloyds Bank, 2019) highlights that 71 per cent of those considered to be 'offline' (defined as not having used the internet in the last three months) have no more than secondary school education and 47 per cent are from low-income households.

Although an in-depth discussion of digital exclusion is beyond the scope of this chapter, the 'Digital Divide', defined as the 'gap between those able to benefit from the digital age and those who are not' (Chan, 2021: 4), must be borne in the qualitative researcher's mind. A lack of access to technology, to the internet, and/or limited digital literacy leads to economic, social, and educational inequalities, and, when employing digital methods in qualitative research, may result in the experiences, perspectives, and opinions of the offline population not being heard.

Access to technology and the internet is the not the only factor that must be considered; the researcher must also explore the preferences of their participants. Author RS recently conducted a qualitative study with participants over the age of 65, none of whom wanted to participate in online focus groups during the Covid-19 pandemic. When the pandemic began, they were given the choice to move the focus groups from being conducted in-person to an online platform. However, they were all happy to wait until restrictions had eased and have in-person focus groups, as they felt more comfortable with this and were concerned about the use of online platforms. Although their preference for waiting until it was feasible to meet in a shared physical environment delayed the progress of this funded research, it is a stark reminder to the qualitative researcher that although it may be possible to collect data using digital methods, this does not mean their participants will necessarily be amenable to this as an approach.

There may also be difficulties with using technology; the researcher needs to be familiar with their chosen platform and its functionality. For this reason, we would advocate using one of the more common videoconferencing platforms wherever possible, a recommendation echoed by Cohen, Manion, and Morrison (2018). In addition to having access to the suite of software (e.g. Microsoft Office) or the ability to download the platform (e.g. Zoom), participants will also need to have some knowledge of how to use the platform in order to log on and take part in the research. Therefore, it is advantageous to arrange to 'meet' in advance, using the same technology as intended for the interview or focus group. In addition to being able to use this as an opportunity to ensure the participant is fully informed, this approach offers the prospective participant and researcher the opportunity to test the use of the technology prior to collecting data, recognising that preparation is important prior to conducting qualitative research interviews (McGrath, Palmgren, and Liljedahl, 2019). Given that access to and familiarity with technology is often cited as a limitation of digital methods, this should allow any technical difficulties to be addressed prior to data collection. Author HH has found that this informal 'meet' also enabled her to begin to build a relationship with the participant, which is beneficial given that rapport is essential when interviewing (Finlay, 2011).

Internet connectivity could be an issue if someone has a slow connection (Cohen, Mannion and Morrison, 2018), if their internet signal 'drops out', or if there is poor-quality audio or video quality. Poor-quality audio can result in issues with recording and subsequent transcription of data. As noted previously, we would recommend testing the platform and ensuring wherever possible that participants are able to connect prior to scheduling the actual interview or focus group itself. It is important to acknowledge that despite one's best efforts and plans, the unexpected can also happen. For example, during an online focus group conducted by author RS, one of the participants had a power cut at their home, and so they disappeared from the focus group in the middle of speaking. They were unable to log back in and sent an email to explain this after the event. Author HH also had technological difficulties with one of her interviews. There was an echo during the interview which was resolved when she and the participant wore headphones. The interview progressed well; however, the recording of the interview failed, with only the researcher being audible, meaning she was unable to hear or transcribe the participant's talk. Following a discussion with her research supervisors, she approached the participant to explain the situation and ask if they would be willing to be interviewed again, which they were. Such technical difficulties were an important reminder to HH that one must be familiar with all technological aspects of the interview process in order to adopt digital methods effectively.

Scheduling Considerations

The scheduling of online interviews and focus groups is also different from meeting face-to-face in a shared physical environment. Conducting research interactions over a secure videoconferencing platform may offer welcome flexibility in terms of scheduling for both participant and researcher, with opportunities to conduct research at mutually convenient times (e.g. in the evening or at the weekend) and around other commitments (e.g. caring responsibilities or employment). When interviewing educators employed at higher education institutions, author HH noted that Microsoft Teams enabled her to schedule interviews around the busy diaries of her participants without needing to incorporate travel and contingency time.

Conversely, arranging interviews or focus groups in-person requires a suitable location to be planned, such as a room booked at the university, hospital, or organisation in which the study is being conducted. Whilst this can present logistical challenges, it may ensure that the research is conducted in a suitably professional setting. Nevertheless, a location deemed professional by the researcher may have a negative effect upon the participant, as perceived power differentials may have an impact upon the way in which the participant views the researcher (Hinton and Ryan, 2020) and, subsequently, the information they are willing to share. Offering the participant the opportunity to participate online enables them to choose a location in which they feel comfortable and at ease. However, in enabling participants to choose to take part from their home or their workplace, there are potential distractions and other issues. The participant could be called away and may not give the interview/focus group their full attention as they would if they were in a neutral setting in-person. There may be distractions in the background, and this can be off-putting to both

researchers and participants. Author HH found that two of her participants became distracted during the interviews she conducted on Microsoft
Teams. Whilst working from the spare room of her home during the
pandemic, the corner of a wrought iron bedstead was visible. One of her
participants mistook this for a music stand and proceeded to enquire about
which instrument she played. On another occasion her dog jumped onto
the bed, becoming visible on the screen. This caused the interview to go off
on a tangent, with the participant asking about the researcher's dog and
talking about her own. Whilst these were only minor interruptions, they
served to disrupt the flow of the conversation within the interview. Author
RS has also experienced participants being distracted as they were taking
part in an online focus group from their place of work, so on occasions they
were speaking to colleagues or were called away from the screen. This
meant that they were not able to give the focus group discussions their full
attention. There were also items visible in the background at their place of
work. This highlights two areas for consideration: privacy and professionalism. Whilst the appearance of author HH's dog was not overly problematic, one must consider what background items are visible to the
participant, as well as the professionalism this conveys. For example, we
would argue that neither interviews nor focus groups conducted by health
care professionals should be undertaken in a clinical area where confidential patient information may be visible to the participant. In addition, and
wherever possible, a simple background effect should be employed: for
example, both Microsoft Teams and Zoom offer the option to blur the
background.

One of the benefits of conducting interviews and focus groups using an
online platform is the reduction in travel time and costs for both
researchers and participants. This may also result in easier recruitment of
participants as the time they need to commit may be reduced and hence
participation may be more convenient for them. As a researcher this could
potentially have a positive impact on the study, especially if funding is
a concern, as online interviews and focus groups will be less costly for all
involved.

Data Collection and Management

To video record or not to video record? As previously noted, interviews and
focus groups are routinely audio recorded to capture the richness of the
participant's words, thus facilitating accurate, verbatim transcription.
Whilst video recording may be used to aid the researcher in evaluating

non-verbal communication during data analysis (Coolican, 2019), the capture of video data must be justified.

Videoconferencing platforms such as Zoom and Microsoft Teams enable simultaneous audio and video recording of the interview or focus group. Whilst the relative ease with which this is possible may appear to be advantageous, both audio and video recording require the informed consent of the participant. We would encourage the researcher to consider whether they could justify video recording the interview or focus group had it taken place in person. Author RS used both audio and video recording in her study, as the non-verbal communication and interactions were seen to be important for the online focus group and as part of the data collected. We would argue that video capture is more useful for focus groups than one-to-one interviews, as group interactions are part of the data collected. Author HH chose only to audio record her online interviews as video recording would not form part of her data analysis and thus could not be justified. Furthermore, this enhanced the privacy of the participant and enabled her to uphold the third principle of the Data Protection Act 2018, in which the data collected 'must be adequate, relevant and not excessive in relation to the purpose for which it is processed' (Data Protection Act 2018).

These practical aspects need to be considered before commencing data collection in order to ensure that the interview or focus group is effective.

Ethical Considerations

In this section, we discuss the initial ethical approval process, before exploring issues of ethical research practice in relation to digital methods. It is worth noting that the qualitative researcher must satisfy the requirements of the relevant Research Ethics Committee (REC) or Institutional Review Board (IRB); thus, the authors strongly encourage the reader to discuss individual requirements with their research supervisor and/or local research and development office. For research undertaken in the National Health Service (NHS) in the United Kingdom, the Research Ethics Service (RES) is one of the core functions of the NHS Health Research Authority (HRA). There is a wealth of guidance available on their website:

Ethical Approval

Ethical and appropriate use of digital methods requires meticulous planning. Although time consuming, one must not be tempted to rush this preparatory stage as subsequent amendment to the methods employed will likely require you to return to the ethics panel for further consideration. This can result in unwanted delays for the research student with a limited period of registration, as well as the researcher in receipt of a time-bound research grant.

The Covid-19 pandemic caused widespread disruption around the world, with the United Kingdom entering lockdown in March 2020 to reduce the risk of coronavirus transmission. Fluctuating government restrictions continued for many months, preventing face-to-face inter-views and focus groups from being conducted in a shared physical environment. Although videoconferencing platforms such as Zoom, Microsoft Teams, and Skype had been utilised by qualitative researchers prior to the pandemic, like many others, author HH sought to adopt digital methods of data collection for her Professional Doctorate in Healthcare Education. Necessitated by periods of varying local and national restrictions, using a secure videoconferencing facility (Microsoft Teams) enabled her to undertake semi-structured interviews in a timely manner whilst avoiding risk to both herself and her participants. Author RS also needed to adapt data collection methods for two funded projects that were undertaken during the pandemic, when the United Kingdom was in lockdown and therefore participants could not travel to attend a focus group conducted in-person. She used Microsoft Teams for these two studies, undertaking focus groups with groups ranging in size from three to six participants for one study and one-to-one interviews for the other study.

Undertaking a Risk Assessment

Researchers must seek to minimise potential harm to their participants (Iphofen, 2011), as well as to themselves and members of the wider research team, where applicable (Goodwin, Mays, and Pope, 2020). RECs and IRBs will expect the researcher to demonstrate that they have examined the potential risks and have sought to control (or at least reduce) the hazards as part of their research design and their ongoing commitment to upholding the ethical principle of non-maleficence (meaning to do no harm). For an accessible yet detailed discussion of the ethical principle of non-maleficence, as well as the principles of autonomy, beneficence, and justice, we direct you towards Beauchamp and Childress (2019). Whilst focussed specifically on biomedical ethics, their explanations of moral and ethical principles are illustrated with real-life scenarios, which serve to challenge the qualitative researcher to question and, if necessary, refine their approach.

A formal risk assessment is undertaken and submitted as part of the ethical approval process, evaluating a range of hazards affecting the participant and the researcher. For example, qualitative research interviews often involve the exploration of sensitive issues, and thus there is a risk of psychological distress. Mitigations often include debriefing and the provision of counselling or other forms of support should it be needed. As discussed earlier, author HH found supporting a distressed participant more challenging online. It is our opinion that researchers must consider the focus of the research and the population of interest when deciding whether to adopt digital methods of data collection.

At the time of writing, Covid-19 virus transmission remains a risk associated with in-person interactions, including research interviews and focus groups. Employing strategies such as social distancing, improved ventilation, and regular lateral flow testing may help to reduce the risk to health; however, the use of videoconferencing platforms eradicates the risk of the participant or researcher becoming infected during the data collection process. With fluctuating infection rates and varying national and local government restrictions on movement and social interaction, we would argue that digital methods offer a safer approach.

As previously acknowledged, the risk assessment should identify and mitigate hazards for the researcher as well as the participant. Collecting data may expose the researcher to potentially dangerous situations, including travelling alone at night or conducting interviews in unfamiliar locations (e.g. a participant's home) (Goodwin, Mays and Pope, 2020). Videoconferencing platforms enable the participant to avoid high-risk locations or situations and may be a safer alternative to in-person interviews or focus groups.

Ethical Research Practice

Research ethics extend beyond the initial approval process (Israel and Hay 2006). Professional bodies, learned societies, and organisations expect their members and employees to uphold the highest of ethical standards throughout their research. For example, the British Educational Research Association (BERA) (2018) has published guidelines to support researchers in educational settings to undertake high-quality, ethical research. Seven responsibilities to participants are emphasised:

1. Consent
2. Transparency
3. Right to withdraw
4. Incentives
5. Harm arising from participation in research
6. Privacy and data storage
7. Disclosure

Such responsibilities are not specific to researchers adopting digital methods; however, the impending discussion focuses on upholding the principles of consent and privacy and data storage when using synchronous videoconferencing platforms to collect qualitative data.

Obtaining Informed Consent

Sharing personal experiences, perceptions, and feelings during research interviews and focus groups – commonly employed methods in qualitative research – can be unsettling for participants (Finlay, 2011). In choosing to explore sensitive issues and/or research vulnerable populations, the risk is heightened.

In gaining informed consent and reducing the risk of harm from participation in research, the researcher must ensure that the participant understands what they are being asked to contribute and that the interview or focus group will be conducted online. This is important given that the experience of participating online is likely to be different from doing so in person. This information must be presented in the participant information sheet (PIS); however, it is good practice to arrange a verbal discussion on this with the participant, enabling them to ask questions and make an informed decision about whether they wish to participate.

When written informed consent is obtained for interviews and focus groups conducted in a shared physical environment, this usually involves a hard-copy consent form signed by the participant (Powell and van Velthoven, 2020) and the researcher. This may not be feasible when adopting digital methods. Following the initial meeting on Microsoft Teams, participants in author HH's study returned a soft copy of the consent form featuring a digitally added signature. The researcher then added a digital version of her signature and returned an electronic copy to the participant, whilst also saving a copy for her records. Each of the statements on the consent form was subsequently reaffirmed verbally before the interview commenced. Author RS employed a similar method:

records were kept of electronic consent forms, and each participant gave verbal consent as part of the recording. Different RECs have different requirements and expectations, some requiring the consenting process to be video recorded or hard-copy consent forms to be posted to and returned by the participant. We would encourage you to discuss the requirements of your local REC or IRB prior to making an ethical approval application. In our opinion, researchers should be able to discuss their proposed research with the REC or IRB rather than simply conforming to their wishes. Often RECs and IRBs are not familiar with qualitative methods, smaller sample sizes, and qualitative measures of rigour, and thus we would recommend attending the REC or IRB meeting, if permitted, so that you can discuss your proposed study with the panel, justifying and expanding upon aspects as required.

A commitment to transparency is closely aligned with that of informed consent. The researcher must be open and honest with the participant regarding the purpose of the study, as well as how their data will be processed and stored (Data Protection Act 2018), yet participants are rarely engaged in any conversation before REC or IRB approval is sought. In healthcare, there is a drive for researchers to involve the public in designing, conducting, and disseminating research, with the arguing that this leads to research which is more relevant, acceptable, and accessible to participants. However, in their initial guidance, RECs and IRBs strongly remind researchers that their study must not commence in any way prior to receiving ethical approval, which raises concerns amongst novice researchers wondering about the preferences of their prospective participants. Participants may have a different opinion about anonymity and may not be concerned about their identity being known; they may be keen to share their perspectives, opinions, and experiences and be identified with them. This could solve some of the issues that occur when reporting on research findings, as fully anonymising data can be a challenge. Yet, as healthcare professionals and educators, this is an uncomfortable option. Confidentiality is engrained in our professional practice, in the regulatory standards and codes we commit to, and the values which we share with our students and uphold for our patients.

Privacy and Data Storage

Some of the factors affecting the privacy of both the researcher and the participant have been explored earlier in the chapter – for example, in considering the background that is visible to the participant online and the decision regarding whether or not to video record the interview or focus group. Secure storage of data is important in all research, and entrenched within UK legislation, namely the Data Protection Act 2018.

The researcher must ensure that the participant's data is secure and only able to be accessed by authorised individuals (e.g. the student's research supervisor or members of the research team involved in data analysis). RECs and IRBs may require the researcher(s) to provide a data management plan as part of the ethical review process. This document explicitly states how data will be managed and is likely to include an explanation of what data will be collected, how and where it will be accessed and stored, and how long for. We would encourage all researchers to formulate a data management plan, even if this is not required by their REC or IEB, in order to systematically and comprehensively consider issues surrounding privacy and data storage.

Storing research data in repositories to facilitate reuse is often a requirement of funding councils (Gibson and Brown, 2009). Although secondary analysis of quantitative data is a well-established approach (Long-Sutehall et al., 2010), access to data and concerns over protecting the confidentiality of the participant initially hindered the proliferation of qualitative data reuse (Tsai et al., 2016). More recent developments in the quantity and accessibility of such data have boosted the popularity of secondary analysis amongst social science researchers (Sherif, 2018), with downloads from the UK Data Service and the number of publications reusing qualitative data increasing in recent years (Bishop and Kuula-Luuma, 2017). Whilst fiscal and time factors are frequently cited as advantages of data reuse, there are social benefits also. Robust designs permit exploration of sensitive issues and elusive populations without the need to collect additional data from participants (Fielding and Fielding, 2000).

In author HH's most recent study, she sought permission from participants to make their data, in the form of anonymised interview transcripts, available for secondary analysis. An explicit statement was included on the consent form: 'I give permission for the anonymised transcript of my interview to be deposited in the UK Data Service research data repository so that it will be available for future research and learning activities by other individuals.' Although it is not feasible to detail every possible scenario for reuse, clarifying the intention to make the data available enabled the participant to make an informed decision. Making the interview transcripts available was an expectation of the institution at which she is enrolled on her professional doctorate programme; however, participants were able to refuse their data being deposited with the UK Data Service, but still participate in the study.

Finally, the researcher must be aware of the legislation concerning transfers of personal data outside of the United Kingdom. To comply with the Data Protection Act 2018, personal data must not be transferred without consent. This must be borne in mind when choosing videoconferencing platforms and storage options. We would encourage researchers to explore this issue further with their research supervisor and/or local research and development office to ensure compliance.

Conclusion

The decisions we made to employ digital methods were in response to the pandemic; however, we would argue that our experiences transcend the current global situation. Whilst there are practical and methodological issues that require careful consideration as online interviews and focus groups cannot be directly substituted for in-person methods, they can still be rigorous and reliable methods to collect qualitative data from participants.

This chapter explores a range of issues to be considered by the qualitative researcher contemplating digital methods. Author RS would like to emphasise the challenges surrounding eye contact, engagement, and rapport; author HH would like to reiterate the need to reflect upon the 'Digital Divide' and the impact on participation from the defined population of interest.

Although we utilised digital methods in response to the Covid-19 pandemic, online interviews and focus groups offer opportunities to facilitate qualitative research that may extend beyond geographical borders, attenuate fiscal limitations, and enable greater collaboration between researchers.

Acknowledgements

Author HH would like to acknowledge her doctoral supervisors at the University of Essex, Dr Caroline Barratt and Dr Chris Green, for their support and guidance during the ethical approval process.

References

Beauchamp, T. L. and Childress, J. F. (2019) *Principles of Biomedical Ethics* (8th ed.) New York: Oxford University Press.

Bishop, L. and Kuula-Luumi, A. (2017) 'Revisiting qualitative data reuse: A decade on'. *Sage Open: Special Issue – Reusing Qualitative Data*: 1–15.

Boddy, R., Gordon, C., MacCullum, F., and McGuiness, M. (2016) 'Men's experiences of having a partner who requires Mother and Baby Unit admission for first episode postpartum psychosis'. *Journal of Advanced Nursing* 73 (2): 399–409.

Bowling, A. (2004) *Research methods in health: Investigating health and health services* (2nd ed.) Maidenhead: Open University Press.

Breen, L. J. (2007) 'The researcher "in the middle": Negotiating the insider/outsider dichotomy'. *The Australian Community Psychologist* 19 (1): 163–74.

British Educational Research Association (BERA) (2018) Ethical Guidelines for Educational Research (4th ed.) (accessed 1 January 2021).

Chan, V. W. S. (2021) 'Initiative on reducing the "Digital Divide"'. *IEEE Communications Magazine* 59 (5): 4–5.

Cohen, L., Manion, L., and Morrison, K. (2018) *Research Methods in Education* (8th ed.) Abingdon: Routledge.

Coolican, H. (2019) *Research Methods and Statistics in Psychology* (7th ed.) Abingdon: Routledge.

Creswell, J. W. (2007) *Qualitative Inquiry and Research Design – Choosing among five approaches* (2nd ed.) London: Sage.

Data Protection Act 2018, c. 12 (accessed 10 September 2021).

Dwyer, S. C. and Buckle, J. L. (2009) 'The space between: On being an insider-outsider in qualitative research'. *International Journal of Qualitative Methods* 8 (1): 54–63.

Fielding, N. G. and Fielding, J. L. (2000) 'Resistance and adaptation to criminal identity: Using secondary analysis to evaluate classic studies of crime and deviance'. *Sociology* 34 (4): 671–89.

Finlay, L. (2011) *Phenomenology for Therapists: Researching the Lived World.* Chichester: Wiley-Blackwell.

Gibson, W. J. and Brown, A. (2009) *Working with qualitative data* London: SAGE.

Goodwin, D., Mays, N., and Pope, C. (2020) 'Ethical issues in qualitative research'. In Pope, C. and Mays, N. (eds.) *Qualitative Research in Health Care* (4th ed.) (27–41) Oxford: John Wiley and Sons.

Health Research Authority (HRA) (2021) Public Involvement (accessed 12 November 2021).

Hinton, L. and Ryan, S. (2020) 'Interviews'. In Pope, C. and Mays, N. (eds) *Qualitative Research in Health Care* (4th ed.) (43–56) Oxford: John Wiley and Sons.

Iphofen, R. (2011) *Ethical Decision-Making in Social Research: A Practical Guide.* Basingstoke: Palgrave Macmillan.

Israel, M. and Hay, I. (2006) *Research Ethics for Social Scientists* London: SAGE.

Jolley, J. (2020) *Introducing Research and Evidence-Based Practice for Nursing and Healthcare Professionals* (3rd ed.) Abingdon: Routledge.

Kitzinger, J. (1996) 'Introducing focus groups'. *British Medical Journal* 311: 299–302.

Kvale, S. (1996) *Interviews: An Introduction to Qualitative Research Interviewing.* London: Sage.

Larkin, M. & Thompson, A. (2012) 'Interpretative phenomenological analysis'. In Thompson, A. & Harper, D. (eds.) *Qualitative Research Methods in Mental Health and Psychotherapy: A Guide for Students and Practitioners* (99–116). Oxford: John Wiley & Sons.

Lloyds Bank (2019) The UK Consumer Digital Index 2019 (accessed 10 September 2021).

Long-Sutehall, T., Sque, M., and Addington-Hall, J. (2010) 'Secondary analysis of qualitative data: A valuable method for exploring sensitive issues with an elusive population.' *Journal of Research in Nursing* 16 (4): 335–44.

McGrath, C., Palmgren, P. J., and Liljedahl, M. (2019) 'Twelve tips for conducting qualitative research interviews'. *Medical Teacher* 41 (9): 1002–6.

Office for National Statistics (ONS) (2021a) Internet access – households and individuals, Great Britain: 2020 (accessed 1 September 2021).

Office for National Statistics (ONS) (2021b) Internet access users, UK: 2020 (accessed 4 September 2021).

Powell, J. and van Velthoven, H. H. (2020) 'Digital data and online qualitative research'. In Pope, C. and Mays, N. (eds) *Qualitative Research in Health Care* (4th ed.) (97–109) Oxford: John Wiley and Sons.

Sherif, V. (2018) 'Evaluating pre-existing qualitative research data for secondary analysis'. *Forum: Qualitative Social Research* 19 (2): 3–18.

Tsai, A. C., Kohrt, B. A., Matthews, L. T., et al. (2016) 'Promises and pitfalls of data sharing in qualitative research'. *Social Science and Medicine* 169: 191–8.

Unluer, S. (2012) 'Being an insider research while conducting case study research'. *The Qualitative Report* 17 (58): 1–14. http://nsuworks.nova.edu/cgi/viewcontent.cgi?article=1752&context=tqr (accessed 4 January 2018).

Walker, C., Mills, H., and Gilchrist, A. (2017) 'Experiences of physical activity during pregnancy resulting from in vitro fertilisation: an interpretative phenomenological analysis'. *Journal of Reproductive and Infant Psychology* 35 (4): 365–79.

CHAPTER 7

Lessons Learned Conducting Online Qualitative Interviews during Covid-19

Sally Lindsay, Hiba Ahmed, Vanessa Tomas, and Abirami Vijaykaumar

Introduction

Over the last twenty years, technological advancements have provided unprecedented opportunities to utilize virtual platforms to conduct qualitative research that extend beyond traditional in-person methods (Namey et al., 2019; O'Connor and Madge, 2017). Online qualitative methods have been categorized as either asynchronous or synchronous in nature (O'Connor and Madge, 2017). For instance, asynchronous methods are predominantly text-based, sometimes including images, and can involve analyses of online discussion forums, email correspondence, and social media platforms, where participants contribute to discussions in their own time and at their convenience (Namey et al., 2019; O'Connor and Madge, 2017). Synchronous methods (real-time communication) can involve solely text-based communication, such as live chat rooms, or audiovisual communication via web-conferencing platforms; some web-conferencing platforms offer both audiovisual and text-based communication modes. Examples of web-conferencing platforms include Skype, Google Hangouts, Citrix GoToMeeting, Cisco WebEx, and, more recently, Zoom (Archibald et al., 2019; Gray et al., 2020; Lobe, Morgan and Hoffman, 2020; O'Connor and Madge, 2017). Synchronous methods are comparable to in-person techniques such as real-time interviews and focus groups. While online qualitative research is not novel, due to the COVID-19 pandemic methods are being further developed, explored, and validated to understand their usefulness and applicability as most researchers have encountered restrictions in face-to-face data collection and have turned to online methods to address the restrictions in physical contact.

Despite online approaches becoming ubiquitous and recognized as a legitimate means for qualitative data collection, there are still diverging opinions and skepticism regarding the overall suitability and reliability of thematic content collected online (Namey et al., 2019; O'Connor and Madge, 2017). However, researchers studying in-person versus online qualitative data, in terms of thematic content, data quality, and quantity, have showcased comparable findings between in-person and online focus groups and interviews (Namey et al., 2019; Shapka et al., 2016). For example, in a study conducted by Namey and colleagues (2019), the researchers utilized a quasi-experimental design to compare four modes of qualitative data collection with 171 participants (in-person, synchronous online audiovisual, synchronous online text-based [chat], and asynchronous online email). Within each mode, participants took part in either focus groups or interviews. Namey and colleagues found that for interview methods, the online audiovisual mode not only contained comparable themes to the in-person data, but actually had more unique themes.

Disadvantages of Online Qualitative Research

While positing that online qualitative data is comparable to in-person data, there are some issues and drawbacks associated with online qualitative research. First, technical difficulties may occur, such as challenges with internet connectivity and lag (Howlett, 2021; Moloney et al., 2003; O'Connor and Madge, 2017). These technical difficulties can pose challenges because slow connection speeds and loss of internet connectivity can result in unsaved data, as well causing frustration amongst both researchers and participants (Gray et al., 2020; Moloney et al., 2003). Second, depending on the software or platform used, online research may be costly, which may deter researchers from using them (O'Connor and Madge, 2017). Older adults and those with low household income are less likely to have access to technology to participate in online research (Archibald et al., 2019; Wilkerson et al., 2014). Furthermore, studies relying on text-based data collection (i.e., online interview with chat-based functions) may deter participation of those with limited typing skills, dyslexia, or visual impairments (Clark, 2007). For online text-based interviews, participants are often expected to reply, read, and process questions and conversations fairly quickly. As a result, this may hinder participation from those who are less familiar with technology or have cognitive impairments (Campbell et al., 2001). Finally, there is a possibility that total anonymity and/or confidentiality cannot be guaranteed, despite data security measures (Lobe, Morgan, and Hoffman, 2020; O'Connor and Madge, 2017; Wilkerson et al., 2014). If participants are using their own computers, researchers do not have control over who else might be listening or who has access to the data. For instance, participants can save the study data files from to their own computer without the knowledge of the research team (Kazmer and Xie, 2008).

Advantages of Online Qualitative Research

There are several benefits of online research methodology. First, online research is more accessible and flexible compared to in-person methodologies (Archibald et al., 2019; O'Connor and Madge, 2017; Wilkerson et al., 2014). Due to vast improvements in technology and global access to the internet, individuals interested in participating in research can do so by the click of a button on their electronic device. As such, researchers can connect to more diverse populations, including more geographically dispersed and vulnerable populations (e.g., persons with disabilities or chronic health conditions) (Gray et al., 2020; Wilkerson et al., 2014). Logistical components to conducting and participating in research (including distance, geographical location, and funding needed for travel) are ultimately eliminated (Deakin and Wakefield, 2014; Gray et al., 2020; Salmons, 2012). Further, while there is limited research focusing on the inclusion of people with disabilities in online qualitative research, evidence and experiential accounts are emerging (Best et al., 2019; Wilkerson et al., 2014; Zolyomi et al., 2019). Built-in technological supports in some web-conferencing platforms can enable and enhance inclusion of persons with disabilities, such as closed captioning, screen-reader support, automatic transcripts, screen sharing, and speaker spotlight. Although not specific to qualitative research, persons on the autism spectrum discussed experiences around web-conferencing and related platforms due to remote working (Zolyomi et al., 2019). Adults with autism spectrum disorder highlighted the benefits of web-conferencing, such as enhanced comfort due to being in their home environment, and mitigation of distractions due to screen sharing and/or speaker view/mode to focus on the task at hand or the person talking (Zolyomi et al., 2019).

Another advantage to online research methodologies includes greater disclosure, particularly around sensitive or taboo topics (e.g., mental health, sexuality, gender identity, etc.), in comparison to in-person methods, due to the ability to preserve one's identity and increased anonymity (i.e., turning off camera, changing name) (Ayling and Mewse, 2012; Wettergren et al., 2016). For example, greater discussion around sensitive topics is portrayed in mental health (i.e., suicide) (Han et al., 2019), sexuality (Wettergren et al., 2016; Wilkerson et al., 2014), and domestic violence literature (Douglas et al., 2021). Wettergren and colleagues (2016) explored the feasibility and usefulness of synchronous, online focus groups with young people with cancer to discuss sensitive topics (sexual activity and fertility issues). They found that participants were more comfortable discussing sensitive topics due to the ability to use a pseudonym and remain anonymous (Wettergren et al., 2016).

Finally, online research methods have the potential to enhance participation amongst youth and young adults (Han et al., 2019; Elmir et al., 2011). Young people more often engage and communicate with peers via online platforms and technological devices, and thus are typically more familiar and comfortable with the virtual world. Upadhyay and Lipkovich (2020) conducted cognitive interviews with youth and young adults using Zoom; they found that use of Zoom facilitated greater diversity amongst young participants, engaged those who would not have participated in-person, allowed for flexible scheduling (e.g., accommodating school schedules), and provided a sense of safety and security amongst youth (e.g., participating from the comfort of their home, could keep the camera off).

To date, most studies exploring online interviews used web-conferencing platforms such as Skype, and there are few existing studies outlining the lessons learned using Zoom. Given the predominance of Zoom during the COVID-19 pandemic (i.e., more than 300 million users at the time of writing) and the increasing reliance on it for online qualitative data collection (Burstynsky, 2020), it is worthwhile to describe the barriers, disadvantages, and lessons learned. Here, we assess the data quality of online Zoom interviews compared to phone interviews in a sample of youth with and without disabilities.

Methods

The purpose of this chapter is to understand the advantages, barriers, and lessons learned in using Zoom to conduct online interviews. The chapter draws on a study that focused on barriers and facilitators for employment during the COVID-19 pandemic among youth with and without disabilities (Lindsay et al., 2021). In the larger study we used a qualitative design to conduct in-depth, semistructured interviews, which was approved by a research ethics board at a pediatric hospital.

Data Collection and Analysis

For the larger study, we used a purposive sampling strategy to recruit participants through flyers, advertisements, and social media. Participants had to meet the following inclusion criteria: aged between 15–29, with a disability or without a disability, who are currently employed or have recent work experience. Those interested in taking part received an information package from a researcher. After obtaining consent, the researchers conducted interviews from July to November 2020. The majority of participants were recruited from the Greater Toronto Area, Ontario, Canada, which was considered a "hot zone" for COVID-19 cases and deaths (Government of Ontario, 2021). At the time of data collection for this study, face-to-face interviews were not permitted due to the pandemic. Zoom was the only platform approved by our ethics board for conducting online interviews.

For this chapter we draw on 30 of the 35 interviews from our larger study, which was conducted online using Zoom (see Table 7.1). Five interviews were conducted by telephone, which we do not report on here. Interviews were audio recorded and transcribed verbatim, and we used an interpretive descriptive methodology to guide the analysis (Creswell and Poth, 2017). The thematic analysis of the larger study is described in detail elsewhere (see Lindsay, Ahmed and Apostolopoulos, 2021). For this chapter, we describe our experiences with conducting the interviews, drawing on our field notes and observations, and on participants' responses to taking part in the study. We used a narrative, thematic analysis of our field notes and participant transcripts to understand the barriers to and advantages of conducting online Zoom interviews (Reissman, 2008).

Sample Characteristics

The sample that we draw on for this chapter involved 30 youth and young adults, aged 16–29 (mean age 23), comprising 5 men and 25 women (see Table 7.1 for overview of participants). Sixteen participants had their camera on, 14 chose to have it turned off.

Zoom

Zoom is a videoconferencing service offering features such as online meetings, a messaging facility, and secure recording of sessions (Archibald et al., 2019). This online platform provides the ability to communicate in real time

Table 7.1 *Overview of participants*

Participant ID	Age	Gender	Disability	Zoom Participant Camera On or Off
1	24	Man	Yes	On
2	29	Woman	Yes	Off
3	22	Woman	Yes	Off
4	19	Woman	Yes	Off
5	22	Woman	Yes	On
6	23	Woman	Yes	Off
7	20	Woman	Yes	On
8	25	Man	Yes	On
9	29	Woman	Yes	On
10	23	Man	Yes	On
11	27	Woman	Yes	On
12	26	Man	Yes	Off
13	19	Woman	Yes	On
14	21	Woman	No	On
15	18	Woman	No	On
16	16	Woman	No	Off
17	26	Man	No	Off
18	23	Woman	No	Off
19	25	Woman	No	Off
20	18	Woman	No	On
21	25	Woman	No	Off
22	20	Woman	No	Off
23	19	Woman	No	On
24	17	Woman	No	On
25	24	Woman	No	On
26	16	Woman	No	On
27	24	Woman	No	On
28	25	Woman	No	On
29	23	Woman	no	On
30	29	Woman	No	Off

and to have online synchronous conversations with participants on a computer, tablet, or mobile device (Archibald et al., 2019; Salmons, 2012). Other features include real-time encryption of meetings. Zoom does not require participants to have an account or download a program (Gray et al., 2020). There are screen-sharing capabilities for both participants and researchers. They can also display other images and videos. Additionally, Zoom has a password protection function that is unique to each scheduled meeting, and it has the ability to record video and audio. With both audio and video functions, participants can decide what level of contact they would like, which affords them greater autonomy.

Results

We noted several barriers, advantages, and lessons learned in conducting online Zoom interviews.

Barriers to Online Interviews

Barriers to conducting online Zoom interviews in our study included recruitment and ethics procedures, technical difficulties, and building rapport.

Recruitment and Ethics

We started the recruitment process a few months into the pandemic, and thus recruitment occurred online using various recruitment strategies (i.e., the hospital volunteer listserv, advertising through the hospital's social media accounts). Initially, we had greater interest from youth without disabilities and hence we were able to reach our desired sample size for youth without disabilities quickly. However, this was not the case for youth with disabilities, which required our team to take a more targeted recruitment approach using snowball sampling and emailing additional organizations.

Ethical Challenges

The research ethics board at the hospital where this study was approved was constantly changing its processes, especially regarding participant consent, data collection, and specific features within Zoom. At the start of the pandemic, it was difficult to obtain consent from some participants because not everyone had a scanner or e-signature facilities. The research ethics board responded quickly to this issue and adapted a process whereby participants could complete an e-consenting process through Research Electronic Data Capture (REDCap). This is a secure web platform for building and managing online databases and surveys, and can also be used for obtaining signed consent from participants.

We encountered some challenges with using Zoom because of limitations imposed by our research ethics board. At the time of conducting the interviews, we were not allowed to use the Zoom chat function. We later requested that this could be turned on, and it was approved, but we were not allowed to record or save the conversations with participants within the chat section.

An additional challenge was that our research ethics board required all the interviews be saved to a secure, shared drive, while the researchers also had to adhere to specific COVID-19 guidelines set by the hospital. This was challenging because once the researchers completed the recording of the interview it would automatically save to the hard drive of the computer. Additionally, interviewers needed be on site at the hospital or have virtual private network (VPN) access to conduct interviews. VPN is an encrypted and secure connection between your internet and the shared network where you can access restricted content remotely. Disadvantages of VPN include that the connection to your internet may be slower when it is encrypted and routed through the VPN server. At the time only one member of our team had access to a VPN laptop, due to the rapid onset of the pandemic combined with the limited supply of laptops, while the other researcher was using Citrix software, which allows you to interact with applications (i.e., shared drive) from your work computer remotely while using a personal laptop.

Technical Issues with Online Interviews

While conducting interviews over Zoom, we ran into some technical issues, including audio cutting out, the audio stopping unexpectedly all together, video lagging, and freezing. First, accessing a reliable internet connection, for both researchers and participants, was challenging at times. The researchers conducted most of the interviews while they were onsite at the hospital, which did not have a stable and reliable internet connection. This made it unclear whether participants had any connectivity or technical issues at their end. In some interviews, the participant's or the interviewer's internet connection would briefly cut out, which sometimes created frustration for participants. For example, one particular participant asked the interviewer to repeat the question a few times and their responses also cut out throughout the interview. Unreliable internet for the interviewer sometimes made it challenging to hear participants clearly, which impacted the flow of the interview. To illustrate:

INTERVIEWER: *Okay, and can you describe what you do in a typical day? . . . sorry did you hear me?*

RESPONDENT: *Yeah, I can hear you. Sorry, are you hearing the noise in the background?*

RESPONDENT: *It must have cut out, I didn't hear the question the first time.* (#21, no disability)

RESPONDENT: *Sorry, it cut out. Could you repeat the question please?*

RESPONDENT: *Sorry, I'm just going to clarify the question because it cut out a few times"* (#21, no disability)

Some participants had slow internet connectivity, which sometimes made it difficult to hear their responses because lagging and/or being cut off. Additionally, participants may not have access to devices such as headphones and speakers, or only have access to poor-quality devices. For instance, one soft-spoken participant faced barriers when participating in the interview, including lagging internet and not having access to good-quality speakers. Although the interviewer was using earphones throughout, those barriers made it a demanding interview to conduct.

INTERVIEWER: *Oh can you hear me? I think it froze for a second*
RESPONDENT: *Yeah, I think it is a bit laggy*
RESPONDENT: *Sure, do you want to see if I can turn my mic a little? (#14, disability)*
INTERVIEWER: *Yes, please*
RESPONDENT: *Okay. It is on the highest, so I guess I will just have to talk a bit louder.*
INTERVIEWER: *Okay thank you. I will let you know if I can't hear you or if I miss something"* (#9, disability)

Other technical challenges included a participant mentioning midway through the interview that they could not hear anything even though the interview had started without any technical issues. The interviewer managed to resolve the problem within a few minutes. The Zoom recording continued; however, for some reason it did not pick up on parts of the audio from the interviewer for a small portion of the recording, though it did manage to record the participant's responses.

RESPONDENT: *Um, I don't hear you*
RESPONDENT: *No, I can't hear you …*
RESPONDENT: *Yeah, yeah I can hear you, that's okay …* (#6, disability)

The video quality was occasionally poor when conducting interviews over Zoom, which depended on the quality of the webcam used. Some interviews were conducted using a laptop and therefore researchers used the built-in webcam. At other times an external webcam was connected to a desktop computer. We found we had better video quality and resolution on the interviewer side when we used an external webcam. However, we were unable to control the video quality of participants who were using devices such as laptops and phones.

For participants who turned on their cameras, it was sometimes challenging to gauge their facial expressions and reactions when there were internet delays. Some participants opted to join by dialing in (audio only). For example, three participants had difficulties in joining the Zoom video call.

The interviewer asked one participant to join the video call by dialing the Zoom phone number and we were then able to conduct the interview, but the interview started approximately 15 minutes after the scheduled time and we had to wrap-up abruptly. Another participant had difficulties joining the Zoom interview and we had to reschedule their interview. For the interview for another participant, Zoom was offline in the hospital for the entire day. The researcher was able to access the back-up recorders and asked the participant to call their landline. Fortunately, they were responsive to emails and willing to accommodate the last-minute change.

The equipment that participants used throughout the interview posed another barrier, sometimes leading to the researchers not hearing the responses properly. Some participants had limited access to their own computer or laptop, and having shared equipment sometimes presented further challenges (i.e., they were not familiar with the settings on the device). An additional challenge was that researchers had no control over the environment or setting in which participants chose to do their interview. Therefore, there was a potential increase in distractions and background noise for participants who did not have access to a quiet space.

Building Rapport

One of the challenges of online interviews is building rapport with participants. Online interviews can be potentially awkward for participants, who may not feel comfortable or at ease interacting through a computer screen. For youth who chose to do a Zoom interview with their video off (n=14), perceiving their nonverbal communication was not possible, which affected the ability to build rapport. It was difficult to gauge how participants felt about certain questions when we were unable to see their facial expressions, which made it challenging to probe further about their experiences. Thus, it is important for interviewers to be attentive to the participant's tone of voice and other nonverbal communication cues (e.g., nods) if they are unable to perceive their facial expressions. This was evident when some participants gave short responses even after probing further or re-phrasing the question.

Advantages to Online Interviews

The benefits of conducting online Zoom interviews included efficiency and flexibility of scheduling for conducting the interviews, technical advantages, and perceived anonymity and privacy.

Efficiency and Flexibility of Scheduling and Conducting the Interviews

Conducting interviews online was time efficient for the researchers, as well as for participants as they did not have to travel to the hospital. Further, the process of scheduling and conducting interviews was very efficient in terms of the researcher's time and necessary resources because we were able to schedule interviews with participants soon after they expressed interest. For example, there were times when the researchers would schedule three or four interviews in one day, and they could accommodate individuals who might have had time constraints.

Online interviews offered several potential advantages for participants, particularly those with disabilities, who reported that they preferred the remote option because it saved them having to travel and arrange transportation.

> I unfortunately do not have a driver's license beyond a G1, so I've been taking public transit, which is about an hour commute versus like driving which would have only taken maybe half an hour. (#5, disability)

Another facilitator of online research was being able to reach and recruit diverse participants that we would typically not have been able to reach if conducting interviews in-person. For instance, we were able to include participants that lived in cities further away who reported having difficulty accessing public transport and traveling to our hospital, where we would typically have conducted in-person interviews.

We were able to enhance the diversity and inclusivity of participants through online interviews, especially those with disabilities, because they could use their own equipment and software adapted to their specific needs (e.g., accessible features, closed captioning [displaying the text of what is said]), and they were in a setting they were comfortable with. For example, some participants explained that having an online option allowed them to participate more easily:

> Transportation is a really big barrier for me because I can't drive. I would either have to get a ride or use transit which those options I mean are good options. But with even with my family, I hate having to schedule rides. (#6, disability)

This sentiment was shared by both youth with and without disabilities, in that not having to commute to an in-person interview made it easier for them to participate in the study. For instance, one participant explained:

> Now that I'm at home, um, I have a bit more time. I'm able to fulfill a lot, a lot of the tasks that I normally wouldn't be able to fulfill in that, in that amount of time. (#27, no disability)

Moreover, we were able to reach individuals who told us that they would be less likely to participate in the interview in-person, especially if the conversation touched on sensitive topics.

Another advantage of online Zoom interviews included being able to reach out to a broader range of potential participants because of online recruitment methods (e.g., social media). An important feature of Zoom is that it includes closed captioning, which can be helpful for participants with disabilities. This feature is beneficial because it produces a transcript at the end of the interview (saving the researchers both time and money).

Flexibility of Scheduling and Conducting Interviews

By conducting interviews online, we could quickly recruit participants over a short period of time, unlike recruiting for studies involving in-person interviews. For example, if a potential participant emailed us, we were often able to give appointments as early as the next day or within the same week. Had the interviews been in-person, this would often involve more coordination of factors, including arranging for and booking a room, and participants arranging time to commute to the hospital. In addition, we were able to synchronize the Zoom interview time with their personal electronic calendar using a calendar invite, which helped to avoid no-shows or participants forgetting what time the interview was.

We were able to accommodate participants' schedules because of the flexibility of online interviews. For example, several participants had busy schedules that would have made it more challenging to find a mutually available time if they had to come onsite for an in-person interview. Holding interviews online allowed the researchers to be more flexible and accommodating around the participant's schedules. In the same vein, we were able to adapt when participants had last-minute scheduling changes. Further, the flexibility of online interviews was beneficial for the research team and allowed us to schedule multiple, back-to-back interviews in one day. Having back-to-back interviews in-person was often challenging because of onsite logistics (e.g., you may have to switch rooms or wait for participants who may be running late).

Consenting Process

Another benefit associated with recruitment for the study was being able to host our research ethics board–approved consent form online through the REDCap platform, which allows participants to read the consent form onscreen and enter an e-signature. We found that many participants preferred submitting online consent versus sending back a scanned or mailed hard copy. Many participants filled out the forms immediately after we sent them the link, which facilitated the recruitment process. This platform was beneficial because we did not need to follow-up multiple times for their consent form.

Technical Advantages of Zoom

We found that Zoom has several benefits for conducting online interviews. First, Zoom is a secure platform because files are automatically encrypted and we were able to record the interviews and save them directly onto our secured drive, which made the process of conducting interviews and uploading files much more efficient. Further, Zoom has several favorable features, including password protection and a user-friendly platform for participants. Other features our team did not use but that are user-friendly include the chat function, screen sharing, and annotations.

The majority of participants interviewed for this study did not experience challenges in joining the interview, which highlights the accessibility of this platform. Further, we found that the sound quality of the Zoom audio file was much clearer compared to the audio recorder audio we typically used for in-person interviews, which was an additional advantage and made the transcription process easier.

To facilitate the engagement and development of rapport with participants, researchers made sure to have their camera on for all of the Zoom interviews. For participants who had their cameras on during the interview, this helped to develop rapport and keep participants engaged. When participants had their camera on, researchers could recognize nonverbal cues, including whether the participants had heard them properly, had understood the question, or if they were engaged in the conversation. For example, on a few occasions when the internet cut out briefly, researchers could communicate with notes and gestures such as nodding yes or no. It was helpful to be able to see when participants' internet or audio cut out so they could pause and/or repeat the question. We noticed that Zoom interviews with the camera on were slightly longer in duration than interviews where participants had the camera off, perhaps because it was easier to develop rapport with the participant when you could see them.

Anonymity/Participant Privacy

Conducting online Zoom interviews helped participants to feel confident that their identity and information would remain anonymous and confidential. The topic of the interviews focused on the impact of the pandemic on employment, so participants were required to share their personal experiences. Some participants expressed frustrations and fears around employment and their future, which may have been uncomfortable for them if the interviews had been held in person. Participants also had the option of having their cameras turned off, which was something mentioned ahead of time when the interview was scheduled. We felt that having the choice to turn their camera on/off as preferred made participants more comfortable and thus it was more likely for them to discuss sensitive, personal information.

Lessons Learned

There were several important lessons learned in conducting online Zoom interviews during the pandemic, including how to build rapport with online participants, providing participants with detailed instructions for how to join the Zoom meeting, discussion of technical requirements with participants prior to the interview, and ethical considerations.

1.   *Building Rapport with Online Participants*

It is important at the beginning of the interview to allocate time to building a strong rapport with participants and ensuring that they are comfortable, which is particularly important for younger participants who may feel apprehensive about sharing their personal experiences online. Although this is necessary for all interviews, it is even more important when conducting online interviews, where you lack in-person interaction. For instance, when interviews are in-person you would greet the participant in the lobby, then create some small talk while walking the participant to the interview room, whereas when meeting online, the participant shows up at their designated time and they may be reserved because they are meeting you for the first time in a virtual format. As a researcher you can build rapport by ensuring your camera is turned on, greeting participants with a smile, and introducing yourself, explaining your role, and discussing the study details in an informal way. You can even ask the participant if they would like to introduce themselves or if they have any questions before you start. We recommend providing the interview questions in advance or having them available on PowerPoint slides through a shared screen. This helps to avoid having to repeat the question while giving them an opportunity and time to reflect.

2   *Provide Participants with Instructions on how to join the Zoom Meeting*

Although joining a Zoom call is generally a straightforward and user-friendly process, it is important to provide step-by-step instructions for participants because it might be a new experience for some people. For example, let participants know to click the Zoom link and to enter the password when prompted. If they do not already have Zoom installed on their computer, let them know that it could take a few minutes to install the program or set up the audio before they can join the call. It is also important to make them aware of the "dialing in option" in case they do not want to download the software.

3   *Discuss Technical Requirements with Participants Prior to the Interview*

We recommend making a plan with participants prior to the interview regarding how they will access the interview and the basic technical requirements (e.g., check audio and video are working, etc.). You should have a plan for how you will handle any technical issues that may arise and what they would like to do if the Zoom software is not working (e.g., reschedule or use an alternate format). All of the steps involved in accessing Zoom and setting up any technical aspects should be provided along with the introductory information and consent form.

An important lesson is the significance of investing in and having access to a good-quality internet connection because many of the technical concerns were attributed to poor Wi-Fi. Additionally, ensuring that interviewers and participants had access to a microphone, webcam, and earphones was critical. It helps to pilot test the equipment and to conduct a mock interview with the research team prior to starting the interviews to identify any potential technical issues. We ensured that we used earphones that had a built-in microphone so the sound was clearer and there was no background noise. Finally, consider having a "tip sheet" of common technical difficulties and sharing it in advance so participants can refer to it throughout the interview.

4   *Ethical Considerations*

When conducting online interviews it is important to know what is allowed by your research ethics board (REB) (e.g., recruitment process, consent, software you can use and the functions within it). For example, in our study we were not permitted to use the chat function due to privacy concerns. Our REB required us to have alternate options (e.g., phone) for those who may not have internet or may not be interested in online interviews. Additionally, research teams should consider whether they intend to save the audio and video files and have plans for where to store them, and the type of secure and encrypted devices they plan on using.

Discussion

This study explored the barriers to and benefits of using Zoom for remote interviews. Barriers to conducting online Zoom interviews included technical difficulties and some challenges with building rapport. Our experience in conducting online interviews is similar to that of others who report the commonality of technical issues such as internet delays (Krouwel, Jolly and Greenfield, 2019) and developing rapport with participants (Gray et al., 2020). It is important to consider that offering online interviews may exclude people who do not have reliable access to the internet (Lindsay, 2010).

The advantages of conducting interviews online included greater efficiency and flexibility, technical advantages, and perceived anonymity and privacy. Other research focusing on conducting Skype interviews shows that conducting interviews online can actually help with building rapport with participants, and they are often comfortable disclosing personal and sensitive information online (Shapka et al., 2016). Some studies also report that within focus groups, participants are more comfortable sharing information online than in-person (Mann and Stewart, 2000). This suggests that online modes may facilitate a safe space for participants to create experiences within a perceived anonymous and private environment (Woodyatt, Finneran, and Stephenson, 2016). Other research shows that online interviews can provide time and cost savings and allow for greater flexibility compared to other interview formats (Archibald et al., 2019).

Our experience in conducting online interviews showed more benefits than barriers. We noted that it seemed to be a preferred method by youth in our study, which is something that researchers should consider in the future. Online interviews have the potential to increase the inclusivity and diversity of participants (e.g., geographical reach, marginalized groups) (Archibald et al., 2019; Upadhyay and Lipkovich, 2020) who might otherwise have difficulty traveling to an in-person interview, such as people with disabilities (Gray et al., 2020; Neville, Adams and Cook, 2016). Additionally, using online data collection methods could be particularly useful for youth, who have embraced online communication technology more than any other age group (Mason and Ide, 2014). Some research indicates that online interviews may be preferred by youth because it is considered a natural communication environment for them (Mason and Ide, 2014).

Limitations and Future Research

This study is limited in that assessing the barriers to and benefits of online interviews was not the primary goal; rather, this was a secondary analysis. The findings should therefore be interpreted with caution, and future research should consider exploring the impact of online interviews (e.g., type of device, internet connection) on data quality. Additionally, many participants chose not to have their video camera switched on, which could have impacted the development of rapport and interview length. Future research should explore differences between camera on versus camera off in terms of data quality.

Conclusion

This study explored the barriers to, advantages of and lessons learned in conducting online interviews during the pandemic. The barriers included technical difficulties and some challenges with building rapport. The benefits we included greater efficiency and flexibility, technical advantages, and perceived anonymity and privacy. Conducting qualitative interviews online could help to increase the diversity and inclusivity of participants. Further research should consider exploring how different types of devices and quality of internet access affects data quality.

References

Archibald, M., Ambagtsheer, R., Casey, M., and Lawless, M. (2019) "Using Zoom videoconferencing for qualitative data collection: Perceptions and experiences of researchers and participants," *International Journal of Qualitative Methods*, 18. https://doi.org/10.1177/1609406919874596.

Ayling, R. and Mewse, A. (2012) "Evaluating internet interviews with gay men," *Sage Internet Research Methods*, 19(4), 566–576. https://doi.org/10.1177/1049732309332121.

Best, P., McConnell, T., Davidson, G., Badham, J., and Neill, R. (2019) "Group based video-conferences for adults with depression: Findings from a user-led qualitative data analysis using participatory theme elicitation," *Research Involvement and Engagement*, 5(40). https://doi.org/10.1186/s40900-019-0173-z.

Burstynsky, J. 2020. Zoom shares pop after users grow from 200 million to 300 million in a matter of days. *CNBC News*. www.cnbc.com/2020/04/23/zoom-shares-pop-after-users-grow-from-to-300-million.html.

Campbell, M., Meier, A., Carr, C., et al. (2001) "Health behaviour changes after colon cancer: A comparison of findings from face-to-face and online focus groups," *Family & Community Health*, 24(3), 88–103.

Clark, G. (2007) "Going beyond our limits: Issues for able and disabled students," *Journal of Geography in Higher Education*, 31(1), 211–218.

Creswell, J. and Poth, C. (2017) *Qualitative Inquiry and Research Design: Choosing Among Five Approaches*. London: Sage.

Deakin, H. and Wakefield, K. (2014) "Skype interviewing: Reflections of two PhD researchers," *Qualitative Research*, 14(5), 603–616.

Douglas, E., Hines, D., Dixon, L., Celi, E., and Lysova, A. (2021) "Using technology to conduct focus groups with a hard-to-reach population: A methodological approach concerning male victims of partner abuse in four English-speaking countries," *Journal of Interpersonal Violence*, 36(9–10), 5257–5280.

Elmir, R., Schmied, V., Jackson, D., and Wilkes, L. (2011) "Interviewing people on potentially sensitive topics," *Nurse Researcher*, 19, 12–16.

Government of Ontario (2021) All Ontario: Case numbers and spread. Available at: https://covid-19.ontario.ca/data (Accessed: May 3 2021).

Gray, L. M., Wong-Wylie, G., Rempel, G., and Cook, K. (2020) "Expanding qualitative research interviewing strategies: Zoom video communications," *The Qualitative Report*, 25, 1292–1301.

Han, J., Torok, M., Gale, N., et al. (2019) "Use of web conferencing technology for conducting online focus groups among young people with lived experience of suicidal thoughts: Mixed methods research," *Journal of Medical Internet Research Mental Health*, 6(10), e14191.

Howlett, M. (2021) "Looking at the field through a zoom lens: Methodological reflections on conducing online research during a global pandemic," Qualitative Research. https://doi.org/10.1177/1468794120985691.

Kazmer, M. and Xie, B. (2008) "Qualitative interviewing in internet studies: Playing with the method," *Information, Communication & Society*, 11(2), 257–278.

Krouwel, M., Jolly, K., and Greenfield, S. (2019) "Comparing Skype (video calling) and in-person qualitative interview modes in a study of people with irritable bowel syndrome: An exploratory comparative analysis," *BMC Medical Research Methodology*, 19, 1–9.

Lindsay, S. (2010) "Disability and the digital divide: Gaps and future directions," in Evans, C. (ed.) *Internet Issues: Blogging, Digital Divide and Digital Libraries* (pp. 215–20). New York: Nova Science Publishers.

Lindsay, S., Ahmed, A., and Apostolopoulos, D. (2021) "Facilitators for coping with the COVID-19 pandemic: A qualitative study comparing youth with and without disabilities," *Disability and Health*, 14(4), 10113.

Lobe, B., Morgan, D. and Hoffman, K. (2020) "Qualitative data collection in an era of social distancing," *International Journal of Qualitative Methods*, 19. https://doi.org/10.1177/1609406920937875.

Mann, C. and Stewart, F. (2000) *Internet Communication and Qualitative Research: A Handbook for Researching Online*. London: Sage.

Mason, D. and Ide, B. (2014) "Adapting qualitative research strategies to technology savvy adolescents," *Nurse Researcher*, 21(5), 40–45.

Moloney, M., Dietrich, A., Strickland, O., and Myerburg, S. (2003) "Using internet discussion boards as virtual focus groups," *Advances in Nursing Science*, 26(4), 274–286.

Namey, E., Guest, G., O'Regan, A., et al. (2019) "How does mode of qualitative data collection affect data and cost? Findings from a quasi-experimental study," *Field Methods*, 32(1), 58–74.

Neville, S., Adams, J., and Cook, C. (2016) "Using internet-based approaches to collect qualitative data from vulnerable groups: Reflections from the field," *Contemporary Nurse*, 52(6), 657–668.

O'Connor, H. and Madge, C. (2017) *The Sage Handbook of Online Research Methods*. London: Sage.

Reissman, C. (2008) *Narrative Methods for the Human Sciences*. California: Sage.

Salmons, J. (2012) "Designing and conducting research with online interviews," in *Cases in Online Interview Research*, Sage [Online]. https://methods.sagepub.com/book/cases-in-online-interview-research.

Shapka, J., Domene, J., Khan, S., and Yang, L. (2016) "Online versus in-person interviews with adolescents: An exploration of data evidence," *Computers in Human Behavior*, 58, 361–367.

Upadhyay, U. and Lipkovich, H. (2020) "Using online technologies to improve diversity and inclusion in cognitive interviews with young people," *BMC Medical Research Sage. Methodology*, 20(159), 1–10.

Upadhyay, U. and Lipkovich, H. (2020) "Using online technologies to improve diversity and inclusion in cognitive interviews with young people," *BMC Medical Research Methodology*, 20(159), 1–10.

Wettergren, L., Eriksson, L., Nilsson, J., Jervaeus, A., and Lampic, C. (2016) "Online focus group discussion is a valid and feasible mode when investigating sensitive topics among young persons with a cancer experience," *Journal of Medical Internet Research Protocols*, 5(2), e86.

Wettergren, L., Eriksson, L., Nilsson, J., Jervaeus, A., and Lampic, C. (2016) "Online focus group discussion is a valid and feasible mode when investigating sensitive topics among young persons with a cancer experience," *Journal of Medical Internet Research Protocols*, 5(2), e86.

Wilkerson, J., Iantaffi, A., Grey, J., Bockting, W., and Rosser, B. (2014) "Recommendations for internet-based qualitative health research with hard-to-research populations," *Qualitative Health Research*, 24(4), 561–574.

Woodyatt, C., Finneran, C., and Stephenson, R. (2016) "In-person versus online focus group discussions: A comparative analysis of data quality," *Qualitative Health Research*, 26(6), 741–749.

Zolyomi, A., Begel, A., Waldern, J., et al. (2019) "Managing stress: The needs of autistic adults in video calling," *Proceedings of the ACM on Human-Computer Interaction*, 3, 1–29.

CHAPTER 8

Virtual Interviewing in the Age of Covid-19
Considerations for Qualitative Research
Charles Edmund Degeneffe

Introduction

Covid-19 refers to a type of coronavirus, SARS-CoV-2, first publicly identified on December 1, 2019 (Sauer, 2021). Public awareness and professional understanding of Covid-19 is continually evolving. Persons become infected with Covid-19 primarily through inhalation of droplets expelled by infected persons; in some cases it may be transmitted via contact with surfaces contaminated by the virus (Centers for Disease Control and Prevention [CDC], 2021a). Covid-19 is a public health challenge faced by countries across the globe. As of July 20, 2021, at 9:42 am GMT-7, there were 190,671,330 confirmed Covid-19 cases and 4,098,758 deaths worldwide (World Health Organization [WHO], 2021). Covid-19 is not restricted within geographic borders and was therefore declared a pandemic by the WHO on March 11, 2020 (Cucinotta and Vanelli, 2020).

From a public health perspective, a particularly challenging aspect of Covid-19 concerns its range of severity, with some infected persons experiencing no symptoms while others encounter a disparate set of outcomes such as coughs, fever, or chills; shortness of breath or difficulty breathing; muscle or body aches; sore throat; loss of taste or smell; diarrhea; headaches; fatigue; nausea or vomiting; and congestion or runny nose (Sauer, 2021). With asymptomatic transmission, infected persons can transmit Covid-19 with no awareness such as they might have with other coronaviruses with perceivable symptoms occurring early and often in the disease process. Hence, public officials struggle with how to minimize risk while ensuring access to public entities such as workplaces, schools, sporting events, and other areas where the public congregate. The public health challenges of Covid-19 sometimes result in personal and political conflicts regarding how to balance personal rights as regards individual choice (e.g., mandatory mask-wearing) versus collective social action to reduce Covid-19 transmissions.

As industries and employers continually need to adapt to Covid-19, higher education has dramatically altered how work tasks are performed. Most colleges and universities rapidly transformed on-campus teaching to teaching via virtual platforms with little to no preparation and expertise. Instead of meeting in person with colleagues for committee meetings, faculty searches, and student advising, faculty shifted to performing these activities virtually, with a concomitant loss of the informal collegiality commonly associated with these types of interactions. Rite-of-passage events such as commencements and dissertation defenses became virtual, and universities struggled with how to hold these events with no frame of reference to draw from. Another key core higher education activity affected by Covid-19 concerns person-to-person research in qualitative studies.

In the social sciences, extant research largely relies on utilizing a quantitative versus a qualitative approach. These traditions differ on several dimensions, guided by the underlying epistemology of each approach (Gelo, Braakmann, and Benetka, 2008). Quantitative research relies on assumptions of human behavior evaluated through surveys, experiments, standardized instruments, and statistical analyses. In contrast, qualitative research follows an idiographic approach by attempting to gain an individualized and subjective understanding of participants' unique perspectives by such means as interviews, focus groups, and naturalistic observations – approaches that were compromised by Covid-19 given their reliance on a researcher–participant personal connection. Due to health and safety considerations, many qualitative researchers needed to unexpectedly shift their data collection approaches to a virtual format.

This chapter is written from my perspective as a faculty member at San Diego State University (SDSU) who conducts qualitative research and supervises doctoral students utilizing qualitative methods in our EdD program in Community College Leadership. As SDSU shifted most operations online in March 2020, many research projects likewise moved to virtual formats. Several of my doctoral advisees who had been planning on conducting interviews and focus groups in person immediately changed their data collections to an online format. We lacked knowledge about the challenges of and best methods for collecting qualitative data online and adopted a "learn as you go" approach. Our initial assumption was that virtual data collection would be inferior to in-person approaches; however, over the past year and a half, we have acknowledged possible unanticipated advantages and benefits to online data collection.

At the time of this writing (July 2021), it is unknown how long Covid-19 will continue to limit the qualitative data collection process. When Covid-19 no longer requires researchers to collect data online, some may continue to use virtual formats as their preferred approach to interviews, focus groups, and naturalistic observations. This chapter provides a primer on virtual approaches to qualitative research interviewing to aid faculty members, students, and practitioners considering virtual methods due to necessity and/or choice. The chapter addresses the following sections: (a) describing virtual interviewing, (b) researcher and participant perspectives, and (c) best practice considerations.

Describing Virtual Interviewing

While Covid-19 necessitates a move to online approaches among qualitative researchers, it is important to note that online data collection has been available for many years, going back to the early days of the Internet as a means of human communication (Lobe, Morgan, and Hoffman, 2020). Virtual interviewing occurs through an asynchronous exchange of information. Asynchronous communication takes place when researcher and participant are engaged in non-real-time and nonlinear interactions. Synchronous communication occurs "in the moment" and more often focuses on the spoken rather than written word to convey thoughts and opinions (James and Busher, 2009). Qualitative researchers familiar with in-person interviews and focus groups likely regard visually based, synchronous communications as approximating their usual approach (Lobe et al., 2020).

Qualitative researchers can utilize several asynchronous data collection approaches. Email interviews involve the researcher sending the participant question(s) and waiting for a response. Researchers can ask follow-up questions based on the participant's initial responses. Email interviews present several disadvantages, such as not being able to assess facial expressions/body language and uncertainty about when (and if) participants will respond to questions (Redlich-Amirav and Higginbottom, 2014). However, email interviews allow participants the opportunity to consider their responses more deeply, and give researchers more ability to adapt their interview approach and questions by being more able (compared to synchronous communications) to carefully evaluate participant responses (Topping, Douglas, and Winkler, 2021). Email interviewing does not require a high degree of computer literacy among both researchers and participants (Neville, Adams, and Cook, 2016). Email interview responses can be populated automatically into data files, thereby avoiding the time-consuming task of data entry (Neville et al., 2016).

The second type of asynchronous data collection approach is website-administered surveys. Several commercially available software programs can generate online surveys, such as Qualtrics (2021) and SurveyMonkey (2024). Like email interviews, website surveys allow participants more time to reflect on their responses, make sample recruitment easier for hard-to-reach populations, do not require advanced computer skills, and automatically generate data files. However, as with email interviewing, participants possess control over when (and if) their responses will be submitted (Neville et al., 2016). Another major disadvantage of online surveys is that they limit researchers' ability to ask follow-up questions (e.g., Grenawalt, Degeneffe, and Kessselmayer, 2020). Because the researcher is not able to probe into responses, participants' responses can sometimes appear superficial or incomplete.

In addition to asynchronous data collection, qualitative researchers can utilize several methods to interact with research participants in real-time, synchronous communications. Like face-to-face interactions, online synchronous communications allow researchers an opportunity to ask spontaneous follow-up questions. Online synchronous data collection occurs through both nonvisual and visual means. Nonvisual synchronous communication is facilitated through text-based means, including instant messaging (Redlich-Amirav and Higginbottom, 2014), chat rooms, and conferencing sites (Neville et al., 2016). Compared to email communications, instant messaging more closely approximates the flow of an oral discussion by not allowing research participants time to revise or reconsider their responses (Redlich-Amirav and Higginbottom, 2014). Likewise, chat rooms and conferencing sites facilitate the immediate transmission of information and allow more control over the flow of the interview with the researcher. In contrast, email communications and online surveys give more control to participants than to researchers since the participants possess greater control over when and how they respond to questions. Another difference between synchronous and asynchronous text communications is the need for participants to demonstrate the higher-level Internet skills necessary for instant messaging, chat rooms, and conferencing websites (Neville et al., 2016).

With the onset of Covid-19, visual synchronous communication has become part of life across various demographic groups and industries. Internet-mediated visual communication and other forms of distance-learning are part of the educational experience for children worldwide

(World Bank, 2020). For example, the K–12 online education technology market in China increased by 37.6 percent from 2019 to 2020 (Khan and Kang, 2020). Likewise, many employers shifted work tasks online. For instance, in its "Household Impacts of Covid-19 Survey" of February 2021, the Australian Bureau of Statistics (2021) estimated that 41 percent of employed Australians worked from home at least once per week. In healthcare, Covid-19 has necessitated moving assessments, consultations, and interventions to an online visual medium through the practice of "telemedicine." Telemedicine has been used by practitioners for many years, but never to the extent now seen with Covid-19. In the United States, the shift to telemedicine was facilitated in part by changes in federal laws and policies. For example, in March 2020 the Centers for Medicare and Medicaid Services allowed health providers to charge the same reimbursement rates for video and in-person visits (Contreras et al., 2020).

Like these sectors, in response to Covid-19 much qualitative research data collection is now performed via visual and synchronous approaches. However, in vivo visual communications have been discussed in qualitative research for many years. As early as the year 2000, Mann and Stewart speculated about the future use of synchronous visual communication with the expected growth of the Internet:

> But Internet communication need not be limited to text. As the capacity of the Internet itself and the connections to it increase, voice and video communication will become possible, eliminating the obstacle of the keyboard. From a research point of view, it could be argued that this simply gets us back to where we are now because it is difficult to see any substantial differences between voice communication on the Internet and voice telephony. Video communication may be a different matter since, although the technology for non-Internet video conferencing currently exists, its inflexibility (and cost) means that it has rarely been used for qualitative research. Cheap miniaturized cameras that can stick on a monitor are already available, and it may before long become the norm to include a video feed of oneself as part of any real-time CMC [computer-mediated communication]. (p. 217)

Qualitative researchers possess a variety of Voice over Internet Protocols (VoIP) (Archibald et al., 2019) to facilitate online discussions, including Zoom, Webex, Skype, GoToMeeting, Adobe Connect, and Microsoft Teams. Lobe and associates (2020) provide an exhaustive review of seven commercially available applications that all facilitate video communication, audio-only discussions, chats, screen sharing, and video recording. They also noted important differences with these platforms, including their level of compliance with HIPPA (the Health Insurance Portability and Accountability Act), a United States federal statute passed in 1996 that protects the privacy of health information. Common VoIP applications also differ in term of the types of features available through free versus paid accounts.

While each application presents unique elements, VoIP programs are accessed in similar ways (Gray et al., 2020, p. 1293): "Video conferencing software programs may have different requirements but generally will require access to specific software, hardware, and high-speed Internet access. Researchers and participants can connect to their chosen platform using their computer, mobile telephone, or tablet and have the choice of using wireless Internet or hardwiring their computer to the Internet."

Researcher and Participant Perspectives

With the dramatic and unexpected turn toward virtual interviewing qualitative researchers worldwide made in response to Covid-19, most likely did so with no understanding of its research efficacy. In my own experience with my SDSU doctoral students, a core assumption was that virtual forms *could only* be inferior to face-to-face communications. Undergirding this belief was our assumption that communication facilitated by email, instant messaging, and VoIP platforms could not capture the nuances of human communication and would likely diminish the ability to establish rapport. We assumed clients would always prefer in-person interactions over the remoteness inherent in Internet-mediated discussions.

Upon an examination of the extant literature, a more fine-grained understanding appears. As noted, virtual approaches to interviewing in qualitative research date back to the global emergence of the Internet. Also, various industries outside of academic research have used the Internet to facilitate communication, especially for telemedicine. Despite this long-standing use of virtual interviewing approaches, limited scholarship exists examining its use in qualitative research.

Scholarship on the use of virtual approaches to qualitative data collection frequently presents first-person narratives from researchers and participants offering opinions and perspectives. One of the primary arguments made for virtual interviewing concerns advantages in sampling and data collection. Several authors stress that virtual interviewing approaches allow access to populations not accessible via or agreeable to in-person research. For example, Redlich-Amirav and Higginbottom (2014, p. 5) argue that email interviews expand the pool of prospective study participants for "people who would otherwise be excluded from research because of geographical distance, different time zones, or wanting to keep their anonymity for various reasons." Likewise, Neville et al. (2016) suggest that website administered surveys increase access to hard-to-reach populations.

Further, Neville and colleagues argue that it is important for researchers to create a safe space for vulnerable and marginalized populations. These populations are defined as persons that are "hidden/invisible, stigmatised, or difficult to access" (Neville et al., 2016, p. 658). Online research environments can help create a safer and more accessible environment for vulnerable and marginalized groups due to the Internet's greater capacity for facilitating participant anonymity and conducting research not limited to aligning participant and researcher proximity (Smith and Pitts, 2007). Hence, virtual approaches to qualitative interviewing help to empower and give voice to populations neglected in social science research. In the age of Covid-19, Topping et al. (2021) advanced this point for research with persons with disabilities. Persons with disabilities are disproportionately impacted by Covid-19 and face reduced access to healthcare compared to the general population (CDC, 2021b). For many persons with disabilities, online interviews might be their only viable means of research participation. For persons with acquired brain injury (ABI), for example, Topping and associates noted that it is common for researchers to talk with professionals or persons close to individuals with ABI (rather than persons with ABI themselves) since individuals with ABI can experience a range of cognitive and communicative impairments, which can make interviewing difficult. With the expanded data collection approaches that create enhanced accessibility through virtual means (e.g., interviewing via email, where participants with ABI have more time to process answers to questions), Internet-facilitated research provides opportunities that give voice to participants with ABI.

Additionally, several articles describe the research experience of virtual interviewing specific to synchronous VoIP data collection. Counteracting a view that research participants would naturally view Internet-mediated communications negatively, several studies document a more balanced perspective. For example, UK-based researchers Deakin and Wakefield (2014) reported on the recruitment outcomes in their respective doctoral dissertation research projects. Deakin's study focused on academic networking for learning and teaching, while Wakefield's research examined student work placement mobility in Europe. The authors gave participants the choice of engaging in interviews either face to face or via Skype; they reported greater participant selection of Skype. Across both studies, 44 percent of participants chose face-to-face interviews, while 56 percent selected Skype. Both authors were able to recruit participants from within and outside the United Kingdom, an outcome they felt would not have been possible without the use of virtual interviewing. In contrast, Weinmann et al. (2012) reported lower participant preference for a Skype interview compared to a phone interview. The authors invited 300 persons aged 18–24 years in Landsberg, Germany, to participate in an epidemiological study identifying potential risk factors for brain tumors; 150 were invited to participate via Skype and 150 were invited for a telephone interview. From these totals, only 10 percent were interviewed by Skype, while 21 percent were interviewed by phone.

Beyond simply documenting participant preferences, several authors describe the virtual interviewing research experience as reported by participants and researchers. This area of literature focuses on VoIP-mediated synchronous video communications. Again, reflective of a balanced assessment, participants and researchers acknowledged the strengths and limitations of virtual interviewing. One area examined concerned the technical aspects of virtual interviewing. For instance, Archibald et al. (2019) discussed the experience of qualitative research interviews via Zoom among sixteen practice nurses in the state of South Australia. At the end of an interview on frailty screening administration, care, and treatment, Archibald and associates asked four open-ended questions on participant opinions of Zoom. Participants reported ratings of video quality, sound quality, and lag time (concerning live feed, audio, or video delays) compared to ratings for two of the original study's researchers. Participants rated each domain on a 1 (none of the time) to 5 (all of the time) scale. Ratings on all domains were generally positive. Sound quality ranged from 3 to 5 (for both groups), with a median of 4 for researchers and 5 for participants. More disparity was found with video quality, with participant ratings ranging from 1 to 5 and researcher ratings from 3 to 5. The median score for both groups was 5. With lag time, ratings for both groups ranged from 1 to 5, with a median score of 5.

Similarly, Gray and associates (2020) conducted Zoom interviews with persons who had completed a six-week parenting program. At the end of the interview, the authors asked follow-up questions on their experiences with Zoom. Regarding the ability to use Zoom software, Gray et al. reported the following: "All participants stated they enjoyed the Zoom videoconference capabilities and that they would be willing to participate in a future Zoom interview. They responded that the ease of logging in, and not being responsible for the technical or functional components of Zoom, made their experience stress-free and pleasurable" (p. 1295).

One technical recommendation by participants was for researchers to format their Zoom invitations to allow synchronization with participants' electronic calendars.

Beyond the technical aspects of virtual interviewing, it is likely most qualitative researchers are concerned with gaining the same degree of participant engagement and rapport building in virtual interviewing as is found in traditional face-to-face interactions. Qualitative research aims to understand the inner worlds and unique contextual environments of clients. Therefore, the ability to cultivate a relationship with the participant in the research environment is vital in qualitative research.

There is research evidence to support these concerns. In telemedicine, for example, while several studies document the efficacy of interventions and treatment approaches online (e.g., Mills et al., 2020; Li et al., 2020), a recent study calls into question the capacity of health practitioners to engage patients therapeutically. In a study of 263 physicians from more than 41 specialties in Santiago, Chile, Garcia-Huidobro and associates (2020) reported that 61.8% of their clinical skills were challenged when serving clients via telemedicine. Physicians in psychiatry – a specialty that relies heavily on patient engagement and rapport building – reflected the greatest level of challenge (59.4%), notably higher than for physicians in ophthalmology/otorhinolaryngology (39.8%), internal medicine subspecialties (34.8%), pediatrics subspecialties (33.2%), generalist specialties (33.2%), obstetrics and gynecology (32.3%), and surgery (16.4%).

Specific to virtual interviews in qualitative research, researchers express a variety of opinions on the capacity of VoIP technologies to facilitate rapport with participants. Initially, literature on the use of VoIP technology in qualitative research focused exclusively on Skype, with more recent publications addressing the use of Zoom likely being reflective of the emergence of Zoom as a worldwide leading technology in synchronous video communications in qualitative research and other industries.

Articles addressing the use of Skype in qualitative research offer conflicting opinions on rapport building. Several authors (Hanna, 2012; Janghorban, Roudsari, and Taghipour, 2014; Sullivan, 2012) argue that the video medium of Skype allows participants to present their true selves the same as they would in face-to-face interactions. On this point, Sullivan (2012) argued:

> The presentation of an authentic self or an accurate presentation of self is difficult to gauge in both face-to-face and online interactions. Although the above is about face-to-face interactions and those in virtual communities, it is argued that using a communication program like Skype mimics face-to-face interactions, including the presentation of self in an authentic way, almost as well as those face-to-face exchanges. (p. 56)

While Skype does afford researchers the ability to perceive participant expressions and other forms of nonverbal behaviors, other authors (Lo Iacono, Symonds, and Brown, 2016; Seitz, 2016) suggest that its capabilities are not equivalent to face-to-face communications. In addressing the limited video frame available in Skype, Seitz (2016) argued:

> A significant difference between traditional in-person and Skype interviews is that interviews over the internet do not allow the researcher and participant to be in each other's physical presence, and to see each other entirely. Even when using the full-screen video format, it is not typical to see more than the person's face or upper body via Skype. (p. 231)

Finally, Deakin and Wakefield (2014, p. 610) suggested an alternative view: namely, that the capacity to establish rapport with participants via Skype is largely dependent on participant personality, with some feeling more comfortable in a virtual versus an in-person setting. The authors noted that "in some of the PhD cases, Skype interviewees were more responsive, and rapport was built quicker than in a number of face-to-face interviews."

In contrast to the mixed opinions on Skype, three more recent articles on qualitative interviewing with Zoom all reported positive outcomes in rapport building, possibly due to advances in VoIP technology and/or the pervasive familiarity with video communications as part of daily life for many worldwide. In Gray et al.'s (2020, p. 1295) study with persons who attended a parenting training program, the authors noted participants' appreciation for being able to "see and connect personally" with interviewers when sharing their views on a topic sensitive in nature. In a study on student homelessness in Houston, Texas, Roberts, Pavlakis, and Richards (2021) noted that rapport with participants was improved by working in teams, with one researcher assigned to addressing the technical aspects of the interview while the other researcher conducted the actual interview. In Archibald et al.'s (2019, p. 4) study with sixteen nurses, 69 percent believed Zoom was "useful in forming and maintaining rapport with the researcher," as compared to nonvisual tools such as telephone or email. Several participants also felt that Zoom was the next best option to face-to-face interviews.

While researchers document a capacity to establish rapport with partici-pants through VoIP applications, no degree of technological sophistication can offer a realistic and hands-on understanding of a participant's context-ual world (outside of the video screen) such as occurs in person-to-person interactions. In their study on student homelessness, Roberts and associ-ates (2021, p. 8) described how, before Covid-19, they aimed to reduce the "social distance" between themselves and their participants by spending time "extensively in areas of the city that were the focus of our data collection to develop a foundational sense of the neighborhoods and spaces in which our study was embedded." However, due to safety concerns during the pandemic, researchers were not able to gain a contextual understanding of participants' lived spaces through in-person contact as planned.

Best Practice Considerations

This chapter concludes with a presentation of best practice considerations for virtual interviewing in qualitative research. In my research and future doctoral student advising, these domains will be incorporated into meth-odological planning for conducting Internet-mediated data collection. In the short term, these lessons will be applied due to the necessity of keeping both the researcher and the participant protected during data collection. Long-term, however, past the era of Covid-19, researchers will need to choose between virtual and in-person interviewing based on the advantages and disadvantages of each approach. These practice recommendations may guide the efforts of qualitative researchers who chose a virtual approach. Three domains of practice considerations are offered: technical prepar-ation, participant engagement, and ethical sensitivity.

Technical Preparation

Any application of technology in virtual interviewing carries the risk of unanticipated problems. When utilizing any type of asynchronous and synchronous Internet-mediated interview, there may be a range of problems – for example, the functioning of the computer, the availability of an Internet connection, and the expected purpose of the email, instant message, web-based survey, or VoIP program. These types of challenges adversely impact the flow of the interview and the researcher's ability to establish rapport with the participant.

Because of its technological sophistication, multiple authors describe potential difficulties with VoIP technology. Most of the problems concern the use of Skype. Some of these challenges likely reflect technological limitations (at the time of these publications), lack of user (researcher and/or participant) experience in visual Internet communication, and reduced public access to high-speed Internet. In their experience of using Skype during their dissertation research studies, Deakin and Wakefield (2014) noted that interviews were sometimes interrupted by poor sound quality, and that technological and signal problems hurt participant rapport building. In her discussion of Skype, Sullivan (2012) mentioned the possibility of malfunctioning microphones and webcams. Also, she emphasized that the most common issue interfering with interview flow was lag time in communications between both parties. Seitz (2016) discussed the problem of dropped calls and pauses in Skype-mediated interviews due to poor Internet connections. Seitz noted that these problems negatively impacted rapport and the quality of research partnerships with participants. More recently, in their Zoom interviews with sixteen practice nurses in South Australia, Archibald and associates' (2019) reported that technical challenges were sometimes due to the lack of digital literacy among participants.

There are several practical approaches qualitative researchers should consider when responding to these challenges. Researchers should assume that technical problems will occur rather than be surprised or frustrated when challenges emerge. To limit the likelihood that a technical glitch will take place, the researcher and the participants should ensure the latest versions of the VoIP or other types of virtual interviewing software are downloaded on their devices. Also, devices used to facilitate interviews, such as smartphones, should be fully charged to prevent communication lags and connection loss (Seitz, 2016). When technical problems do occur, the researcher needs to have backup plans in place (Sullivan, 2012). For example, a researcher planning on conducting a Zoom interview could prepare multiple computer devices (e.g., computer, tablet, smartphone) should the primary computing device malfunction.

To avoid user errors, the qualitative researcher and the participant should be thoroughly familiar with and trained to correctly use the virtual interviewing software (Mirick and Wladkowski, 2019). For instance, Seitz (2016) interviewed forty-five student researchers on their use of Skype to facilitate qualitative research interviews. Seitz shared the example of a student who stated she practiced using Skype with a friend before conducting her interviews.

Participant Engagement

Qualitative researchers should not assume that an interview protocol planned for in-person interactions will seamlessly transfer to a virtual environment. Rather, it is necessary to prepare for and account for the unique features of Internet-mediated interviews and consciously employ strategies designed to maximize participant engagement.

Qualitative researchers should attend to multiple considerations when using Internet data collection methods. Participants are likely to feel more empowered and engaged in the interviewing process when given a choice of technology. Hanna (2012) offered participants the choice of telephone, face-to-face, or Skype interviews, while Deakin and Wakefield (2014) let participants decide if they wanted to be interviewed in person or via Skype through video and audio or audio-only discussions. Hanna (2012) noted that part of giving participants choice over the interview modality was responding to their individual needs. In choosing remote interviews, Hanna tried to avoid discomfort among participants not wanting Hanna to travel many miles from his home on the south coast of England. Also, participants might have perceived less encroachment of their physical space due to the virtual rather than in-person interaction. Finally, the choice of virtual method is especially important when researching with vulnerable populations to create a sense of trust in and respect for the interview process (Neville et al., 2016).

Virtual interviewing requires particular attention to rapport building. The online environment sometimes creates barriers to participants' willingness to share information or to feel comfortable. Several recommendations are offered. Because of the many technological requirements of virtual interviews, the ability of the researcher to develop rapport and engagement with the participant can be compromised. To respond to this challenge, in their study on student homelessness, Roberts and associates (2021) deployed two-member research teams. One member of each team was assigned the duties of note-taking and technical management, while the other member applied their full attention to the dynamics of the interview, such as appropriately responding to participants nonverbal behavior. A second strategy was offered by Deakin and Wakefield (2014). Face-to-face interviews naturally allow space and time for the researcher to engage in small talk and rapport-building before initiation of the actual interview. To recreate this dynamic in a virtual environment, both researchers exchanged several emails with participants before the Skype interviews to build a pre-interview connection and address participants' questions.

Attaining a full and accurate perspective in qualitative research can also incorporate a contextual understanding of participants' lived spaces. For example, while Roberts and associates (2021) were not able to physically spend time in Houston, Texas (the setting of their study on student homelessness) due to travel restrictions presented by Covid-19, they remained committed to gaining this understanding by alternative online means:

> by exploring neighborhoods via online interactive maps, attending virtual public lectures about current local issues, setting alerts for relevant news media, and curating reading lists about Houston's history, neighborhoods, and public policies. For example, virtual lectures hosted by a local university on the state of housing in Houston helped us better understand how shifts in housing stock and affordability were driving evictions and homelessness in the area. (p. 8)

Ethical Considerations

Virtual interviewing requires qualitative researchers to not assume one's in-person interview approach will automatically apply virtually; hence, the consent process likewise needs to incorporate factors unique to a digital setting. In drafting consent documents, qualitative researchers need to anticipate a range of threats and establish risk mitigation procedures to ensure participants' rights are honored in the research process. The first consideration is acknowledging possible violations of participant confidentiality and anonymity. Participants should know the privacy policies for companies offering VoIP and other Internet-based data collection approaches. Archibald et al.'s (2019) review of Zoom's data collection policies (as of March 19, 2019) reveals that the company automatically stores information on user data such as IP addresses, device type, and name and contact details. Also, in Zoom, cloud-based session recordings of video, audio, and text transcriptions can be saved or transferred to world-wide servers. Because of potential data collection vulnerabilities, US-based researchers collecting protected health information need to ensure the virtual technology is HIPPA compliant (Lobe et al., 2020).

An additional privacy consideration is the unanticipated sharing of private information with individual interviews and/or focus groups. With video-based interviews, many participants will choose to log on from home and may unintentionally share information about their lives beyond what they intended when details (e.g., family pictures) in their video backgrounds are visible. To address this problem, Lobe et al. (2020) suggested the use of a virtual or blurred background. Lobe and associates (p. 6) also noted that maintaining participant privacy in online focus groups is particularly difficult, and suggested the following informed consent language: "Be aware that your confidentiality cannot be guaranteed in a group setting such as this. Please respect one another's privacy by not discussing who attended this meeting or repeating anything that was said." Qualitative researchers must also contemplate the distinction between public versus private spaces when considering what Internet users might regard as private (e.g., email communication) versus public (e.g., posting to a website). Facilitating an informed consent process in nonprivate Internet settings can be difficult or infeasible (Redlich-Amirav and Higginbottom, 2014).

Qualitative researchers need to also consider different options for obtaining informed consent in a virtual environment. An early publication on video-based interviewing (Sullivan, 2012) offered the option of gaining consent verbally. More recent publications appear to stress a more documented approach. Lobe et al. (2020) suggested adding a scanned signature to a Microsoft Word consent document or using signature software programs such as Docusign. Roberts and associates (2021) described how they obtained electronically signed consent documents via Qualtrics and noted the program's capacity to accept signatures through various types of devices such as smartphones and laptops. Regardless of the approach used, Roberts et al. stressed the importance of assessing participants' "digital literacy" in understanding how to correctly navigate the online consent process.

Conclusions

The Covid-19 pandemic necessitated dramatic and immediate modifications in how humans interact with and relate to each other. Because much qualitative research depends on human interaction and engagement, how data is collected has increasingly shifted to virtual environments. Someday Covid-19 will no longer present a public health danger to researchers and participants. When that time comes, will qualitative research shift back to in-person data collection for most, or has the current scenario permanently changed perceptions about the role of the Internet in qualitative data collection?

This chapter highlights how virtual interviewing is neither superior nor inferior to face-to-face interviews. Rather, it is simply a different approach that offers a range of possible advantages and disadvantages. In my research and my advising of SDSU doctoral students, this chapter reminds me that choosing to move one's interview approach from in-person to online involves an array of technical, conceptual, and ethical considerations, each of which must be discussed and debated.

The continued development of the Internet will provide researchers with an expanded and more sophisticated set of research tools to conduct interviews in an online environment. It is hoped that future scholarship will continue to critically evaluate this unique approach to data collection so that researchers will be well informed and properly trained in this use of emerging virtual interviewing technologies.

References

Archibald, M. M., Ambagtsheer, R. C., Casey, M. G. and Lawless, M., 2019. Using Zoom videoconferencing for qualitative data collection: Perceptions and experiences of researchers and participants. *International Journal of Qualitative Methods, 18,* 1609406919874596.

Australian Bureau of Statistics. 2021. A year of Covid-19 and Australians work from home more. www.abs.gov.au/media-centre/media-releases/year-covid-19-and-australians-work-home-more (accessed 30 July 2021).

Centers for Disease Control and Prevention [CDC]. 2021a. How Covid-19 spreads. https://www.cdc.gov/coronavirus/2019-ncov/prevent-getting-sick/how-covid-spreads.html (accessed 20 July 2021).

Centers for Disease Control and Prevention [CDC]. 2021b. People with disabilities. https://www.cdc.gov/coronavirus/2019-ncov/need-extra-precautions/people-with-disabilities.html (accessed 9 August 2021).

Contreras, C. M., Metzger, G. A., Beane, J. D., et al. 2020. Telemedicine: Patient-provider clinical engagement during the COVID-19 pandemic and beyond. *Journal of Gastrointestinal Surgery, 24*(7), 1692–1697.

Cucinotta, D., and Vanelli, M., 2020. WHO declares COVID-19 a pandemic. *Acta bio-medica: Atenei Parmensis, 91*(1), 157–160. https://doi.org/10.23750/abm.v91i1.9397.

Deakin, H. and Wakefield, K., 2014. Skype interviewing: Reflections of two PhD researchers. *Qualitative Research, 14*(5), 603–616.

Garcia-Huidobro, D., Rivera, S., Chang, S. V., Bravo, P. and Capurro, D., 2020. System-wide accelerated implementation of telemedicine in response to COVID-19: Mixed methods evaluation. *Journal of Medical Internet Research, 22*(10), e22146.

Gelo, O., Braakmann, D. and Benetka, G., 2008. Quantitative and qualitative research: Beyond the debate. *Integrative Psychological and Behavioral Science, 42* (3), 266–290.

Gray, L. M., Wong-Wylie, G., Rempel, G. R. and Cook, K., 2020. Expanding qualitative research interviewing strategies: Zoom video communications. *The Qualitative Report, 25*(5), 1292–1301.

Grenawalt, T. A., Degeneffe, C. E. and Kesselmayer, R. F., 2020. Perceived career impacts from specialized instruction in cognitive disabilities: A phenomenological study. *Rehabilitation Research, Policy, and Education, 34*(4), 235–249.

Hanna, P., 2012. Using internet technologies (such as Skype) as a research medium: A research note. *Qualitative Research, 12*(2), 239–242.

James, N. and Busher, H., 2009. Engaging with research participants online. In *Online Interviewing*, pp. 19–29. SAGE. http://dx.doi.org/10.4135/9780857024503.

Janghorban, R., Roudsari, R. L. and Taghipour, A., 2014. Skype interviewing: The new generation of online synchronous interview in qualitative research. *International Journal of Qualitative Studies on Health and Well-Being, 9*(1), 24152.

Khan, Q., and Kang, Z., 2020. Promising post-Covid-19 future of China's online K12 market: An overview of the nascent industry. https://equalocean.com/analysis/2020123115340 (accessed 30 July 2021).

Li, H. L., Chan, Y. C., Huang, J. X. and Cheng, S. W., 2020. Pilot study using telemedicine video consultation for vascular patients' care during the COVID-19 period. *Annals of Vascular Surgery, 68*, 76–82.

Lo Iacono, V., Symonds, P. and Brown, D. H., 2016. Skype as a tool for qualitative research interviews. *Sociological Research Online, 21*(2), 103–117.

Lobe, B., Morgan, D. and Hoffman, K. A., 2020. Qualitative data collection in an era of social distancing. *International Journal of Qualitative Methods, 19*, 1609406920937875.

Mann, C. and Stewart, F., 2000. *Internet communication and qualitative research: A handbook for researching online.* Sage.

Mills, E. C., Savage, E., Lieder, J. and Chiu, E. S., 2020. Telemedicine and the COVID-19 pandemic: Are we ready to go live? *Advances in Skin & Wound Care, 33*(8), 410–417.

Mirick, R. G. and Wladkowski, S. P., 2019. Skype in qualitative interviews: Participant and researcher perspectives. *The Qualitative Report, 24*(12), 3061–3072.

Neville, S., Adams, J. and Cook, C., 2016. Using internet-based approaches to collect qualitative data from vulnerable groups: Reflections from the field. *Contemporary Nurse, 52*(6), 657–668.

Qualtrics. 2021. How we roll. www.qualtrics.com/about/ (accessed 27 July 2021).

Redlich-Amirav, D., & Higginbottom, G. 2014. New emerging technologies in qualitative research. *The Qualitative Report, 19*(26), 1–14.

Roberts, J. K., Pavlakis, A. E. and Richards, M. P., 2021. It's more complicated than it seems: Virtual qualitative research in the COVID-19 era. *International Journal of Qualitative Methods, 20*, 16094069211002959.

Sauer, L. M., 2021. What is coronavirus? Health. www.hopkinsmedicine.org/health/conditions-and-diseases/coronavirus (accessed 20 July 2021).

Seitz, S., 2016. Pixilated partnerships, overcoming obstacles in qualitative interviews via Skype: A research note. *Qualitative Research, 16*(2), 229–235.

Smith, A. and Pitts, M., 2007. Researching the margins: An introduction. In A. Smith and M. Pitts (eds.) *Researching the Margins* (pp. 3–41). London: Palgrave Macmillan.

Sullivan, J.R., 2012. Skype: An appropriate method of data collection for qualitative interviews?. *The Hilltop Review*, *6*(1), 10.

SurveyMonkey. 2024. Create your own surveys. www.surveymonkey.com/mp/take-a-tour/ (accessed 16 February 2024).

Topping, M., Douglas, J. and Winkler, D., 2021. General considerations for conducting online qualitative research and practice: Implications for interviewing people with acquired brain injury. *International Journal of Qualitative Methods*, *20*, 16094069211019615.

Weinmann, T., Thomas, S., Brilmayer, S., Heinrich, S. and Radon, K., 2012. Testing Skype as an interview method in epidemiologic research: Response and feasibility. *International Journal of Public Health*, *57*(6), 959–961.

Wilson, D. and Neville, S., 2009. Culturally safe research with vulnerable populations. *Contemporary Nurse*, *33*(1), 69–79.

World Bank. 2020. Remote learning, EdTech & Covid-19. www.worldbank.org/en/topic/edutech/brief/edtech-covid-19 (accessed: 30 July 2021).

World Health Organization. 2021. Coronavirus disease (COVID-19) pandemic. www.who.int/emergencies/diseases/novel-coronavirus-2019 (accessed: 20 July 2021).

CHAPTER 9

Minimizing the Impact Technology Has on Interviewer–Interviewee Rapport
An Existential-Phenomenological Analysis

Patrick M. Whitehead and Gary Senecal

Introduction

Many years ago, a friend explained that they had created a website to collect interview data for their qualitative dissertation. Prospective participants were asked by e-mail to complete a short questionnaire and, if they qualified, were prompted to answer a series of questions in order to be entered into a drawing for a gift card. All this friend had to do was wait for the data to trickle in.

Fishing for data on the internet is very different from sitting across the table or office from a person who has gone to the trouble of getting there. This difference is the central question of the present chapter. It is argued here that, with a little planning and fidelity to the research participant(s), the qualitative researcher can rely heavily on the internet and other digital technologies during the research process without worrying that they have abandoned the objectives of qualitative research.

Human relations today are mediated by digital technology; it is inescapable. News, correspondence, work meetings, and visits from relatives are piped in by way of smart phones, tablets, laptops, and computers. Qualitative researchers themselves find their practices of data collection, analysis, storage, and publication are increasingly mediated by technology – something evident throughout books such as this.

The specific question the authors ask in this chapter is as follows: does using technology to conduct qualitative research interfere with the goals of qualitative research? In the words of German philosopher Martin Heidegger, who has inspired many qualitative researchers and whose work is called on later in the chapter; Does technology impair the researcher's ability to "let that which shows itself be seen from itself in the very way in which it shows itself from itself" (Heidegger defining phenomenology; 2008, p. 58)?

Technology is not merely used by humans. The relationship is reciprocal – that is to say, humans are changed by the technologies they use. For example, an interviewer might use a tape recorder to make interview transcriptions easier. With the recorder, the interviewer is free to become absorbed in the conversation without fumbling over pen and paper. But a change has taken place. With pen and paper, the interviewer writes "this is what I understood." With the tape recorder, there is a record of "what was actually said." The pen and paper capture interviewer intuition; the recording captures words.

The authors do not wish to question the use of recording devices. The latter is simply an example of the reciprocally influential human–technology relationship. If, however, the tape recording example is magnified a few hundred times, a troubling future in qualitative research appears.

It is not difficult to imagine a scenario where technology transforms the process of qualitative research to such an extent that the latter becomes unrecognizable. In a hypothetical and exaggerated way, technology could be applied to qualitative healthcare research by increasing the quantity of participants, the volume and accuracy of transcripts, and the ease of analysis. A digital personality (such as Apple's Siri or Amazon's Alexa) could conduct thousands of interviews while simultaneously transcribing and computing out of them chunks of meaning and organizing those chunks into a narrative that corresponds to the writing and storytelling style of *The New York Times*. In this (hopefully) fictional example, there is no researcher–participant relationship. There are no insights or intuitions, at least not in the human sense of those terms. There is no meeting or sharing of time and space. There is nothing personal. There is only information.

If it can be concluded that this hypothetical scenario is a troubling one, then a boundary must be identified – somewhere beyond tape-recorders yet shy of researcher-free data analysis programs. To accomplish this, the authors will more carefully examine the human–technology relationship as it has been encountered, explored, and criticized by phenomenological philosophers and scholars. The discussion will then turn to the practice of phenomenological research in healthcare, and conclude with an analysis of an international study concerning posttraumatic stress disorder (PTSD) in military combat-ants – a study which relied heavily on technology (Senecal & Mcdonald, 2021).

Phenomenological Inquiry and Technology

It would be impossible to imagine an area of qualitative research more divided about the use of technology than phenomenology. Phenomenology is home to the exciting and boundary-pushing research of postphenomenology which celebrates technology, but it is also home to Martin Heidegger and his followers, who regard technology with contempt and suspicion.

Postphenomenology's Celebration of Technology

Postphenomenology began with the work of American philosopher Don Ihde, specifically his *Technology and the Lifeworld* (1990). Ihde explains how technology, which is anything that mediates between human and world, is inescapable. Like all mediating factors, technology transforms what it mediates. This reciprocal relationship can be seen in simple technologies, such as a pair of primitive sandals. Sandals protect the sole of the human foot, which is already thick with calluses for standing and walking. The leather sandal sole makes it possible to cross gnarly terrain without worrying whether a jagged rock will tear the plantar fascia of the sandal-wearer. Soon the network of footpaths expands, owing to an expansion of walkable surfaces. This changes the environment by wearing away shrubs alongside riverbeds, up rocky slopes, and through dense ground-cover. It also changes the body of the sandal-wearer, whose walking gait is adjusted slightly to allow for the few millimeters of added sole, an adjustment which is absorbed throughout the rest of the body (to say nothing of the weakened muscles and calluses in the feet, which are no longer worked as they had once been).

The changes brought about by sandal-wearing are small but easy to see. The digital technologies examined by Ihde and his followers are substantial yet often hidden. It is not immediately apparent how a social media application changes the environment, because the warehouse-sized server-farms are hidden away and out of sight. Postphenomenology examines technologies for their impact on human and world, such as how cell phones change human cognition (Wellner, 2015), how screens and earbuds weave technology seamlessly into daily life (O'Neal Irwin, 2016), and how cochlear implants (and other audial devices) shape human awareness (Idhe, 2012).

It is not difficult to imagine how medical technologies have changed humans. Statins have transformed the diets and lifestyles that people can pursue without worrying about collapsing in the hallway clutching dramatically at their chests. Sunscreens and skin creams have made habitable previously uninhabitable climates. Hotels and resorts have followed closely behind.

Postphenomenologists have chosen their moniker carefully. Among other reasons, Rosenberger and VerBeek (2015) have explained that the "post" indicates a step past what might be called traditional phenomenology, particularly with respect to phenomenology's criticism of technology.

Heidegger's Criticism of Technology

Following Martin Heidegger's many criticisms of technology, students of phenomenology acquire a degree of skepticism regarding the role played by technology. This position is further intensified by the living conditions of the great German philosopher during his later years: isolated in an electricity-free and unplumbed cabin on the side of a mountain in the Black Forest, which was accessible only by hiking. Combining Heidegger's philosophy with his practice, the Heidegger scholar assumes that the purest experiences occur only in the absence of technology.

Heidegger (1977) compares the changes brought about by technology (*techne*) with those brought forth naturally (*physis*). Understanding the difference is essential to understanding Heidegger's criticism of technology. A trail through the forest, for example, can be created by either *techne* or *physis*. If deer continually use the same pathway through the trees, then they create a network of trails by yielding to the forest (*physis*). If a committee of fell runners use chainsaws and bucket trucks to create the line through the trees that corresponds to what they had drawn on their maps, then they are making the forest yield to them (*techne*).

Heidegger further divides technology into two categories: Greek and modern. Given his fondness for the Greeks and his disapproval of modernity, the comparison is an easy one to anticipate. The Greeks, Heidegger explains, were not without technology. But, in Heidegger's estimation, the pre-Modern style of technology works *with* nature – it is a means of bringing about the essences with which nature is pregnant. This would be like the fell running committee spending time with the forest and learning which pathways were already suggested by the rhythm and flow of the vegetation, and only then using the chainsaws and bucket trucks to help these existing pathways become more pronounced. In this case, the trail is developed without violating the essence of the forest. In the modern version, however, the fell running committee forces the trail on the forest, ignoring and possibly violating the forest's essence. Such a trail would be susceptible to washout, eroding the trailside shrubs along with it. It is the modern form of technology that Heidegger cautions against because, like the practice of modern science, it transforms things (such as forests and persons) into objects (natural resources and bodies, respectively).

Jacques Ellul (1964) contributes to Heidegger's criticism of modern technology. He defines technology as anything done with the goal of maximizing efficiency. Waiting for deer to create a walkable path would be minimally efficient, whereas bull-dozing the entire forest would be maximally efficient. Staircases descending into the recesses of the Mammoth Cavs National Park in the United States is an example of maximum-efficiency-spelunking. Doing so, however, violates the integrity of the caves, making them subject to collapse. This is why steel I-beams and braces have been constructed to reinforce the cave's walls and ceilings. In a few decades, perhaps the entire cave system will be as accommodating as the New York City subway (thereby violating the wild essence of the cave).

To summarize, Heidegger's criticism is directed at the modern iteration of technology, which, for him, violates the essences of things as it changes them. In healthcare, this would be like extending the lifespan by five or ten years without wondering what (or who) is being preserved. The meaning of living is discarded, replaced by measures of improvement. This is the familiar criticism of medicalization (Aho, 2018; Illich, 2000; Svenaeus, 2018; Szasz, 2007; Whitehead, 2019; Whitehead & Groth, 2019).

Problems with Technology in Healthcare

In order to appreciate how technology changes the essence of human being, we must examine the distinctly *homo sapient* process (i.e., thinking). Heidegger (2004) describes two types of thinking: meditative and calculative. Calculative thinking is the process of actively breaking things down into their simplest units, separating the units into categories, and working with them on that level to achieve predetermined objectives. Calculative thinking can be seen in the auto mechanic who examines the battery, alternator, and starter before solving the ignition problem. Meditative thinking, by comparison, begins with an openness to what is possible. The meditative thinker is not actively searching for answers to problems, but waits for answers and insights to come. This is like Leonardo DaVinci staring at a mural for hours or days before it occurs to him that what is missing is a dab of paint (Capra, 2007).

In a letter to Médard Boss, Heidegger (2001) explains how technology can only be implemented in a calculative way. More transportation methods (trains, ships, airplanes) means greater ease of product distribution, and, calculatively speaking, greater ease is always better. Ease of distribution increases exponentially until only a few companies remain and a handful of people own the majority of wealth. With calculative thinking, there is no asking "Good for whom?" There is only "good." In this fashion health, which is merely the state of well-being (Gadamer, 1996), has been turned into a consumer good. The healthy person is the person for whom medical health is the furthest thing from awareness.

The dangers of technology in healthcare are somewhat revealed by the use of pedometers to encourage exercise in normally sedentary people. This is because the hourly or daily walks up and down hallways and around office buildings are done with no other intention than accumulating steps – a goal that would otherwise be preposterous. For Hans Georg Gadamer, filling the schedule with so-called healthy activities is the antithesis to health, because they disrupt ordinary routines and well-being.

Perhaps the best Heideggerian criticism of medical technology comes from Fredrik Svenaeus (2018), who gives the example of how the technology of psychiatric drugs has changed what it means to live and feel:

> [B]y relieving symptoms like feelings of hopelessness, anxiety, and restlessness – [drugs] also may separate the person from his or her true self. When the pills flatten the life moods of the patient, he or she is no longer forced to challenge himself or herself on the true meaning of his or her life: what he or she wants to accomplish and who he or she wants to be. By producing health the drugs would therefore – at least in some cases – alienate the patient from his or her true self. (p. 143)

In each of these examples, the problem is when technology (and technique) alienates persons from their experience: human being is replaced with measurable objects.

The Essence of Qualitative Research and Its Violation

Heidegger finds in modern science the same kind of violation that occurs in modern technology. In order to subject humans, rivers, and insects to the scientific method, these must first be converted into objects – that is, they must be viewed not as humans, rivers, or insects, but as bundles of measurable properties. Anything unmeasurable is discarded. In psychology, this means discarding mind, consciousness, belief, feeling, inspiration, purpose, spirituality, meaning, and so on (e.g., Watson, 1930). This practice results in a chilling psychology of sex (e.g., Masters & Johnson, 1966).

In the modern practice of medicine, the human body is broken into cells, tissue, organs, organ systems, and so on. This has led to breakthroughs in the understanding and treatment of infectious diseases, but it has also created unsolvable problems such as conditions of unknown medical origin (ambiguously called "chronic" or "idiopathic"; Slatman, 2018). Patients complain of pain, discomfort, difficulty, and suffering, but the technologies of medical science can provide no explanation. Viruses and broken bones can be viewed with the tools of modern science, but suffering cannot. Modern science can see the what, but never the who.

Midcentury Swiss doctors became aware of Heidegger's critique of modern science, and invited him to their hospital to teach the doctors how to recover some of what medicine had lost to the scientific approach (Heidegger, 2001). Heidegger compared for them the two German words for body: Körper, which is the body in its inert and corporeal form, and Leib, which is the body thanks to which we tie our shoes and jog along forest trails. While jogging, for example, the body is absorbed in being: legs disappear from awareness until fatigue sets in or an ankle is sprained. Only then do the legs announce themselves as objects with tendons and ligaments that are susceptible to strain. During this episode a shift in perspective takes place from Leib to Körper. While rolling along the trail's undulations, there is no body; there is only being-a-jogger. During and after fatigue or injury, the body is transformed into an object, divided into parts with specialized functions: elastic fascia, sturdy bones, powerful muscles. These functions describe body parts in general as if they belong to nobody.

It is only with the body as object (Körper) that one can say "my leg is broken" or "the tumor has metastasized." These cannot predict how the information is received or lived by a person. Modern science cannot view the body as it is lived (Leib), and therefore cannot view the essence of having cancer or a broken leg. Understanding illness requires a different approach (see Kleinman, 1986). For Heidegger (and the authors), the different approach is phenomenology.

Heidegger (2008) reminds us that phenom*enology* is not a science of phenomena the same way that the*ology* is the science of Gods, bi*ology* is the science of life, or cosm*ology* is the science of the universe. He explains,

> Those terms designate the objects of their respective sciences to the subject-matter which they comprise at the time. Phenomenology neither designates the object of its researches nor characterizes the subject-matter thus comprised. The word merely informs us of the "*how*" with which what is to be treated in this science gets exhibited and handled. To have a science "of" phenomena means to grasp its objects *in such a way* that everything about them which is up for discussion must be treated by exhibiting it directly and demonstrating it directly. (pp. 58–59)

This means that the practice of phenomenology must begin with a singular instance of experience, which, for Heidegger, is "being" or "existence." In order to keep the essence or nature of the experience intact, the experience can neither be divided into objects with discrete properties nor scrubbed clean of the meaning or significance it has for the person.

The foregoing description of phenomenology is familiar to qualitative researchers who do not wish to take hold of objective properties, but who hope to better understand the nature of medical conditions and their treatment as they are encountered by living persons.

Phenomenological Research and Existential Medicine

Preparing a phenomenological study in medicine is not as easy as picking up the closest book. Owing somewhat to a careless use of the word in the middle of the century (see Spiegelberg, 1967), there remains disagreement and uncertainty about what phenomenology is and how it should be practiced. Consequently, there are a diversity of phenomenological methods to follow. Whichever method is followed, the researcher can be sure that they are probably doing it wrong. Over the last few years, for example, leading phenomenological theorists Max van Manen (2019) and Dan Zahavi (2019) have had a public and acrimonious exchange about how the other has abandoned their guiding philosophy – an exchange that has taken place primarily in the pages of qualitative research in nursing journals. To wit, this exchange has included the title "On Getting it Quite Wrong," where Zahavi (2018) lists the phenomenological blunders committed by van Manen (2016).

Recognizing the need for direction in qualitative and phenomenological research, SAGE publications has developed a book series. The series editor writes, "[t]he proliferation of articles on qualitative research methods and the disagreement among researchers as to how to conduct certain types of research have led to the development of this [Methods in Nursing] research series" (Brink, 2000, p. vii). Scholars have written essays clarifying the methodological differences that follow from Heidegger's (2008) hermeneutic phenomenology or Edmund Husserl's (1970) transcendental phenomenology (e.g., Laverty, 2003).

Heidegger has received recent attention in healthcare research (Aho, 2018; Whitehead, 2019), including a new collection of Heidegger's Zollikon seminars and letters on medicine not yet available in English (Heidegger, 1962). Existential medical research examines the lived body (Leib), which has peculiar consequences in healthcare research. Gadamer

(1996) explains that health cannot mean the absence of disease. To experience the absence of disease requires that one first think of one's body as an object, and only then imagine that said body is unhampered by virus or injury. Instead, Gadamer explains, health may be understood existentially as the experience of being fully absorbed in life. Anything that draws one out of this absorption in one's life violates the essence of health, transforming it into something that can more easily be manipulated and measured. Counting steps to increase health draws one out of one's everyday routine, asking one to view one's body as a machine in need of routine maintenance.

Research in existential medicine follows a case-study approach where, as quoted earlier, "discussion must be treated by exhibiting [medical conditions] directly and demonstrating [those same conditions] directly." In his follow-up to Heidegger's medical lectures, psychiatrist Médard Boss (1979) provides an example of what this would look like by examining the peculiar psychosomatic symptoms of a patient (Regular Zurcher). In such analyses one finds no broken bones, viruses, or infections, but only disruptions to living. Whitehead (in press) provides a case study approach for applying Heidegger's insights to the social sciences and healthcare.

Not Losing Sight of Human Being: Heidegger's Existentials

Heidegger's criticism of technology is reason for researchers to be cautious of relying on technology to conduct their qualitative research. But in the foregoing discussion of this critique, there is also evidence of an antidote – a sort of inoculation against technological violence (i.e., when technology violates the essence of things). To avoid violating the essence of humans and their experience, care must be taken to preserve these. To do so, we turn to those qualities that are unique to human existence: Heidegger's existentials.

Humans, Heidegger (2001, 2008) tells us, are not merely here and there the way that houseplants and bricks are here and there. Wherever humans are found, they are always *being* there. This is why Heidegger has used the peculiar word *Dasein* ("being there") to describe the unique being of humans. Dasein can be understood through (at least) five existentials: body, space, time, relatedness, and mood. Readers are directed elsewhere for a complete discussion of these (Aho, 2018; Boss, 1979; Whitehead, 2019). In short, this list of existentials represents what humans *are*, and not what they have. A teacher is a teacher through their body – capable of shushing classrooms or communicating understanding through bodily movements.

The authors propose the existentials as a test for preserving the human side of qualitative health research. In order to avoid violating the essence of humans, qualitative researchers must acknowledge as many of these existentials as possible.

Figure 9.1 shows the interconnection of Heidegger's existentials. When encountering humans, we are only ever given the center of this figure – that is, existence, which has components that can be abstracted into body, mood, and so on. (The figure is imperfect, however, because it suggests that Body can only be related to Time through Space, and so on.) When looking after human being, the qualitative researcher is encouraged to notice all five existentials.

For example, a slipped disc or pinched nerve can occur in a person's lower back. X-rays and CT-scans can verify this. These descriptions, however, remain at the level of an inert and corporeal body, not the body of a middle-aged dad. The attending physician might say "I see you have a slipped disc between the L4-L5 vertebrae." This statement of fact occurs only at the level of the body (Figure 9.2a). The same event can be described by examining relatedness: to dad, there is no slipped disc. What dad experiences is a nagging discomfort that keeps him from playing catch in the front yard (Figure 9.2b). Dad may also experience a growing concern that the pain won't get any better, and that extra hours at the factory may no longer be feasible (Figure 9.2c). These experiences cannot be found in

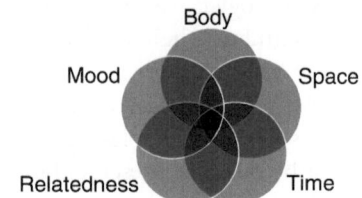

Figure 9.1 Heidegger's existentials

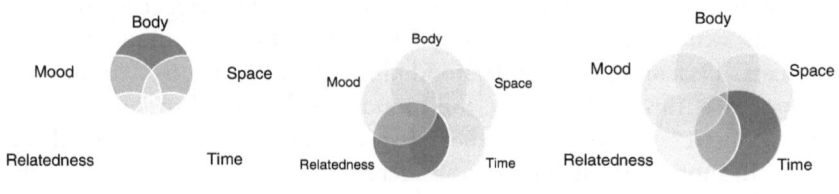

a: Body only   b: Relatedness only   c: Time only

Figure 9.2 Slipped disc x existential

the lower back. They occur in this man's daily life, and are exhibited in a slight limp, an uncomfortable posture, and the occasional grimace – these are moments when the injury announces itself to the injured man, and anybody else around to take notice.

In order to capture the essence of the slipped disc, the phenomenological researcher is encouraged to explore the impact on all five existentials. Consequently, part of the resulting medical prognosis might involve something unusual in medicine, such as working with the patient to explore alternative activities to enjoy with his children.

Heidegger's existential phenomenology asks that the medical researcher considers the broader implications of a medical injury, and to realize how there is more at stake than the lower back region.

Noticing Heidegger's five existentials is unusual in ordinary encounters with others. Even in a face-to-face conversation, much of the other person's life is going to be invisible. When interviewer and interviewee are sitting face-to-face, they are sharing space and time, but that does not mean that the interviewer is aware of either. A distracted or inexperienced interviewer is going to be limited to the interview questions written in front of them. Using technology to conduct interviews further complicates this process. Once the researcher becomes familiar with the interview process and, if necessary, the technology used, a greater sensitivity to the interviewee can occur. This requires a period of learning, wherein the researcher obtains familiarity and facility with the technologies used. An example of this can be found in the two-year qualitative study conducted by author Senecal and his colleagues (2021).

In what follows, researchers report interview limitations imposed by video-conferencing software and hardware. Using smart phones and desktop computers inhibited the establishing of interviewer–interviewee rapport to which the researchers had become accustomed in dealing with the military veteran population. Through patience, practice, and a series of adaptations, these limitations shrank until they were scarcely noticeable at all.

Application to Qualitative Healthcare Research: A Study of Veteran Reintegration

To better understand the high incidence of PTSD and suicide among American veterans, colleagues and I (Senecal) organized a study where we would interview military veterans from the United States as well as other NATO countries. The selection of NATO allies as comparison countries allowed us to control for factors such as site deployment (e.g., Afghanistan) as well as frequency and length of deployment.

The sampling strategy called for selection of participants who were not within driving distance, so a nonlocal interviewing platform was necessary. Half of the participants lived in Canada, England, Germany, Norway, or Israel and, due to specific demographic issues of persons likely to serve in the American military, very few participants were located in our region of research (New England). A second and unplanned limitation was the social distancing protocols put in place during the COVID-19 pandemic, making ordinary recruiting and interviewing procedures were impossible.

Drawing on nearly a decade of personal research, the greatest challenges to qualitative research with veterans are the establishment of interpersonal rapport and the choice of an environment that facilitates sincere reflection and candor. It is imperative that the researcher remain open to the subjective nuance and lived experience of the participant. Technology certainly has its effects on this process.

One clear example of how technology limited the openness of the researcher and the human connection between researcher and participant was eye contact. Eye contact was limited through Zoom and WhatsApp, which are internet-based video-conferencing programs. Making eye contact on Zoom is bizarre. This is because it is impossible for the eyes of the person on screen to coincide with the "eye" of the video camera, which is usually situated on the top-center of the computer screen. For the participant to have the experience of being looked at eye-to-eye, which is an invaluable element of building interpersonal rapport, the researcher must focus on the video camera at the top of the computer screen. If, instead, the researcher looks into the eyes of the participant on screen, the participant will see a researcher who is looking at their shoulders or stomach. Though looking into the camera may comfort and support the participant, it can be deeply distracting to the researcher and, thus, cause one to lose a sense of flow and spontaneity in the interview process.

This results in a double bind. The researcher must choose between looking at a disembodied techno-eye and appearing to look their participant in the eyes, or actually looking their participant in the eyes and appearing to be distracted by something else.

Though Zoom had benefits over WhatsApp (discussed later in the chapter), both platforms impaired the researcher–participant relationship. Through both mediums, the ability to read body language and keep eye contact with participants was hindered. This was far more limiting via WhatsApp, which is only available as a smartphone application. Interference occurred due to screen size, camera size, and the constant need to keep the smartphone upright throughout the interview, which requires an orientation to the screen that is unusual for a face-to-face conversation (the unusual quality may diminish as familiarity with smartphone use for video-conferencing becomes more common, as it did due to periods of compelled isolation). Zoom, which can be used on desktop and laptop computers, provides an interview setting that is more familiar, with interviewer and interviewee sitting opposite one-another in life-size or near life-size dimensions. For this reason, we scheduled as many interviews using Zoom as was feasible. WhatsApp was used only when veteran participants were limited to smart phones.

In most cases, however, the initial awkwardness of the technological apparatus faded away and rapport was reached. Tried and trusted methods of interpersonal communication were helpful in expediting this process: tone of voice, facial expressions, active listening, and so on. So too with methods of building rapport specifically with the veteran population: using military vernacular and acronyms; understanding rank structure, job specialty, and differences between branches; understanding black or gallows humor; and a care not to bristle at or otherwise communicate nonverbal judgments. All of these interview skills were helpful in minimizing the impact technology had on the interviewer–interviewee relationship. Eye contact, as mentioned earlier, proved to be a recurrent problem that was never comfortably resolved. In the end, we felt that most participants were candid, open, and vulnerable after an initial period of hesitancy. In most cases, it took roughly the first thirty minutes or so to really broach sensitive topics, which is consistent with my experiences of dealing with the military population, regardless of context.

One of the biggest insights we had during our research was the pervasive tendency of American veterans to aggrandize their achievements – to say, for example, that they had experienced action when in fact they had never left training grounds (Senecal & McDonald, 2021). In virtual interviews with me, however, few American veterans admitted to doing this themselves. These same veterans admitted that others were guilty of doing so, but never themselves.

Because it wasn't a controlled study designed to test the effects of technology on self-disclosure, it is impossible to say whether it was technology or some other factor that was responsible for this. It is my suspicion, however, that technology played a role.

Undoubtedly, technology offered some benefits to our research project due to geographical and pandemic-related limitations. However, being in the physical presence of the veteran participant allows for more fluid and candid investigation of the participant's experience. So much of doing research with veterans involves laying the early groundwork of building trust, and even solidarity, with the participant. Without some level of interpersonal connection, there is too much resistance and skepticism and any authenticity is lost. It doesn't help that veterans are skeptical of civilians to begin with (a distinction that is particularly strong among American veterans). In-person, we are able to pick up on subtle body-language cues that give us insight into how to ask follow-up questions. When utilizing Zoom or WhatsApp, there were no effects on one's ability to speak with clear control of military vernacular and support veteran participants' dark humor and provocative rhetoric. In future research projects where the use of technological mediums is required, it would benefit qualitative researchers to look into the camera lens when asking questions to participants to provide a representation of eye contact for the participant. When the participant is responding, the greater benefit would be to pay attention to the screen while making periodical glances into the camera lens. The priority during the participant's response should be on perceiving body language. Another suggestion would be asking the participant, if they are comfortable to do so, to sit further away from the camera so that body posture or bodily gestures are visible.

Conclusion

The impact of technology on the interview process is inescapable, but that doesn't mean that it has to be negative. The same qualities that mark good qualitative research can be used in technologically mediated qualitative research. We do not think a Heidegger-inspired skepticism of technology should be used to denounce the use of technology in qualitative healthcare research. As demonstrated in the study on veteran reintegration, problems imposed by technology can be diminished by minimizing the size and effect of its impairment. This can happen by following the same solutions as for problems in face-to-face communication.

Problems that result from unfamiliarity with technology will fade as its usership increases. Conversations with others through smart phones held at arms' length are evident at universities and shopping malls around the world. Perhaps, in a few years' time, smartphone-based video-conferencing programs will replace desktop-based programs.

What cannot be corrected by familiarity and habituation might be corrected by the software platforms and hardware apparatus themselves. Cameras are inching their way closer and closer to the viewing screen. Perhaps, in time, the apparent disparity in eye contact will be diminished to nothing.

References

Aho, K. (2018). *Existential medicine: Essays on health and illness.* Rowman & Littlefield.

Boss, M. (1979). *Existential foundations of medicine and psychology* (S. Conway & A. Cleaves, Trans.). Jason Aronson.

Brink, P. J. (2000). Series editor's foreword. In M. Z. Cohen, D. L. Kahn, & R. H. Steeves (Eds.). *Hermeneutic phenomenological research: A practical guide for nurse researchers,* vii–viii. SAGE.

Capra, F. (2007). *The science of Leonardo: Inside the mind of the great genius of the Renaissance.* Doubleday.

Ellul, J. (1964). *The technological society.* Vintage Books.

Gadamer, H. G. (1996). *Enigma of health: The art of healing in a scientific age* (J. Gaiger & N. Walker, Trans.). Stanford University Press.

Heidegger, M. (1962 [1927]). *Being and time.* Harper.

Heidegger, M. (1977). *The question concerning technology* (W. Lovitt, Trans.). Harper & Rowe.

Heidegger, M. (2001). *Zollikon seminars: Protocols – conversations – letters.* M. Boss (Ed.). (F. Mayr & R. Askay Trans.). Northwestern University Press.

Heidegger, M. (2004). *What is called thinking?* (J. G. Gray, Trans.). Harper Perennial.

Heidegger, M. (2008). *Being and time* (J. Macquarrie and E. Robinson Trans.). Harper Perennial.

Heidegger, M. (2017). *Gesamtausgabe: Zollikoner seminare.* P. Trawny (Ed.). Verlag Vittorio Klosterman.

Husserl, E. (1970). *The idea of phenemenology.* Nijhoff.

Ihde, D. (1990). *Technology and the lifeworld: From garden to earth.* Indiana University Press.

Ihde, D. (2012). *Listening and voice: Phenomenologies of sound* (2nd ed.). SUNY Press.

Illich, I. (2000). *Limits to medicine: Medical nemesis, the expropriation of health.* Marion Boyars Publishers.

Kleinman, A. (1986). *The illness narratives: Suffering, healing, and the human condition.* Basic Books.

Laverty, S. M. (2003). Hermeneutic phenomenology and phenomenology: A comparison of historical and Methodological Considerations. *International Journal of Qualitative Methods,* 2(3), 21–35. https://doi.org/10.1177/160940690 300200303.

Masters, W. H., & Johnson, V. E. (1966). *Human sexual response.* Little, Brown, & Co.

O'Neal Irwin, S. (2016). *Digital media: Human-technology connection.* Lexington Books.

Rosenberger, R., & VerBeek, P. (2015). *Postphenomenological investigations: Essays on* human-technology relations. Lexington Books.

Senecal, G., & McDonald, M. C. (2021). *American and NATO veteran reintegration: The trauma of social isolation and cultural chasms.* Lexington Books.

Speigelberg, H. (1967). https://link.springer.com/chapter/10.1007/978-94-010-16 70-4_13, 219–241.

Slatman, J. (2018). Reclaiming embodiment in medically unexplained physical symptoms, in K. Aho (Ed.). *Existential medicine: Essays on health and illness*, Rowman & Littlefield, 101–114.

Svenaeus, F. (2018). Heidegger's philosophy of technology and the perils of medicalization. In K. Aho (Ed.). *Existential medicine: Essays on health and illness*. Rowman & Littlefield, 131–144.

Szasz, T. (2007). *The medicalization of everyday life*. Syracuse University Press.

Watson, J. (1930). *Behaviorism*. W. W. Norton & Co.

Wellner, G. (2015). *A postphenomenological inquiry of cell phones: Genealogies, meanings, and becoming*. Lexington Books.

Whitehead, P. (2019). *Existential health psychology: The blind-spot in healthcare*. Palgrave Macmillan.

Whitehead, P. (2021). Applying Heidegger to case study research in the medical and social sciences. *The Qualitative Report, 26*(10), 3014–3028.

Whitehead, P., & Groth, M. (2019). *Resituating humanistic psychology: Finding meaning in an age of medicalization, digitization, and identity politics*. Lexington Books.

van Manen, M. (2016). *Researching lived experience: Human science for an action sensitive pedagogy*. Routledge.

van Manen, M. (2019). Rebuttal: Doing phenomenology on the things. Qualitative Health Research, 1–18. https://doi.org/10.1177/1049732319827293

Zahavi, D. (2018). Getting it quite wrong: Van Manen and Smith on phenomenology. Qualitative Health Research. https://doi.org/10.1177/1049732318817547.

Zahavi, D. (2019). The practice of phenomenology: The case of Max van Manen. Nursing Philosophy. https://doi.org/10.1111/nup.12276.

CHAPTER 10

Participatory and Invasive Online Worlds
Exploring the Research Method of Qualitative Digital Ethnography

Adele Phillips and Shane Blackman

Introduction

This chapter seeks to advance the debate on digital research methods beyond the opposition between 'face to face' or online ethnography. Our focus will be on the practical experience of doing online ethnography, alongside how traditional and online ethnography can be integrated through the ideal of 'being there' (i.e., direct observation). Technology in ethnography has been a part of the approach since the time of Malinowski in the early 1900s, and virtual methods have been used in ethnographic fieldwork for decades (Pink et al. 2016). Christine Hine (2008: 257) notes that 'the study of Internet interactions became popular in the 1990s'. We explore what is understood as authentic ethnography between the online and the offline through critically observing what is comfortable and uncomfortable in both worlds to argue that, as a method and a theory, ethnography adapts over time.

Firstly, we look at authenticities and crises in traditional and online ethnography through the 'myth' of 'being there'. Secondly, we explore what happens when the private space becomes an ethnographic field. Thirdly, we assess the power dynamics of control beyond the screen, which will lead into a critical discussion about the value of what we call 'online pocket ethnography'. Finally, we conclude with practical reflections on doing traditional and online ethnography within a health care setting.

'Being There': Authenticities and Crises in Traditional and Online Ethnography

Ethnography as a research approach is highly adaptative and moves through challenges from 19th century 'armchair anthropology' to contemporary online ethnography. The research methodologies of ethnography have a long and complex history, and the key principle of contemporary authentic ethnography has been based on the notion of 'being there' in the field. Ethnography originated historically as an anthropological research technique and was closely linked to the expansion of colonialism during the nineteenth century. Marcel Mauss (1947/2007), when writing his *Manual of Ethnography*, states: 'the present book ... is intended for administrators and colonists who lack professional training' (p. 11). Mauss is writing within the colonial period, which reflects the everyday concordance of ethnography and Empire at the time. The ethnographer's mask of scientific neutrality and compassion concealed their complicit relation with the forcible imposition of control over people, land and resources and their exploitation by an imperial power. Thus, Bejarano, Mirian, García, and Goldstein (2019) call for a decolonisation of ethnography.

During the nineteenth century, anthropology was dominated by 'armchair anthropologists,' including James Frazer and Edward Burnett Tylor (Sera-Shira 2014). The revolution for ethnography came when Malinowski (1922/1932: 14) argued that fieldwork was 'the ethnographer's magic.' Clifford Geertz (1988: 4) sees this magic as deriving from the concept of 'being there'. The debate between the value of traditional and online ethnography can be subject to what Christine Hine (1994: 4) calls 'cheap tricks'; elaborating, she states that 'Virtual ethnography is not put forward as a new method to replace the old.' We agree: our argument is that this binary opposition between one type of ethnography or another is a false construction. We see 'being there' as a key part of online ethnography as well, through a blending of traditional and online forms of data collection where authenticity is based on immersion, empathy, and exchange.

Ethnography has always involved technological communications, and 'digital ethnography', 'netnography', 'webnography', 'cyber-ethnography,' and 'online ethnography' represent only the most recent changes (Isomaki and Silvennoinen 2013). Electronic methods of data collection are not new to ethnography (Lee 2004). Firstly, from 1915 to 1918, Malinowski collected many photographs of his research participants and made black wax cylinder recordings of his participants singing. Secondly, at the Chicago School, Park and Burgess directed the early studies by Charles Johnson (1922) (*The Negro in Chicago*), Frederic Thrasher's (1927) (*The Gang*), and Clifford Shaw (1930) (*The Jack-Roller*), who used stenograph recordings 'concealed behind a screen' (George Payne, 1932: 246), and those studies contained numerous visual representations and maps of locations and photographs.

Before online ethnography emerged, during the late 1980s and early 1990s postmodern criticism of ethnography calling for reflexivity created new opportunities for ethnography to focus on locality, multiple voices, participation and exchange, dialogue, emotion, involvement, and biography. The authenticity of 'being there' in traditional ethnographic studies was questioned by James Clifford and George Marcus (1986) in the collection *Writing Culture*. Ethnography was accused of writing fixed representations of truth as universal. The assertion was that ethnographic studies were presented as 'fact' through the very act of 'being there', and that this exaggerated authorial power resulted in questioning the trust of the ethnographer's account. The criticism was understood by John Brewer (2000: 24–5) as a challenge related to 'truth claims'. The accusation against traditional ethnography was based on lacking neutrality and a failure to recognise the ethnographer's own role in the creation of the study and how it was written. Karen O'Reilly (2005: 219) argued that this resulted in an immediate 'crisis of representation,' where 'analysis of how we write led to a fear that we can retain no validity and that we should therefore scrap everything.' James Clifford's criticism of ethnography was interpreted by Clifford Geertz (2000: 116–18) as an attack on fieldwork and the ideal of 'being there,' which would be replaced by 'walk-through research' and 'freestyle anthropology.' However, the crisis of representation brought new forms of textuality linked to digital technologies and advanced the idea of reflexivity.

Our argument is that crisis within ethnography is not new. In 1967 Bronislaw Malinowski, the founder of contemporary ethnography and the notion of 'being there,' had a selection of his fieldwork diaries published posthumously which contested the full extent of 'being there'. In *A Diary in the Strict Sense of the Term* (1967), Malinowski talked about his failures and uncertainties in fieldwork, his hostile attitude towards some informants, how he was preoccupied reading novels at the expense of fieldwork, how he lusted after the young women he found, and how he was bored by fieldwork and sexual tension. Clifford Geertz (1967: 12) lamented that it was Malinowski himself who 'destroyed' for us the myth of empathy and 'being there'. This is taken further by Lauren Angelone (2018: 280), who explores the possibilities of not 'being there' in virtual ethnography to argue that 'being there is no longer a guarantor of validity'.

Both traditional and online ethnography evoke representations of the social world containing research subjects' voices selectively orchestrated by an author: the ethnographic description tells one story under the guise of another. On this basis, it is argued that ethnographic texts are based on a partial truth through interactive dialogue (Lumsden 2019). From the time of Malinowski and the Chicago School, we see that ethnography traditionally takes place in physical spaces, both rural and urban, and where ethnographers can also travel with their research participants (Pink 2008). This physical space is also transcended and augmented by electronic screen-based cultures of film, music, and art. Virtual ethnography can be both local and international, and has created opportunities for ethnographic research to migrate into online realms: emails, chatrooms, webinars, social media (e.g., Facebook, Instagram), and smartphone apps. Screen-based mediated contact tends to be two dimensional. A weakness of virtual ethnography we found is that that sensual aspects can be lessened in terms of direct sound, smell, touch/feel, aura, and ambience of locations and people. Media technologies can offer degrees of sensitivity, which may be similar to and different from traditional ethnographies, although the latter favours the physical world (but even in traditional ethnographies participants may not act as themselves).

Our aim is to address the value of screen-mediated social interaction. We see 'face to face' or online ethnography as integrative not exclusive. Ethnography is defined by space, and our understanding is that online and offline communities represent another multi-sited potential for ethnography. We identify the critique of online ethnographic as lacking authenticity, which parallels an emergent trend to ascribe measurement to ethnography. This prescriptive measuring takes on a positivist perspective in terms of counting the number of ethnographic notebooks to be filled, or how many hours of observation will occur. This preoccupation with numeration is hegemonic and is counterproductive to the very nature of ethnography as both an art and an emotional experience (Evans-Pritchard 1951: 85). Therefore, we afford corresponding and respective value to 'face to face' and online ethnography as different and complementary ethnographic methods. Our assertion is not that online ethnography should be seen as replacing face-to-face connections, but that online ethnography can be used in combination with ethnographic fieldwork to enhance the research imaginary.

Face and Screen: Beyond the Power Dynamics of Control

The onset of the global COVID-19 pandemic forced social restrictions in the United Kingdom from March 2020 onwards, creating a sudden and unexpected conundrum for qualitative social sciences researchers – namely, removal of the traditional research field (Christin, 2020). The 'temporary' hiatus on face-to-face contact with participants has posed significant challenges for ethnographic researchers who seek to prioritise the generation of a 'thick description' (Geertz, 1973) of people's everyday lives and the fostering of rapport and intimacy with participants. For ethnographers researching vulnerable people in healthcare settings, the restrictions are likely to be particularly stringent and may be of some duration. This is a particular problem when considering the role that ethnographic work could play in understanding people's health-related experiences. Here we will explore issues of contemporary inclusion and exclusion throughout the ethnographic journey. Using reflections from the researchers' lived experience of online ethnographic work, it is argued that virtual and physical spaces can be integrated to promote inclusive research, whilst retaining the hallmarks of ethnographic tradition.

The visual and usability aspects of the online platforms, apps, or sites used to communicate with participants can influence entrée, as these determine how the researcher gains access to the research field. While traditional fields may feature formal gatekeepers who need to be approached to gain this authorisation, online ethnographies can necessitate liaising with informal gatekeepers (Bailey, 2018). This may require demonstrating an authentic commitment to the research topic that goes beyond academic credentials, such as disclosing personal experiences and openness about researcher positionality to the participants.

During my own research, I found it useful to consider my positionality to participants when deciding which tools and platforms should be used to contact them. For example, when interacting with participants using the business communication platform Microsoft Teams that I use professionally, I felt that I was entering the field in 'work mode'. The language that I initially used when interacting with these participants was more likely to adopt a professional tone. My professional role became more salient, rather than my personal qualities. Conversely, when communicating with participants using less formal apps (such as WhatsApp, Facetime, and Facebook), I was more likely to feel that I was in 'friend mode' and these spaces were characterised by the use of emojis, memes, humour, and Internet slang. I felt that I could be more personally authentic through 'being there' with the latter participants, was more comfortable being honest about my feelings, and was more likely to be critical about the research. Despite this, several of my participants occupied senior professional roles and I therefore felt that it was more appropriate to use a professional platform such as Microsoft Teams, as I wanted them to realise that this was a research project that I was taking seriously and conducting properly. At the same time, we see a valuable place for less formal apps as these retain a personal and intimate capacity to gather data.

Hart (2017) argues for the importance of online ethnographers making adequate preparations to 'travel' to virtual spaces in the same sense that traditional ethnographers would physically travel to the field, by learning how to use the digital tools that will be needed. To balance the power dynamic between myself and participants from the outset, I initially attempted to co-navigate a favourable online space with them. I found that initially asking participants which platforms or software they preferred or could access meant that the interview was more likely to go ahead and run smoothly on a practical level. Contingency planning with alternative platforms was also an effective means of accessing participants (e.g., 'how about if we use Skype if Teams doesn't play ball?'). With participants' permission, I also audio-recorded video conferencing sessions, which proved necessary in one instance where a participant and I were unable to access the videorecorded session. These open-ended and flexible approaches can be burdensome for the researcher if they do not have wide access to or expertise in using these technologies, and in my case I found that quite a lot of time was spent up-skilling myself on using different technologies and running tests to ensure that my devices would support these on the day. However, this was worth the investment, as both researcher and participant were able to control the means of building rapport in a flexible way from the outset.

In the Field: The Private Space of the Home and Ethics

Within both traditional and online ethnography, doing insider research through 'being there' allows the researcher to enter participants' private space and is akin to personal intimacy (Hodkinson 2005). This may encourage both voyeurism and possible exploitation, defined as 'invasive ethnography', which could intensify the power differential between patient and practitioner. During fieldwork it was found that some participants remain outside of online contact, not only because they are hard to access, but due to material factors that arise where participants do not possess effective gadgetry or lack IT literacy. Through the pandemic, data collection that would typically have taken place within traditional ethnographic fields – such as hospitals and other health care services, participants' homes, and community-based spaces – is now occurring in rooms in the private space of the researcher's own home. This shift to utilising a private space as the research field raises several methodological considerations that will be discussed here. Additionally, it is argued that despite ongoing challenges, embracing the private space of the home as a research field can facilitate the elicitation of health service users' voices and enable a more inclusive research culture (Murthy 2008).

Traditional ethnographic work would closely examine the relationships between participants within their environments, as well as their relationships to the researcher through the notion of 'being there'. Online ethnography within the home for both researcher and participants is influenced by partners, children, pets, and the constraints and affordances of the physical environment. Researchers should be mindful that these influences can shape processes of data collection and analysis, rapport building, and ethics. During my own research, I found that the presence of pets had the potential to facilitate essential rapport building with participants and can provide a humorous or therapeutic element during emotional conversations. For example, during one instance where a participant became visibly angry and upset as he recounted his negative experiences of using a healthcare service, his dog crept on to his lap and stared down the camera, obscuring the participant from view. As well as providing a comfort to the participant, the dog's actions amused us both and we laughed as we pretended that the dog was the one being interviewed instead. The participant was able to continue recounting his experiences, but more comfortably, and I was no longer concerned that our interaction was creating an unsafe space.

Despite this, it was that found some family members and pets demonstrated annoyance at the participant's lack of attention to them during some of the interviews conducted. I tried to remain composed as I overheard a woman yelling at her husband to 'get off the damned phone', saw children crying for dinner to be cooked, and watched a participant being smacked in the face by his own cat as he disclosed his lifelong battle with drug addiction. My own frustrations as a researcher mounted at times, as I tried to concentrate on a participant interview while construction workers dug up the road outside my window, or when the post arrived and I had to leave the room to answer the door. I found that 'being there' online became a near distraction from the data collection, as with traditional ethnography you sometimes find yourself in a setting which is uncomfortable and would prefer to be elsewhere (Blackman 2016: 73–4)!

In addition to some of the practical barriers of researching online from home spaces, there are ethical issues concerning confidentiality, which may be relevant when researching highly stigmatised topics such as domestic violence, drug and alcohol use, and gambling. Andrejevic (2006) highlights the phenomenon of 'lateral surveillance': a term used to describe the process whereby citizens feel compelled to monitor one another, particularly friends, family members, and potential love interests. These activities are facilitated by use of networked, online technologies and devices and can include finding out information about a person by examining their Facebook profile, covert audio and video recording, checking Internet search histories, and use of specialist 'spying' software. Further, participants may not always have access to confidential spaces in their home where they can engage in an online interview without being overheard by others. In my own research concerning health professional employment issues, I interviewed a participant from his work office who disclosed stories that involved him making criticisms of his employer. Throughout the interview, he spoke in anxious, hushed tones and visibly leapt into the air in fright when a colleague walked into the room to borrow a stapler. In these instances, organisational arrangements for online meetings, as well as ethical review processes, should consider how both research and participant confidentiality can be maintained throughout the research journey.

Avoiding voyeurism, understood as exploitation of participants that may be of a sexual nature, has long been an important consideration within traditional ethnography. There are notable examples of controversies surrounding the ethics of research that examines spaces where sexual activity takes place, such as public toilets (Humphreys, 1970) and semi-public spaces hired for parties (Moser, 1998). The more recent shift to online ethnography has resulted in researcher's and participant's private spheres merging; during the pandemic this has become the intimate (and often sexual) site of the bedroom. Early sociological work that examined 'bedroom culture' (McRobbie and Garber, 1976) argued that the bedroom provided a site for teenage girls to enhance their agency but, according to Lincoln (2012), one that was open to exploitation by powerful commercial interests, such as the music and fashion industries. Several decades on, the bedroom is now a space of 'being there', where people spend significant proportions of their time engaged in online activities, and thus this has developed into a site where media and identity intersect (Bovill and Livingstone, 2001). This may potentially jeopardise participants' well-being, as digital spaces have been characterised by consumerism, surveillance, and voyeurism; therefore, online interactions, particularly those that involve a degree of anonymity or deception, are at risk of posing significant mental health issues, or even trauma, to users (Kavanaugh and Maratea, 2020). As ethnographers seek to discover 'real worlds', there is a difficult balance to be struck between maintaining intimacy and avoiding exploit-ation (Bain and Nash, 2006).

Virtual Backgrounds: Unreal, Fantasy or Scary?

When I began conducting ethnographic interviews online, I was initially in a quandary about whether to make use of the array of virtual backgrounds that are free and widely available when using video conferencing software such as Zoom or Microsoft Teams. Virtual backgrounds are simulated environments that are displayed behind the user and cause them to appear as though they are in an alternative environment, so can be used to conceal the user's location, environment, and other people within it (Conti et al., 2021). These provide opportunities for participants and researcher to re-present themselves by masking their reality and replacing it with a new one (Hay, 2020). In my case, a virtual background could have been used to mask the private space of my bedroom. We did casually wonder how the University ethics committee would respond if I were to state on the application form that I was 'letting 16 participants into my bedroom'! What would I replace this scene with, in any case?

To resolve this within my own research, the matter of virtual versus real background was a deliberate and conscious decision, and I took the advice of academics such as Markham (2017) and Cocq (2019), who suggest that researchers should focus on the reasons why they are carrying out the research, rather than be driven by the instrumental aspects of the research. As my topic involved examination of the tensions posed in healthcare services when motivations for policy and treatment development are non-transparent, any notion of concealment on my part did not align well ideologically with the research purposes. Therefore, in the spirit of authen-ticity, I invited sixteen participants into my bedroom. I was curious to see whether they would invite me in return. Several participants invited me into their bedrooms (and some directly into bed); others invited me into their place of work, one into the centre of a cat activity playground, and a few into their fully kitted-out home office spaces. In one instance a participant had changed his home background into a virtual professional-looking office space. Every now and again the graphics would 'glitch' slightly to reveal sudden glimpses of a living room in a house. This made me, as a researcher, feel a bit unnerved at what might lie behind the graphics, and I was glad that I had opted for an unmasked space after all. The weirdness of screen-image distortion can make for an unsettling experience whereby blurring and exaggeration make participants seem unreal, like funfair amusement arcades, and slightly scary! Ultimately, I emphasised that all participants were free choose their own space and modify it how they wished in the interests of them being in control of their own area.

Co-creating Ways of 'Being There'

Further to virtual backgrounds enabling participants to mask and control what others see, these can also enable them to build virtual realities for *themselves* (Hay, 2020). Virtual backgrounds are sometimes presented to users in terms of them being able to make a personal choice to customise the image that they present. The emphasis here is on user control. Research demonstrates that providing participants with the means of controlling the visual aspects of their environment can foster a sense of empowerment, enable full immersion with their environment, and benefit mental health and wellbeing. MacDonald et al. (2021) conducted a study that documents musicians' experiences of using Zoom software to facilitate online, synchronous improvisation sessions during COVID-19 social restrictions. It was shown that as sessions progressed, participants would personalise this creative space by altering their virtual backgrounds and tailoring what other participants could see on their screen (MacDonald et al., 2021: 10). By enabling participants to gain a sense of creative control, they felt that they could engage in building their own individual 'stage' on which to perform.

From my own online ethnography there was evidence of an increase in personal control for participants who felt that the democratic co-creation of a virtual space led to genuine feelings of connectedness and being alive. This is supported by Kozinets (2002), who argues that although online communities may be termed 'virtual', their existence does indeed have real-life consequences and will affect the behaviour of participants in the real world. Many communities have both online and offline elements to them and this creates a fusion that combines ways of 'being there' (Cocq, 2019). In addition to the control that researcher and participants can exert through adaptations to the virtual background, communicating with others online is also a bodily experience. In traditional, face-to-face ethnography, the opportunity to observe the face and body is set in the context of the physical location and surrounding environment. In contrast, online ethnography may involve a direct and sustained focus on the face in an intimate and sometimes intimidating manner. Therefore, both researcher and participant are likely to adapt, consciously or unconsciously, particularly if this is an unfamiliar context. For example, as a researcher, I became a lot more conscious of what my face might look like in close-up when I knew that was what participants would be forced to focus on. I chose my makeup carefully (nothing too bright or 'unprofessional') and tied my hair back so that my facial expressions could be clearly observed. Similarly, MacDonald and coleagues's (2021) study showed that women who never normally wore makeup did so in the online space as a means of augmenting their reality and enhancing performance through bodily adaptations.

These experiences can be likened to those of researchers within trad- itional fieldwork settings who experience anxiety about what to wear in the field, as they are aware that even the tiniest aspects of how they dress and present themselves will immediately impact their positionality with parti- cipants and have implications for blending in, sexual expression, and general interactions (Bain and Nash, 2006). Hine (2015, p. 32) conceptual- ises ethnography for the Internet as *embedded* in various contexts, an *embodied* experience, and that use of Internet is an unremarkable aspect of people's *everyday* lives. This framework provides researchers with a context for considering multiple ways of 'being there'. We found that being allowed into some participants private and bedroom spaces brought with it an intimacy of 'carefulness' in terms of both clothing worn and other items of clothing left observed within the frame. The eye-to-eye contact on screen and the wider visualisation of a private space required human sensitivity, respect, and joint recognition of closeness.

Reconfiguring Inequalities

Online ethnographic work has enabled researchers and participants to co- create new ways of 'being there', and this demonstrates a need to reconfig- ure our understanding of traditional power dynamics within health and social research. Power inequalities are a feature of the relationships between researchers and participants within the field during the data collection process, as well as influencing who can access the field in the first instance. Hine (2015) argues that one element of the embodied experience of online worlds is that we are socially situated bodies and, consequently, types of privilege have emerged that can include or exclude particular groups of people from digital experiences. These 'digital inequalities' are under- pinned by four key areas: the technical means (includes hardware, software, and Internet access), autonomy of use, social support networks enabling use, and experience of gaining benefits from use (Beaunoyer et al., 2020).

The prevailing discourse around digital inequalities has tended to focus on the technical means aspect – that is whether people can materially afford the technology to engage. It has been suggested that there is a growing 'digital divide' between those who have access to digital technologies and the concomitant opportunities, knowledge, services, and goods, and 'non-Internet users' who experience inequalities in these areas (Office for National Statistics, 2019).

Our fieldwork suggests it is important to consider where digital and traditional inequalities intersect, especially as social inequalities are at the heart of social sciences research (Robinson et al., 2015). Somewhat paradoxically, the research field can act as a site in which both participant and researcher unwittingly reproduce existing power relations that are the subject of study. For example, institutional research settings have historically positioned women as subordinate to men, due to many professions, particularly medicine, being rooted within patriarchal power hierarchies (Balcom, Doucet and Dubé, 2021). This has been shown to be problematic, as female participants are then inclined to use the language of male authority figures to explain their experiences, even if these are inauthentic. Additionally, within medicalised institutional settings that require service users to be compliant with internal policies and processes to gain a desired treatment outcome, service users have been found to construct a particular role that can reproduce power imbalances, such as playing the role of 'junkie' (Radcliffe and Stevens, 2008).

Shifting to online spaces in which less powerful groups can exert a greater degree of control over their physical space, and their appearance within it, are likely to elicit new ways of 'being there' and interacting. For example, global research concerning the health needs of older people found that when left to their own devices in familiar urban spaces, they demedicalised their physical activity requirements by playing the location-based augmented reality game *Pokémon GO*, rather than relying on gyms, clinical treatments, or medication (Hjorth, 2020). This demonstrates that older and socially isolated people, who may traditionally be marginalised from research entirely, are also everyday users of Internet technology who can utilise these assets to vocalise their health needs and understand health and wellbeing on their own terms.

As Beaunoyer et al. (2020) highlight, having the autonomy to engage with digital technologies is embedded in the social and economic circumstances in which people live their lives. The COVID-19 pandemic has illuminated digital inequalities, particularly in terms of how these relate to protected characteristics such as gender. Evidence shows that women across the world, particularly those from Black and Asian ethnic groups, have shouldered an increased share of the domestic duties and childcare during the pandemic (UN Women, 2020). This unjust distribution of labour has negatively impacted the ability of women scholars to engage with research (Gewin, 2020). As well as impeding women's life and career opportunities, the lack of women's research and voices concerning experiences of the pandemic result in a limited picture of the challenges posed and the possible future solutions. Although conducting ethnographic studies (or some aspects of research) online can be more inclusive of participant groups who cannot afford immediate financial costs, such as travel expenses, future research should consider how to increase opportunities for women to engage with research by responding to their social circumstances (Arnout et al., 2020).

Online Pocket Ethnography

One feature of traditional ethnography that can help researchers to examine more covert aspects of participants' lives is personal documents that are given to the researcher, termed 'pocket ethnography' by Valerie Hey (1997, p. 50). In Hey's ethnography of girls' friendships in London comprehensive schools in the 1980's, she discovered that 'illegitimate knowledges' were shared amongst the girls that took the form of secret communications by letter or scribbled notes. Hey (1997) and Blackman (2007) were gifted several items during their ethnographic studies on young women. In Blackman's (1998) ethnography of 'The New Wave Girls' he disclosed that participants gave him notes, letters, badges, and a hand-written poem to express how they felt about their relationship with the research and the researcher. Other researchers have considered the meanings of different documents which may be practically useful to fieldwork; participants in McPherson's (2017) research on the night-time drinking economy in Canterbury provided him with flyers that advertised alcohol-related events. These were useful as they provided the researcher with a valuable source of insider information that documented when and where specific events occurred.

Extending Hey's ideas, this section considers the value and meaning of 'online pocket ethnography' that takes place in online ethnographic work, reflecting on examples of 'digital gifts' that I was given by participants during my research journey. In one instance, before the online meeting took place, one of my participants emailed me a magazine article that he had written about substance misuse treatment. The article demonstrated his positionality relating to a controversial issue that had been discussed heatedly within both academic circles and popular media. When I met with the participant, I therefore already knew what his values were concerning the research topic; he did not know mine, however. After we introduced ourselves, I immediately thanked him for sending me the article, stated that I agreed with his points and the conversation proceeded thus:

RESEARCHER: I wouldn't normally open an interview by saying this, but having read your article . . .
PARTICIPANT: I had a kind of sneaky suspicion and the only reason for me to send you that was to really test out the water, because it would help with the context hugely, and maybe even give us a bit of a head start . . . well then, I think in that respect, we're on the same page.
RESEARCHER: I think we are! *(mutual laughter)*

It was interesting to hear that the participant had wanted to 'test' the researcher before the online meeting took place. 'Trials' are often identified in traditional ethnography, whereby participants set tests for the researcher to prove their authenticity and commitment as a marker of 'being there' (Blackman 1998). The exchange of the article led to an immediately honest conversation whereby each party 'knew where the other stood'. Throughout the research, several participants provided me with the following documents: journal articles, academic reports, or news articles about pertinent issues, some that they had written or taken part in themselves. In these instances, the information contained within the documents was public information and it seemed that participants wanted to showcase their work or communicate a positionality to a specific issue that was important to both parties.

Other documents sent were of a confidential nature and included private email discussions, confidential reports, contact details for other potential participants, and files (e.g., spreadsheets and pictures). In one instance, a participant who was employed as a healthcare worker had spent some time compiling a report containing data that revealed a significant health issue in his local area. He was dismayed when the report was dismissed by his managers and expressed during a conversation that he was pleased that 'someone was finally taking an interest in it'. This demonstrates trust on the part of the participants; in these instances, we swore each other to secrecy, and I felt that a bond of trust was formed through an electronic sense of 'being there'. These transactions demonstrate trust in and a valuing of the research relationship, particularly where confidential and personally exposing documents are shared. The sharing of pocket ethnography poses a significant risk for both traditional and online ethnography, but digital documents create increased risk for ethnography due to the potential for items to be shared to a global audience within a matter of seconds!

In addition to social bonding, the phenomenon of sharing confidential documents can be interpreted as a mechanism for social resistance. Examining the letter sharing of participants through a feminist lens, both Hey (1997) and Blackman (1998) concluded that the girls took subversive pleasure in sending one another secret writings, representing a mechanism of ethnographic authenticity of 'being there' which enabled them to honestly express feelings of dislike or disagreement, from critical assessment of their boyfriends to ridicule of the social pressures to comply with constructing an image of a 'nice girl'. Similarly, digitally shared documents can serve this same function: private expressions of rebellion in the face of a felt need to be a compliant practitioner in health and social care services. As discussed by my healthcare worker participants and I:

PARTICIPANT: I did do a report on x . . . about two years ago now, I've got it somewhere, if I can find it, I'll whack it over to you.
RESEARCHER: Thank you!
PARTICIPANT: But only between you and me, cos I did it for them, all I got was a very patronising pat on the back, so . . . I don't give a fuck; you know what I mean.

The concept of online pocket ethnography may provide further opportunities for researchers to examine expressions of social resistance among groups of people whose voices may otherwise remain hidden.

Conclusions and Practical Reflections

This chapter has argued that online ethnographic approaches are not only valuable per se, they can also be used to further our understanding of hidden worlds by broadening researcher access beyond that of face-to-face interactions. Online methods can add value by providing researchers with access to participants such as older people, people who do not access health and social care services, women with childcare responsibilities, those who cannot travel to meeting sites, and socially isolated people. As well as being more inclusive in this sense, online communications can help to break down hegemonic power relationships between medical practitioner and service user. Despite facing some criticisms around authenticity, conducting ethnographic research online is an embodied experience that can enable the establishment of emotional bonding and trust, thereby enhancing degrees of intimacy between researcher and participants (Blackman, Phillips, and Sah, 2019).

There are several considerations that are specific to online ethnography and differ from those associated with traditional research. Firstly, there are preparations to be made for digital up-skilling, although it is acknowledged that digital inequalities may prevent researchers or participants from accessing various platforms or devices via which to communicate, thus making the ideal of 'being there' difficult. Here, researchers and participants may be able to co-navigate online spaces to reach mutually beneficial arrangements that involve contingency planning in the event of technological difficulties.

Secondly, online ethnographers should also be prepared to manage the merger of their private world with that of the participants to some extent; for example, they may be transported into a participant's bedroom, and have them 'present' in theirs. To maintain an ethical balance between developing intimacy and avoiding voyeurism, researchers should promote participant autonomy by enabling them to be in control of their private spaces. This can be expressed through bodily enhancements, use of virtual backgrounds, personalised display features, and platform choice. The research process may be interrupted by other agents within either the researchers' or the participants' private spaces, such as family members or pets. Within traditional ethnographic settings, interruptions can be a common feature, but, whether face-to-face or through a screen, these can be used as opportunities for building rapport, humorous exchanges, or gaining further insight into the private world of the participant.

Like traditional ethnography, online ethnography is an embodied experience in which researchers and participants consider their physical presentation. Researcher decision-making concerning clothing, hair, and makeup are certainly nothing new for ethnographers, and a shift towards research being conducted in online spaces is likely to raise ongoing debates about how these embodied aspects of the research influence acceptance and power relationships within the field. Similarly, gift-giving within the field is a typical hallmark of ethnography; however, online spaces are likely to encourage digital exchanges of artefacts – what we call here 'online pocket ethnography'. By integrating face-to-face and online worlds, ethnography can maintain its long tradition of utilising adaptive approaches, even in the face of a global pandemic, Ethnographically, 'the show must go on'.

References

Andrejevic, M. (2006) 'The discipline of watching: Detection, risk, and lateral surveillance', *Critical Studies in Media Communication*, 23 (5), 391–407, https://doi.org/10.1080/07393180601046147.

Angelone, L. (2018) 'Virtual ethnography: The post possibilities of not being there', *Mid-Western Educational Researcher*, 31 (3), 275–95. www.mwera.org/MWER/volumes/v31/issue3/V31n3-Angelone-DISTINGUISHED-PAPER.pdf.

Arnout, B. A., Abdel Rahman, D. E., Elprince, M., Arnout, B. A., Abada, A. A., and Jasim, K. J. (2020) 'Ethnographic research method for psychological and medical studies in light of COVID-19 pandemic outbreak: Theoretical approach', *Journal of Public Affairs*, 20 (4), https://doi.org/10.1002/pa.2404.

Arya, D. and Henn, M. (2021) 'COVID-ized ethnography: Challenges and opportunities for young environmental activists and researchers', *Societies*, 11 (58), https://doi.org/10.3390/soc11020058.

Bailey, C. A. (2018) *A Guide to Qualitative Field Research*, 3rd ed. London: SAGE Publications Ltd.

Bain, A. L. and Nash, C. J. (2006) 'Undressing the researcher: feminism, embodiment and sexuality at a queer bathhouse event', *Area*, 38, 99–106.

Balcom, S. Doucet, S. and Dubé, A. (2021) 'Observation and institutional ethnography: Helping us to see better', *Qualitative Health Research*, 31 (8), 1534–41.

Beaulieu, A. (2004) 'Mediating ethnography: Objectivity and the making of ethnographies of the Internet', *Social Epistemology*, 18 (2–3): 139–63.

Beaunoyer, E., Dupéré, S. and Guitton, M. J. (2020) 'COVID-19 and digital inequalities: Reciprocal impacts and mitigation strategies', *Computers in Human Behaviour*, 111, https://doi.org/10.1016/j.chb.2020.106424.

Bejarano, C., Mirian, C. L., García, A., and Goldstein, D. (2019) *Decolonizing Ethnography: Undocumented Immigrants and New Directions in Social Sciences*, Durham: Duke University.

Blackman, S. (1998) '"Poxy Cupid": An ethnographic and feminist account of a resistant female youth culture – the New Wave Girls, in *Cool Places: Geographies of Youth Cultures*, ed. T. Skelton and G. Valentine. London: Routledge, pp. 207–28.

Blackman, S. (2007) '"Hidden ethnography": Crossing emotional borders in qualitative accounts of young people's lives', *Sociology*, 41 (4), 699–716.

Blackman, S. (2016) 'The emotional imagination: Exploring critical ventriloquy and emotional edgework in reflexive sociological ethnography with young people', in ed. S. Blackman and M. Kempson, *The Subcultural Imagination: Theory, Research and Reflexivity in Contemporary Youth Cultures*, London: Routledge, pp. 65–79.

Blackman, S. Phillips, A. and Sah, R. (2019) 'Ethnography and emotions: New directions for critical reflexivity within contemporary qualitative health care research', in *Enhancing Healthcare and Rehabilitation: The Impact of Qualitative Research*, ed. C. Hayre and D. Muller. Mahwah: CRC Press, pp. 379–93.

Bovill, M. and Livingstone, S. M. (2001) 'Bedroom culture and the privatization of media use', in *Children and Their Changing Media Environment: A European Comparative Study*, ed. S. Livingstone and M. Bovill. Mahwah: Lawrence Erlbaum Associates, pp. 179–200 [online]. http://eprints.lse.ac.uk/archive/oo 000672 (accessed 1 September 2021).

Brewer, J. (2000) *Ethnography*. London: Sage.

Chiseri-Strater, E. (1996) 'Turning in upon ourselves: Positionality, subjectivity and reflexivity in case study and ethnographic research', in *Ethics and Representation in Qualitative Studies of Literacy*, ed. P. Mortensen & G. Kirsch. Urbana: National Council of Teachers of English, pp. 115–33.

Christin, A. (2020) 'Algorithmic ethnography, during and after COVID-19', *Communication and the Public*, 5 (3–4), pp. 108–11.

Clifford Geertz, C. (1967) Under the Mosquito Net, *The New York Review*, September 14.

Clifford, J. and Marcus, G. (1986) (eds.) *Writing Culture*. Berkeley: University of California Press.

Cocq, C. (2019) 'The where, how and who of digital ethnography', *Folklore Fellows' Network*, 53, 3–6.

Conti, M., Milani, S., Nowroozi, E. and Orazi, G. (2021) 'Do not deceive your employer with a virtual background: A video conferencing manipulation-detection system', *Cryptography and Security*, https://doi.org/10.48550/arXiv.2106.15130.

Evans-Pritchard, E. E. (1951) *Social Anthropology*. London: Routledge

Fine, G. A. and Abramson, C. M. (2020) 'Ethnography in the time of COVID-19: Vectors and the vulnerable', *Etnografia e Ricerca Qualitativa*, 165–74. https://doi.org/10.3240/97802.

Geertz, C. (1973) *The Interpretation of Cultures*. New York: Basic Books.

Geertz, C. (1988) *Works and Lives*. Stanford. Stanford University Press.

Geertz, C. (2000) *Available Light*. New Jersey: Princeton University Press.

Gewin, V. (2020) 'The career cost of COVID-19 to female researchers and how science should respond', *Nature*, 583, 867–69.

Góralska, M. (2020) 'Advice on digital ethnography for the pandemic times', *Anthropology in Action*, 27 (1), 46–52.

Hammersley, M. and Atkinson, P. (2007) *Ethnography: Principles in Practice*. 3rd ed. Abingdon: Routledge.

Hart, T. (2017) 'Online ethnography', in Matthes, J. (ed.) *The International Encyclopaedia of Communication Research Methods*. Hoboken, NJ: John Wiley and Sons.

Hay, I. (2020) 'Zoom and place: Video conferencing and virtual geography', *South Australian Geographical Journal*, 116 (1), 7–11.

Hey, V. (1997) *The Company She Keeps: An Ethnography of Girls' Friendship*. Buckingham: Open University Press.

Hine, C. (1994) Virtual Ethnography, paper delivered at 3th International Conference on Public Communication of Science and Technology (PCST),

Montreal, Canada, 10–13 April, https://pcst.co/archive/pdf/Hine_PCST1994 .pdf.

Hine, C. (2008) 'Virtual ethnography: Modes, varieties, affordances', in *The SAGE Handbook of Online Research Methods*, ed. N. Fielding, R. Lee, and G. Blank. London: SAGE Publications.

Hine, C. (2015) *Ethnography for the Internet*. London: Bloomsbury.

Hjorth, L. et al. (2020) *Digital Media Practices in Households*. Amsterdam: Amsterdam University Press.

Hodkinson, P. (2005) 'Insider research in the study of youth culture', *Journal of Youth Studies*, 8 (2): 131–50.

Humphreys, L. (1970) *Tearoom Trade: Impersonal Sex in Public Places*. Chicago: Aldine Publishing Company.

Isomaki, H. and Silvennoinen, J. (2013) 'Online ethnographies', in *Information Systems Research and Exploring Social Artefacts*, ed. P. Isaias and J. M. Nunes. Hershey, PA: IGI Global, pp. 124–41.

Johnson, C. (1922) *The Negro* (The Chicago Commission on Race Relations). Chicago: Chicago University Press.

Kavanaugh, P. R. and Maratea, R. J. (2020) 'Digital ethnography in an age of information warfare: Notes from the field', *Journal of Contemporary Ethnography*, 49 (10), 3–26.

Kozinets, R. V. (2002) 'The field behind the screen: Using netnography for marketing research in online communities', *Journal of Marketing Research*, 49, 61–72.

Lee, R. M. (2004) Recording technologies and the interview in sociology, 1920–2000, *Sociology*, 49 (5): 869–89.

Lincoln, S. (2012) *Youth Culture and Private Space*. Basingstoke: Palgrave.

Lumsden, K. (2019) *Reflexivity: Theory, Method and Practice*. London: Routledge.

MacDonald, R., Burke, R., De Nora, T., Sappho Donohue, M. and Birrell, R. (2021) 'Our virtual tribe: sustaining and enhancing community via online music improvisation', *Frontiers in Psychology*, 11, 4076.

Malinowski, B. (1922/1932) *Argonauts of the Western Pacific: An account of Native Enterprise and Adventure in the Archipelagoes of Melanesian New Guinea*. London: George Routledge & Sons.

Malinowski, B. (1967) *A Diary in the Strict Sense of the Term*. Stanford. Stanford University Press.

Markham, A. N. (2017) Ethnography in the digital era: From fields to flow, descriptions to interventions. In N. Denzin, & Y. Lincoln (Eds.). *The Sage Handbook of Qualitative Research, 5th Edition* (650–668). Thousand Oaks: Sage.

Mauss, M. (1947/2007) *Manual of Ethnography*. New York: Berghahn Books

McPherson, R. (2017) Towards a normalisation of young people's drinking practices: A Chicago School ethnographic study in the Canterbury night-time economy. PhD thesis. Canterbury Christ Church University. https://reposi tory.canterbury.ac.uk/item/88wz3/towards-a-normalisation-of-young-people-s-drinking-practices-a-chicago-school-ethnographic-study-in-the-canterbury-night-time-economy (accessed 1 September 2021).

McRobbie, A., & Garber, J. (1976). Girls and subcultures, in *Resistance through rituals: Youth subcultures in post-war Britain*, ed. S. Hall & T. Jefferson. London: Hutchinson, pp. 209–23.

Morse, J. M. (2005) 'Ethical issues in institutional research', *Qualitative Health Research*, 15 (4), 435–7.

Moser, C. (1998) 'S/M (Sadomasochistic) interactions in semi-public settings', *Journal of Homosexuality*, 36 (2), 19–29.

Murthy, D. (2008) 'Digital ethnography', *Sociology*, 42 (5), 837–56.

O'Reilly, K. (2005) *Ethnographic Methods*. London: Routledge.

Office for National Statistics (2019) Exploring the UK's digital divide. www.ons .gov.uk/peoplepopulationandcommunity/householdcharacteristics/homeinter netandsocialmediausage/articles/exploringtheuksdigitaldivide/2019-03-04 (accessed 1 September 2021).

Payne, G. (1932) 'Research problems and trends in educational sociology', *The Journal of Educational Research*, 25 (4/5), 239–52.

Pink, S. (2008) 'The sensory sociality of ethnographic place-making', *Ethnography*, 9 (2), 175–96.

Pink, S., Horst, H., Postill, J., et al. (2016) *Digital Ethnography: Principles and Practice*. London: Sage.

Radcliffe, P. and Stevens, A. (2008) 'Are drug treatment services only for "thieving junkie scumbags"? Drug users and the management of stigmatised identities', *Social Science and Medicine*, 67 (7), 1065–73.

Robinson, L., Cotten, S., Ono, H., et al. (2015) 'Digital inequalities and why they matter', *Information, Communication and Society*, 18 (5), 569–82.

Sera-Shriar, E. (2014) What is armchair anthropology? Observational practices in 19th century British human sciences, *History of Human Sciences*, 27 (2), 26–40.

Shaw, C. (1930), *The Jack-Roller*. Chicago: University of Chicago Press.

Thrasher, F. (1927) *The Gang*. Chicago: University of Chicago Press.

UN Women (2020) Whose time to care? Unpaid care and domestic work during COVID-19. https://data.unwomen.org/sites/default/files/inline-files/Whose-time-to-care-brief_0.pdf (accessed 1 August 2021).

CHAPTER II

Using Online Survey Tools to Improve Access to International Experts
The 'E-Delphi'

Georgina Clutterbuck

Introduction

The e-Delphi method is the modern version of a research method that utilises expert opinions to address complex research questions. The traditional Delphi method was developed in the 1950s as a way of forecasting future events (Dalkey & Helmer, 1963); however, it has undergone considerable transformation over time, with modern application in health sciences including validation of classification systems (Palisano et al., 2008) and frameworks (Culley, 2011; Rahimzadeh, Bartlett, & Knoppers, 2021; Verschuren et al., 2011), and the development of research priorities by both consumers and professionals (Bäck-Pettersson et al., 2008; Hult Khazaie & Khan, 2020; Mackenzie et al., 2017; McIntyre, Novak, & Cusick, 2010; Rankin et al., 2012). The Delphi method is particularly useful when researchers need to address complex problems where there is no source of definitive 'fact' (Linstone & Turoff, 1975).

In the Delphi method, expert opinions become the source of data and are used to establish consensus through a series of iterative surveys. In comparison to a focus group or a single survey, the Delphi method structures and refines expert opinion via anonymous debate by interspersing these surveys with feedback regarding the groups' combined opinions. The series of surveys ('rounds') have two roles: (1) to identify experts' opinions, and (2) to refine them through question repetition and feedback, to reach consensus on a given research question.

1. **Identification of expert opinion** is conducted in the first round (sometimes called 'round zero'). This round includes open-ended questions designed to develop statements or hypotheses based on personal experience and/or opinion. The aim of this first round is to

elicit a range of opinions which subsequently become the basis of future surveys. This step is an essential part of reducing researcher bias. Where individual surveys are constructed by a single researcher or researcher group and may use predefined frameworks or opinions to develop questions, the Delphi method collects diverse opinions to develop comprehensive follow up surveys in subsequent rounds. These surveys are organically constructed based on the collated responses to the first survey round.

2. **Opinion refinement** is conducted from round two onwards. Experts are typically asked to rank items identified in the first round in order of importance. Analysis of round two answers removes options below a predetermined threshold of agreement. Subsequent rounds include feedback on how the expert group responded and may ask experts to either re-rank items in order of importance or use a binary scale to rate items as important or not important. Experts may also be asked to rank their confidence in their answer, which may be used by researchers to decide whether to emphasise a participant's responses when determining consensus.

While all Delphi methods follow these basic principles, there is a lack of consensus regarding key survey characteristics in the literature. Researchers have introduced variations to the Delphi method to meet the specific needs of their research (Keeney, Hasson, & McKenna, 2011; Sackman, 1974). In general, variations relate to *how* the data is collected (e.g. via post, in-person, or electronically), and *what* the method involves (e.g. number and characteristics of experts and surveys).

This chapter will focus on the e-Delphi method, drawing on researchers' practical experiences using a modified e-Delphi method to establish consensus on the definitions of sport and physical recreation for children with disabilities between consumers, rehabilitation professionals, and sport practitioners in Australia. While this chapter provides an overview of traditional Delphi methods, the focus is on highlighting the benefits and challenges of the electronic form and provide practical recommendations for researchers conducting e-Delphi methods.

E-Delphi Method: Survey Characteristics

The modern e-Delphi method follows the principles of the traditional method; however, it leverages the benefits of electronic communication to improve efficiency. Ironically, there is no consensus on the definition of the

Delphi method. The flexibility of both the traditional method and of conducting research in an electronic context invoke a range of important considerations for researchers. This section describes the decisions researchers must consider in relation to survey characteristics in the context of the opportunities and limitations of an electronic collection method. Key characteristics include means and timing of communication, quantity and type of questions and feedback, number of survey rounds, and thresholds for consensus and survey end-points.

Means of Communication

There are three main means of collecting data using the Delphi method: (1) via postal mail, (2) in person, and (3) electronically/online. The Delphi method was originally conducted via the postal service. Now known as 'snail-mail', the significant time taken for each round of surveys to be distributed, completed, and returned led to the development of more timely methods. In-person methods have also been used to expedite the collection of data, with real-time debates reducing the number of survey rounds conducted. However, anonymity – a key tenet of the Delphi method – was significantly impacted. Finally, advances in technology have allowed surveys to be conducted electronically (e-Delphi). An e-Delphi is simply any Delphi method that is conducted using electronic means. Early iterations of the e-Delphi simply mimicked traditional paper-based studies by employing email instead of the postal service. Modern e-Delphi methods take advantage of online survey platforms such as Survey Monkey, Qualtrix, and Redcap. While each method of data collection (postal, face-to-face, electronic) is capable of collecting the same types and quantities of data, they each have different benefits and challenges.

Timing of Communication

A defining feature of a Delphi method is the time period across which the data are collected. Both *traditional* and *e-Delphi* methods use three or more iterative surveys over a designated data collection period (Keeney et al., 2011). The first of these surveys includes open-ended questions so as to elicit a range of opinions; subsequent surveys are then used to refine these opinions and for consensus to be achieved.

The *modified Delphi* method uses a combination of a real-time focus group or interviews to replace the first survey round in one discrete time period (Thorpe & Holt, 2007). In this method, the first round facilitates

Table 11.1 *Types of Delphi method by method and timing*

	Post	In-person	Electronic
Iterative surveys over time	Traditional Delphi	Modified Delphi*	e-Delphi Online Delphi
Real-time	N/A	Modified Delphi* Real-time Delphi OR Consensus conference	Real-time e-Delphi OR Technological Delphi

* The modified Delphi method uses a combination of in-person and either post or electronic methods.

the codification of answers by experts in real-time to facilitate structured knowledge flow. Subsequent iterative survey rounds are performed either via post or electronic methods.

Real-time Delphi methods conduct the entire Delphi process within a discrete time period. In-person, real-time methods are also known as *consensus conferences* as the loss of anonymity threatens this key tenet of the Delphi method. However, the real-time e-Delphi method can also use technology to facilitate real-time sharing of opinion, feedback on others' opinions, and debate, all whilst maintaining anonymity. The use of technological solutions (such as a data input programs used on a computer or tablet) to input data provides instant visibility of responses and feedback. Table 11.1 shows how the interaction of method and timing relates to the Delphi method.

Question Design

The number and type of questions asked should be carefully considered. Long surveys may offer greater opportunities to collect data; however, they increase the risk of expert attrition and may decrease the likelihood of receiving detailed answers in the later parts of the survey. Conversely, short surveys may not collect adequate data, and may necessitate a larger number of rounds to reach consensus. Simulations exploring the salient aspects of the Delphi method have shown that there is no difference in consensus indices when question numbers range from six to forty (Birko et al., 2015). However, this does not account for expert fatigue. Researchers should carefully balance the number and length of questions with the need for detailed, considered answers and demands on expert time.

The type of questions used should always be based on the types of answers required and the type of analysis to be conducted. In the first survey round, questions will primarily be open-ended to provide qualitative data which will undergo thematic analysis to identify and classify the range of opinions held by participating experts. In subsequent rounds, dichotomous or Likert scales with optional open-ended comment boxes are typically used to allow descriptive statistical analysis to be conducted and used to determine if consensus is reached and/or provide feedback to experts in subsequent rounds.

In some cases, researchers may aim to reduce the variation in round one answers, and therefore the number of rounds needed to gain consensus, by using established frameworks to guide answers. While the use of valid and reliable frameworks may facilitate effective communication and early consensus, it limits the identification of novel opinions that may otherwise have been offered, and has a significant risk of introducing bias (Duffield, 1993; Jenkins & Smith, 1994; Keeney et al., 2011). The urge to minimise the number of rounds by introducing frameworks early may be a particular challenge when researchers are time-limited due to limitations in funding, pressure to publish, collaborator time limits (including in student-led research), or expert availability.

Our recent e-Delphi on sport and physical recreation participation for children with disability used a number of well-recognised frameworks to guide the first recruitment survey. These frameworks originated from health (the International Classification of Functioning, Disability and Health,), sport and physical recreation (Physical Literacy), and research (SPORTS Participation Framework) contexts. The frameworks contextualised the questions being asked of experts, who were from varying backgrounds, thereby ensuring questions were properly understood so as to provide relevant data. For example, one question provided a copy of the SPORTS Participation Framework which describes the stages of sports participation children may move through from entry-level to elite sports participation, and asked if this represented all stages of participation, as well as what stages were not represented.

QUESTION: Different levels of sport have been identified that children may progress through as they become more skilled and/or experienced. The following is a suggested method of categorising the levels of participation for children with disabilities:

(cont.)

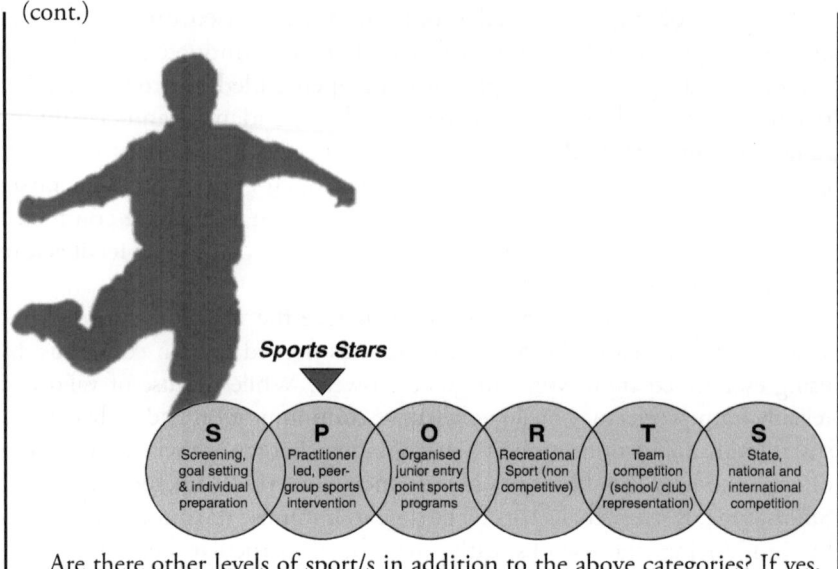

Are there other levels of sport/s in addition to the above categories? If yes, please list.

Feedback Design

Feedback is created by the researcher from the experts' aggregated and anonymous responses. Item refinement is facilitated by allowing experts knowledge of their previous answers, and the summarised answers of other experts (Lewis-Beck, Bryman, & Liao, 2003). Experts reflect on their own opinions within the context of others', and may change, justify or modify their responses in subsequent survey rounds. The iterative process of the Delphi method, offers multiple opportunities to reflect on answers in the context of others' arguments. This reflection of traditional debate is more robust than a single survey that collects isolated opinions at a single time-point (Barrett & Heale, 2020; Rowe & Wright, 1999).

Researchers may choose to provide quantitative feedback, qualitative feedback, or both. The presentation of descriptive statistics such as mean, median and standard deviation facilitates movement towards consensus due to the inclination to favour majority viewpoints (Rowe, Wright, & McColl, 2005). Comparatively, detailed qualitative feedback which describes the reasons behind experts' choices has significantly more impact on experts' subsequent answers than quantitative feedback (Best, 1974). This is particularly important when considering exposure to new viewpoints from a diverse range of experts including minority voices. Feeding back new perspectives has the potential to create divergent thinking, prompting experts to analyse and potentially modify their answers away from the previous majority.

In our recent e-Delphi on sport and physical recreation participation for children with disability, we choose to provide qualitative feedback only. For example, this was the feedback and subsequent question in the round two survey:

Feedback: *In the first survey, we asked if you agreed with the categories of sport put forward by Sport Australia. It was identified that sports such as running, swimming and long jump were not included in the original categories (invasion, striking and fielding, net and court, target, and movement exploration). The category of 'Speed and Distance' has been added to include sports such as running, swimming, frame running, long jump etc.*

Question: In this question, we want to make sure that all sports can be clearly categorised.

Proposed categories include:

Invasion – sports which involve moving into the other team's territory to score a goal (e.g. soccer and rugby).

Striking and fielding – sports that involve hitting a ball to a field and requiring to return the ball to the original place hit (e.g. softball and cricket)

Net and court – sports that include a fixed area separated by a net to score a point (e.g. tennis and volleyball).

Target – sports that include an area to hit to gain the most point(e.g. golf and ten-pin bowling).

Movement exploration – sports that utilise the body to perform a task(e.g. gymnastics or ice-skating).

Speed and Distance – sports that aim to **complete tasks as fast, or as far as possible** (e.g. running, frame running, or wheelchair racing, swimming, long or high jump, and discus, javelin or shotput).

1. Do you believe all sports are included in these categories?
2. Why do you believe these categories don't cover all types of sport?

(cont.)

3. Should the speed and distance category be a separate category as presented above, or a sub category of movement exploration?
4. When assessing a child's sports participation, is it important is it to identify what type of activity they are participating in? (yes/no)
5. If no, why not?

It is important that researchers are objective in terms of managing feedback responsibly and ethically to minimise their influence when phrasing questions. As real-time clarification and elaboration is not possible, researchers must also take care to minimise misunderstandings in the way they write their survey questions. The subsequent survey rounds can be used by researchers to clarify their understanding of answers. Poorly designed research using e-Delphi methods has the potential to report significantly biased findings that adversely affect the progress of the research area (Winkler & Moser, 2016).

Number of Rounds

The strength of using an e-Delphi method is in the speed of the data collection. Faster survey distribution and return may enable a larger number of rounds, especially compared to postal methods. While theoretically researchers may therefore use as many rounds as needed to gain consensus, the risk of expert attrition increases with each round. Researchers should therefore use the smallest number of rounds needed to gain adequate consensus.

The number of rounds used in published research employing Delphi methods varies greatly. While traditional Delphi methods suggest at least three survey rounds, with the same experts asked the same questions at least twice (Thorpe & Holt, 2007), this is not mandatory, and it should not be assumed to have occurred in any study reporting to have used Delphi methods. It is therefore important that researchers justify the number of rounds used. This will typically relate to the predefined research end-point, and analysis of the effects of methodological limitations.

Consensus and End-Points

Unfortunately, there are few guidelines as to what level consensus should be set. In lieu of recommendations, researchers should ensure that they predefine and communicate their justification of consensus levels prior to undertaking the study. Consensus levels will vary based on the similarity of experts' backgrounds (greater consensus is expected between experts of similar backgrounds), the importance of low variation (i.e., in issues where consistency is critical), and associated risk factors (e.g., where significant policy decisions or funding choices will be based on the results of the research). It is important to note that consensus should not be forced and is not a mandatory outcome (Rowe et al., 2005). Higher thresholds for consensus may require a larger number of rounds, leading to issues with attrition.

In the absence of predefined consensus and end-points, research could go on indefinitely, risking high levels of attrition or expert burnout, or end prematurely, risking a lack of meaningful results. These risks can be mitigated by setting clear definitions for consensus and for failure to reach consensus prior to the commencement of research.

Communication of Survey Characteristics

The flexibility associated with e-Delphi methods, along with the absence of consensus regarding optimal survey characteristics, means that researchers must thoughtfully choose how to conduct their research and provide adequate detail and justification of these choices when reporting results. Researchers should provide full justification of the following survey characteristics:

1. Communication

    a. Means (postal, in-person, electronic)
    b. Timing (iterative survey rounds, real-time)

2. Questions

    a. Number of questions
    b. Type of questions (open-ended, dichotomous, scale)
    c. Modifications to traditional methods (replacement of a survey round, use of guiding frameworks)

3. Feedback

    a. Amount of feedback
    b. Type of feedback (descriptive statistics, qualitative explanations)

4. Number of survey rounds
5. Thresholds for consensus and question end-points

Expert Characteristics

The validity of a Delphi method is reliant on the experts who participate in the research, and their participation behaviour in the study. Expert selection and management are therefore of utmost importance, being foundational to the quality, trustworthiness, and reliability of the final results. The e-Delphi method introduces a range of benefits and challenges relating to expert selection and management that are either not relevant to traditional Delphi methods or are emphasised in electronic methods. This section deals with (1) the definition of 'expert', (2) sample size, (3) recruitment, (4), retention and attrition, (5) anonymity in relation to the e-Delphi method, and (6) communication of expert characteristics.

Defining an 'Expert'

The definition of an expert differs between studies. In general, it is accepted that an expert has interest, knowledge, and experience in the area of investigation, and that their level of knowledge and/or experience would be considered sufficient to answer the research question (Adler & Ziglio, 1996). This is a slight variation on what may be accepted as the common definition of 'expert', leading some researchers to use alternate terms such as 'participant', 'respondent', or 'professional' in publications. Regardless of choice of title, the researchers are responsible for determining the level of knowledge and experience required to answer the research question. The researchers are also responsible for establishing clear inclusion and exclusion criteria to ensure that participants have adequate knowledge and/or experience to contribute meaningfully when answering the research question. In this chapter, we use the word 'expert' to indicate the expected specific qualifications that the sample must have in order to answer the research question, above and beyond the level of knowledge expected in a random sample of the general population.

Examples of criteria used to define an expert in health science research using a Delphi method include:

- qualifications (e.g. Bachelor's degree, PhD) (Giltenane et al., 2022; Sun et al., 2015)
- professional registration or titling (e.g. conferred as a specialist by a national professional association) (Forbes et al., 2017; Sun et al., 2015)
- years of experience in a specific context (e.g. >1 year of teaching physiotherapy students) (Sole et al., 2019)
- lived experience (e.g. as an autistic person) (Higgins et al., 2021; Richards et al., 2022).

An e-Delphi method provides opportunities for experts to participate without geographical barriers; however, other barriers are introduced. The lack of geographical restrictions may introduce the possibility that criteria relating to expertise have different meanings in different locations. For example, in Australia, physiotherapists qualify with Bachelor-level qualifications and are first-contact practitioners who can refer patients for medical imaging. In the United States, physical therapists have doctor-level qualifications but typically see patients after referral from a primary physician. Capturing equivalent expertise across countries (and in some cases, even jurisdictions) may require careful consideration of criteria wording.

One challenging component of the expectations of an expert during research is that they should be able to be relatively impartial to the outcome of the research and should be able to represent all sides of an argument (Goodman, 1987; Linstone & Turoff, 1975, 2011). However, selected experts are often personally affected by the topic, or have devoted considerable time and energy into clinical or research work in the area and therefore impartiality may be difficult. The issue of bias introduced by expert selection is addressed later in this section.

Sample Size

The number of experts recruited in Delphi methods is extremely variable. Recommendations vary from less than ten to hundreds (Birko et al., 2015). There are arguments for both small and large samples. Larger samples are better able to mitigate the effects of outliers, increase the likelihood of representing a variety of viewpoints, and increase the likelihood of maintaining anonymity in groups where experts are acutely aware of others' views. In many fields, however, the number of experts is small, and aiming for a large sample size may require the use of broad inclusion criteria, resulting in the dilution of expertise. Larger sample sizes are also associated with high attrition, which impacts reliability of results (de Villiers, de Villiers, & Kent, 2005) as participants are more likely to drop out than provide opinions that differ from the majority. Conversely, small samples allow strict inclusion criteria, which may limit the number of available participants yet ensure relevant expertise in the sample. Therefore, it is recommended that the target sample size is small enough to specifically target experts with the level of expertise required to answer the research question, yet large enough to capture diversity in expert background and opinions. What is considered an adequate sample size should be clearly described and justified in publications resulting from research using Delphi methods and should extend beyond the convenience of the recruitment time-frame.

Expert Recruitment

The Delphi method relies on the presence of 'diverse and subjective judgements, opinions, experiences and intuitions of participants' (Thorpe & Holt, 2007, p. 73). Therefore, well-justified methods of recruitment and retention of experts are of primary importance. E-Delphi methods offer opportunities to recruit larger numbers of experts by improving researchers' ability to identify experts through publicly available information and social media networks. However, an e-Delphi can introduce or emphasise barriers associated with language, literacy, digital literacy, access to technology, or digital presence.

It is not typical for a Delphi method to use a random sample due to the limited numbers of experts available for recruitment. When diverse voices are omitted during recruitment practices bias may be introduced to the sample of experts. Therefore, it is important that researchers implement techniques designed to identify and recruit experts with varied backgrounds, particularly those who are frequently marginalised in research in general or within the particular topic under consideration. People of diverse backgrounds are essential to the Delphi method, as previously mentioned when discussing their value in feedback. Diversity amongst the experts introduces a variety of perspectives in the first survey round that may not be present in existing frameworks and/or mainstream discourse relating to the topic. These perspectives can then be presented to all experts and considered in subsequent survey rounds.

Researchers frequently report contacting known experts and utilising social media to recruit for studies using e-Delphi methods. Therefore, expert selection may be impacted by privilege and (conscious or unconscious) racism, sexism, ablism, or classism. Contacting experts through known networks, while convenient, introduces bias based on the researcher's own attributes. This method of recruitment tends to heavily favour experts who resemble the researchers themselves – for example, location in the native country of the research team, level of education, ethnicity, cultural and/or religious background, and interest in the type of research conducted by the research team. These biases endure even when there are no specific exclusion criteria, simply due to the nature of recruitment strategies. It is essential that researchers acknowledge the risk of these biases and actively recruit minority voices (Rowe et al., 2005).

Bias may also be introduced during recruitment via expert self-selection. Experts may disproportionally accept or decline invitations for studies using e-Delphi methods due to time limitations or workload capacity (frequently increasing with increasing expertise/seniority), or feelings of inferiority or inadequacy relating to the title of 'expert'. Self-selection bias may further prevent those with diverse views from participating in research using e-Delphi methods, whereby individuals with differing views are aware that their views are not consistent with their field and have experienced marginalisation or have been disregarded due to these views.

Judicious use of the e-Delphi method can assist in reducing bias from recruitment strategies. Some strategies for reducing bias include:

1. Using strict inclusion and exclusion criteria which necessitate searching outside of the researchers' networks to identify experts for inclusion. When a pool of potential participants is small and well-defined, it is more likely that all relevant experts can be identified and invited to participate. An extreme example would be a criterion of having won a Noble Peace Prize! Publicly available records streamline identification of eligible participants.
2. Clearly describing inclusion and exclusion criteria to potential participants and explaining the importance of capturing diverse views to minimise self-selection bias. If you are aware of specifically marginalised groups in your area of research, specific recruitment of this group should be prioritised.
3. Identifying key experts through organisations (e.g. children with cerebral palsy on the national register), or publicly available information (e.g. authors of papers included in relevant systematic reviews or government websites listing contact details for all school principals).
4. Identifying key points of recruitment which would target diverse voices (e.g. key contact points in multiple countries, organisations, or networks).

In our e-Delphi on sports and physical recreation participation for children with disability, we targeted recruitment across three groups to ensure that a diverse range of perspectives were collected: (1) people with lived experience of childhood-onset disability; (2) rehabilitation professionals; and (3) sports professionals. Due to their differing contexts, a variety of opinions were introduced to the research.

(cont.)

In each of these three groups, there was a large potential expert group of people with lived experience of childhood-onset disability. Our sampling method of distributing invitations through large organisations and social media was effective in identifying participants; however, it introduced bias as it did not capture potential participants who (a) do not interact with these providers, (b) do not have access to technology, or (c) are not in the networks which shared the invitation online. While our study was national, we found a higher proportion of respondents from our local state due to the networks each researcher used to distribute the survey. This bias introduced during recruitment had the potential to influence the study results.

Expert Retention and Attrition

Expert retention is essential to the Delphi method. Research participation that is difficult, time consuming, or frustrating will frequently lead to a high rate of attrition, which may result in false consensus due to the withdrawal of participants with differing opinions (Buck et al., 1993). Th e-Delphi method facilitates expert retention by fostering a sense of ownership and responsibility for the project and results (McKenna, 1994), reducing geographical barriers, minimising demands on experts', time and enhancing convenience and user experience through optimisation on both desktop and mobile devices. In addition, the immediate availability of data for researchers significantly reduces the time between survey rounds, thus optimising expert's attention for and commitment to the study.

Despite the benefits of being able to complete surveys when and where experts have capacity, the risk that surveys may be rushed or completed when the expert is focussed on another task increases (Rowe et al., 2005). To mitigate the risks of poor attention when using e-Delphi methods, researchers should clearly inform participants of the real-world application of the results and the value of providing detailed answers to questions.

A technique that has been used in the modified Delphi method to reduce attrition, improve expert attention, and increase speed of research is the use of an in-person first round. While e-Delphi methods do not lend themselves to a true in-person round, web conferencing software offers alternative real-time capabilities. Another option for the e-Delphi method is to use a 'recruiting' survey prior to the first e-Delphi round to identify a wide range of potential participants and capture opinions of those unable or unwilling to commit to the full e-Delphi method (Hung, Altschuld, & Lee, 2008).

Mobile optimisation allows participants to complete surveys when and where they have capacity. For example, I participated in multiple rounds of a study using an e-Delphi method while on parental leave. I completed three rounds of surveys during 2am feeds, when my baby was refusing to go back to bed for the rest of the night!

Expert Anonymity

Anonymity is an essential component of the Delphi method. The e-Delphi method using an online survey offers true anonymity, meaning that experts are anonymous not only from each other, but also from the researchers, who are frequently also well-known experts in the field. True anonymity is established in an e-Delphi when data collection is separated from the method used to contact experts. Where traditional and early e-Delphi methods would allow identification based on return postal or email address, modern e-Delphi methods direct experts to an external survey platform. Researchers must ensure that they do not violate anonymity by asking experts identifying questions either during data collection, or before/after data collection, when using the online survey platform.

Anonymity minimises bias in three key ways. First, it reduces self-censorship due to concerns about how an opinion may be perceived by others. Second, it reduces the risk that experts will have preconceived ideas of the value of other experts' opinions, and therefore change their ratings after receiving identifiable feedback. This reduces the halo effect, whereby high-profile or dominant experts views are amplified (Winkler & Moser, 2016). Third, it reduces researchers' bias when analysing data. The introduction of bias is an important consideration when modifying e-Delphi methods. For example, a modified Delphi method, violates anonymity by revealing the identity and opinions of experts in the in-person first round. This introduces the risk of self-editing due to fear of judgement, or a significant change of opinion based on the opinions of other highly respected experts present.

Communication of Expert Characteristics

The importance of experts to the reliability and validity of the results of an e-Delphi mean that it is essential that researchers are thoughtful in identifying expert characteristics relevant to their study, and fully justify these when reporting results. Researchers should provide full justification for the following expert characteristics:

1. Sample size
2. Recruitment strategy

   - Method of identification of experts
   - Efforts to engage with diverse and/or marginalised groups
   - Mitigation of bias through recruitment

4. Maintenance of anonymity
5. Retention methods

Electronic Data Collection, Storage, and Management

One of the most frequently cited benefits of e-Delphi methods is the ability to reduce geographical inequity in the expert sample. However, in the place of geographical inequity, the e-Delphi introduces bias due to lack of digital infrastructure and/or digital literacy. This section addresses the innate challenges of using an e-Delphi method, and how researchers may try to minimise these within their research.

Electronic Access

To participate in research via an e-Delphi method, individuals must have the knowledge, skills, and technology to be contactable for recruitment and survey distribution and then complete electronic surveys. Experts' access depends on the presence of reliable digital infrastructures and access to personal electronic devices with the requisite accessibility functions (e.g. assistive technology integration). Individuals must then have functional digital literacy to be able to use email and survey platforms appropriately.

Digital infrastructure includes the overarching technologies needed to be 'online, ' such as Wi-Fi. Access to digital infrastructure is most significantly impacted in lower socio-economic nations. For example, Eritrea, Somalia, and South Sudan have some of the lowest percent of their population using the internet (1–7%) (The World Bank, 2022). Poor digital infrastructure also affects individuals in OECD nations who live in remote or disadvantaged areas (e.g. remote Aboriginal communities in Australia). Even those with functioning digital infrastructure and skills may be adversely affected. For example, email filters may send research invitations to the 'junk' folder, while virus protecting firewalls may prevent experts from accessing certain online platforms from within their organisation (Keeney et al., 2011).

In addition to having access to overarching digital infrastructures, individuals also need to be able to access and use personal electronic devices (e.g. computer, tablet, or smart phone) effectively. While most people have grown up with technology and use it in their day-to-day work and personal lives, there are people who may have difficulty using both hardware (i.e. the phone, tablet, or computer) and software (i.e. the email program or online survey platform). Individual access to technology and digital literacy are challenges for members of marginalised groups, including people of low socio-economic status, those with disabilities, and the elderly. Access to online platforms using assistive technologies (e.g. screen reading capability, voice to text, translation services) is important to ensure equitable access. Researchers should carefully consider how to engage people from marginalised groups in their research, informing them of the array of assistive technologies available and ensuring engagement with all communication and accessible participation for all. Minimising access issues should be prioritised to enhance inclusion of experts with diverse backgrounds and perspectives.

To enhance access:

1. Use the Web Content Accessibility Guidelines to ensure that content is perceivable, operable, understandable, and robust (see www.w3.org/WAI/standards-guidelines/wcag/).
2. Ensure your digital platform is accessible for screen readers. If using images in your survey, ensure that alt text is enabled and appropriately filled out.
3. Provide simple, clear instructions for survey access.
4. Check in with participants and/or provide contact details for assistance with survey completion.
5. Identify groups who may not be reached by the e-Delphi method and include them via other research methods, or acknowledge the absence of their voices in the study limitations (Education and Outreach Working Group, 2005).

Data Security

Electronic data collection is associated with a range of practical and ethical challenges which should be addressed at the study planning stage. In general, these relate to the security of the survey platform, communication methods, and data storage software, as well as the human aspect of data management.

The security of online platforms is an important consideration, especially when considering potentially sensitive data. One important aspect which ethics committees will be interested in is where data will be stored. Online platforms that are available globally will have servers in a specific country, which may or may not be acceptable for ethics committees. It is important to note that companies may store data on the servers of their parent company: for example, the popular Survey Monkey site has servers managed by its parent company, Momentive Inc., with data stored in the United States, Ireland, and Canada. An internet search for 'server location, *platform name*' or checking the 'Privacy' section on a platform's website will typically give you the information that you need.

It is not a surprise that even for electronic research, humans are a common source of data storage and security failures. In recruitment, anonymity may be impacted when individuals other than the expert have access to the email account used for survey invitations, such as in the case of administrative assistants managing the email accounts of senior staff members (Keeney et al., 2011). While the e-Delphi method reduces the risk of individual data loss through the postal service, the risk of large-scale data loss due to issues relating to inappropriate storage increases. Selecting an approved and legitimate online platform can mitigate such data management risks. Data, once collected, may be exported and saved in a number of ways, including cloud storage, local networks, computer hard drive, or on a mobile storage device such as a USB or external hard drive. Each of these data storage facilities has associated risks which should be reviewed in a well-documented data management plan. Such plans need to be written in line with local (e.g. university), state, and national data security and information privacy legislations. In general, researchers should consider who can access the data, how the data is secured (physically and electronically), and the risks to individuals and organisations from data loss or theft.

Environmental Considerations

Overall, the e-Delphi is an environmentally friendly research method (Keeney et al., 2011), and you could be forgiven for thinking that there are no negative environmental impacts. The e-Delphi method reduces the need for people to travel to a central location for focus groups or for the researcher to travel for individual interviews (reducing carbon emissions from cars, planes, and trains), reduces the use of paper (reducing logging and water use), and reduces the physical storage of non-renewable resources. While using cloud computing for data collection and storage is a more efficient storage method, the sheer volume of data stored globally means that the amount of electricity used to sustain this storage is growing (Markovic et al., 2013). Therefore, care should be taken not to collect all possible information, and to instead carefully curate surveys in a way that collects the most relevant and meaningful information. Not only does this minimise the amount of data that needs to be processed and stored from an environmental perspective, but it streamlines the data analysis and communication process.

Survey Design

The increased accessibility of online survey tools has modernised the Delphi process. Where early e-Delphi methods relied on email as a direct replacement of snail-mail, modern e-Delphi methods utilise email simply as the method of initial contact, and to direct participants to an online survey platform where the majority of data collection occurs. There are many benefits to this, including true anonymity, reduced data loss, streamlined data storage, and a simpler user experience. The researcher still must intentionally make and justify choices in relation to platform and survey design, and acknowledge the effect these choices have on their results.

Online Survey Platform Choice

There are a large range of online platforms that are suitable for research using e-Delphi methods. This section will not recommend specific platforms, but rather will highlight the primary considerations researchers need to consider relating to a platform's feasibility and fitness for purpose.

First, researchers need to identify the limitations of their online platform options. The most common issue is cost. Large institutions frequently subscribe to a limited number of platforms, reducing a researcher's choice while also providing 'pre-approved' and costed options. Without a subscription, the cost of running a single survey can vary significantly. The other common limiting factor is the digital literacy of the researcher. Most online survey platforms are designed for people with basic computer skills and are very user friendly. However, others require substantial technical knowledge, and while they come with increased capacity and flexibility, they may be difficult to use for experts who are unfamiliar with that platform, which introduces an additional barrier to expert retention.

After excluding options that are too expensive, or that do not match the researcher's skills, platform choice is influenced by fitness for purpose. The design of the expert-facing interface will shape their experience of completing the survey. This will influence how easily they can progress through the survey, and subsequently the quality of data collected. A clunky interface means that experts will spend time negotiating the platform rather than considering the content of the questions. In the worst case, experts may simply give up and fail to complete surveys that are not user friendly. Similarly, mobile optimisation is an important feature to allow experts to complete surveys regardless of their available technology; optimising surveys for mobile access will assist in recruiting and retaining marginalised voices, including individuals without access to a computer due to homelessness or poverty, who are away from their computer (e.g. new parents), or who have extensive demands on their time.

Online Survey Platform Features

A key benefit of utilising specialised online platforms is that data collection is efficient. Online platforms are designed with a multitude of tools to enhance understanding, improve survey efficiency, and facilitate the collection of complete data. These tools minimise expert attrition by improving the user experience through help text and an attractive but simple interface that loads quickly and uses minimal internet bandwidth. Commercial platforms facilitate complete data collection by ensuring that users must respond to required questions or with specific data (e.g. numerical, date, time). Based on their answers, experts can be routed past irrelevant questions, allowing them to focus their time and attention on responding to relevant questions.

Conclusion

The e-Delphi method is a modern, flexible research method, which has the potential to return meaningful data while being time- and cost effective. The e-Delphi method enhances expert recruitment and retention by providing a platform for non-synchronous collaboration and debate from anywhere in the world. The onus, however, is on researchers to invite, from within the many accessible relevant experts, a diverse range of experts and to overcome barriers of connectivity to ensure marginalised voices are represented. Researchers are responsible for facilitating the process to maintain true anonymity, and to facilitate flow of information in a way that minimises the introduction of bias and maximises expert buy-in. Rather than trying to develop one standardised method, it is our recommendation that researchers employing an e-Delphi method ensure that they thoughtfully choose and justify choices relating to recruitment strategies, sample size, modification of traditional methods, online survey platform, number of rounds, and consensus and end-point thresholds.

References

Adler, M., & Ziglio, E. (1996). *Gazing Into the Oracle: The Delphi Method and Its Application to Social Policy and Public Health.* Jessica Kingsley Publishers.

Bäck-Pettersson, S., Hermansson, E., Sernert, N., & Björkelund, C. (2008). Research Priorities in Nursing: A Delphi Study among Swedish Nurses. *Journal of Clinical Nursing, 17*(16), 2221–31. https://doi.org/10.1111/j.1365-2702.2007.02083.x.

Barrett, D., & Heale, R. (2020). What are Delphi studies? *Evidence Based Nursing, 23*(3), 68–9. https://doi.org/10.1136/ebnurs-2020-103303.

Best, R. J. (1974). An Experiment in Delphi Estimation in Marketing Decision Making. *Journal of Marketing Research, 11*(4), 448–52. https://doi.org/10.2307/3151295.

Birko, S., Dove, E. S., Özdemir, V., & Dalal, K. (2015). Evaluation of Nine Consensus Indices in Delphi Foresight Research and their Dependency on Delphi Survey Characteristics: A Simulation Study and Debate on Delphi Design and Interpretation. *PLoS One, 10*(8), e0135162–e0135162. https://doi.org/10.1371/journal.pone.0135162.

Buck, A. J., Gross, M., Hakim, S., & Weinblatt, J. (1993). Using the Delphi Process to Analyze Social Policy Implementation: A Post Hoc Case from Vocational Rehabilitation. *Policy Sciences, 26*(4), 271–88. https://doi.org/10.1007/BF00999473.

Culley, J. M. (2011). Use of a Computer-Mediated Delphi Process to Validate a Mass Casualty Conceptual Model. *Computers, Informatics, Nursing, 29*(5), 272–9. https://doi.org/10.1097/NCN.0b013e3181fc3e59.

Dalkey, N., & Helmer, O. (1963). An Experimental Application of the DELPHI Method to the Use of Experts. *Management Science, 9*(3), 458–67. https://doi.org/10.1287/mnsc.9.3.458.

de Villiers, M. R., de Villiers, P. J. T., & Kent, A. P. (2005). The Delphi Technique in Health Sciences Education Research. *Medical Teacher, 27*(7), 639–43. https://doi.org/10.1080/01421590500069947.

Duffield, C. (1993). The Delphi Technique: A Comparison of Results Obtained using Two Expert Panels. *International Journal of Nursing Studies, 30*(3), 227–37. https://doi.org/10.1016/0020-7489(93)90033-Q.

Education and Outreach Working Group & Accessibility Guidelines Working Group (2005). WCAG 2 Overview. www.w3.org/TR/WCAG20/.

Forbes, R., Mandrusiak, A., Smith, M., & Russell, T. (2017). Identification of Competencies for Patient Education in Physiotherapy using a Delphi Approach. *Physiotherapy, 104*(2), 232–8. https://doi.org/10.1016/j.physio.2017.06.002.

Giltenane, M., Sheridan, A., Kroll, T., & Frazer, K. (2022). Identification of Quality Indicators of Public Health Nursing Practice: 'Modified Delphi' Approach. *Public Health Nursing*, *39*(1), 214–28. https://doi.org/10.1111/phn.13000.

Goodman, C. M. (1987). The Delphi Technique: A Critique. *Journal of Advanced Nursing*, *12*(6), 729–34. https://doi.org/10.1111/j.1365-2648.1987.tb01376.x.

Higgins, J. M., Arnold, S. R. C., Weise, J., Pellicano, E., & Trollor, J. N. (2021). Defining Autistic Burnout through Experts by Lived Experience: Grounded Delphi Method Investigating #AutisticBurnout. *Autism*, *25*(8), 2356–69. https://doi.org/10.1177/13623613211019858.

Hult Khazaie, D., & Khan, S. S. (2020). Social Psychology and Pandemics: Exploring Consensus about Research Priorities and Strategies using the Delphi Method. *Asian Journal of Social Psychology*, *23*(4), 363–71. https://doi.org/10.1111/ajsp.12442.

Hung, H.-L., Altschuld, J. W., & Lee, Y.-F. (2008). Methodological and Conceptual Issues Confronting a Cross-Country Delphi Study of Educational Program Evaluation. *Evaluation and Program Planning*, *31*(2), 191–8. https://doi.org/10.1016/j.evalprogplan.2008.02.005.

Jenkins, D. A., & Smith, T. E. (1994). Applying Delphi Methodology in Family Therapy Research. *Contemporary Family Therapy*, *16*(5), 411–30. https://doi.org/10.1007/BF02197902.

Keeney, S., Hasson, F., & McKenna, H. P. (2011). *The Delphi Technique in Nursing and Health Research*. Chichester: Wiley-Blackwell.

Lewis-Beck, M. S., Bryman, A., & Liao, T. F. (2003). *The SAGE Encyclopedia of Social Science Research Methods* (Vol. 3). Thousand Oaks: SAGE Publications.

Linstone, H. A., & Turoff, M. (1975). *The Delphi Method: Techniques and Applications*. Reading, MA: Addison-Wesley Pub. Co., Advanced Book Program.

Linstone, H. A., & Turoff, M. (2011). Delphi: A Brief Look Backward and Forward. *Technological Forecasting & Social Change*, *78*(9), 1712–19. https://doi.org/10.1016/j.techfore.2010.09.011.

Mackenzie, L., Coppola, S., Alvarez, L., et al. (2017). International Occupational Therapy Research Priorities: A Delphi Study. *OTJR (Thorofare, N.J.)*, *37*(2), 72–81. https://doi.org/10.1177/1539449216687528.

Markovic, D. S., Zivkovic, D., Branovic, I., Popovic, R., & Cvetkovic, D. (2013). Smart Power Grid and Cloud Computing. *Renewable & Sustainable Energy Reviews*, *24*, 566–77. https://doi.org/10.1016/j.rser.2013.03.068.

McIntyre, S., Novak, I., & Cusick, A. (2010). Consensus Research Priorities for Cerebral Palsy: A Delphi Survey of Consumers, Researchers, and Clinicians. *Developmental Medicine & Child Neurology*, *52*(3), 270–5. https://doi.org/10.1111/j.1469-8749.2009.03358.x.

McKenna, H. P. (1994). The Delphi Technique: A Worthwhile Research Approach for Nursing? *Journal of Advanced Nursing*, *19*(6), 1221–5. https://doi.org/10.1111/j.1365-2648.1994.tb01207.x.

Okoli, C., & Pawlowski, S. D. (2004). The Delphi Method as a Research Tool: An Example, Design Considerations and Applications. *Information & Management*, *42*(1), 15–29. https://doi.org/10.1016/j.im.2003.11.002.

Palisano, R. J., Rosenbaum, P., Bartlett, D., & Livingston, M. H. (2008). Content Validity of the Expanded and Revised Gross Motor Function Classification System. *Developmental Medicine & Child Neurology*, *50*(10), 744–50. https://doi.org/10.1111/j.1469-8749.2008.03089.x.

Rahimzadeh, V., Bartlett, G., & Knoppers, B. M. (2021). A Policy Delphi Study to Validate the Key Implications of Data Sharing (KIDS) Framework for Pediatric Genomics in Canada. *BMC Medical Ethics*, *22*(1), 1–71. https://doi.org/10.1186/s12910-021-00635-1.

Rankin, G., Rushton, A., Olver, P., & Moore, A. (2012). Chartered Society of Physiotherapy's Identification of National Research Priorities for Physiotherapy using a Modified Delphi Technique. *Physiotherapy*, *98*(3), 260–72. https://doi.org/10.1016/j.physio.2012.03.002.

Richards, K. L., Woolrych, I., Allen, K. L., & Schmidt, U. (2022). A Delphi Study to Explore Clinician and Lived Experience Perspectives on Setting Priorities in Eating Disorder Services. *BMC Health Services Research*, *22*(1), 1–788. https://doi.org/10.1186/s12913-022-08170-4.

Rowe, G., & Wright, G. (1999). The Delphi Technique as a Forecasting Tool: Issues and Analysis. *International Journal of Forecasting*, *15*(4), 353–75. https://doi.org/10.1016/S0169-2070(99)00018-7.

Rowe, G., & Wright, G. Expert Opinions in Forecasting: The Role of the Delphi Technique. In *Principles of Forecasting* (pp. 125–44). Boston, MA: Springer US. https://doi.org/10.1007/978-0-306-47630-3_7.

Rowe, G., Wright, G., & McColl, A. (2005). Judgment Change during Delphi-like Procedures: The Role of Majority Influence, Expertise, and Confidence. *Technological Forecasting & Social Change*, *72*(4), 377–99. https://doi.org/10.1016/j.techfore.2004.03.004.

Sackman, H. (1974). *Delphi Critique: Expert Opinion, Forecasting, and Group Process*. Lexington: Lexington Books.

Sole, G., Skinner, M., Hale, L., & Golding, C. (2019). Developing a Framework for Teaching Clinical Reasoning Skills to Undergraduate Physiotherapy Students: A Delphi Study. *New Zealand Journal of Physiotherapy*, *47*(1), 49–58. https://doi.org/10.15619/NZJP/47.1.06.

Sun, C., Dohrn, J., Klopper, H., et al. (2015). Clinical Nursing and Midwifery Research Priorities in Eastern and Southern African Countries: Results From a Delphi Survey. *Nursing Research*, *64*(6), 466–75. https://doi.org/10.1097/NNR.0000000000000126.

Thorpe, R., & Holt, R. (2007). *The SAGE Dictionary of Qualitative Management Research*. London: SAGE Publications, Limited.

Verschuren, O., Ketelaar, M., Keefer, D., et al. (2011). Identification of a Core Set of Exercise Tests for Children and Adolescents with Cerebral Palsy: A Delphi Survey of Researchers and Clinicians. *Developmental Medicine & Child Neurology*, *53*(5), 449–56. https://doi.org/10.1111/j.1469-8749.2010.03899.x.

Winkler, J., & Moser, R. (2016). Biases in Future-Oriented Delphi Studies: A Cognitive Perspective. *Technological Forecasting & Social Change, 105,* 63–76. https://doi.org/10.1016/j.techfore.2016.01.021.

World Bank. (2022). Individuals using the Internet (% of population). https://data.worldbank.org/indicator/IT.NET.USER.ZS.

CHAPTER 12

Refining Interview Protocols for Online Interviews on the Employment of Persons with Down Syndrome
Insights from a Pilot Test

Md Mizanur Rahman, Abg Safuan, Sharifa Ezat, Razitasham Safii, Chen Yoke Yong, Rosalia Saimon, and Ting Chuong Hock

Introduction

Currently, it is estimated that 15% of the world population, or about one billion people, are people with disabilities (PWD) (The World Bank, 2011). Employment is crucial to PWDs. It provides the prospect of forging meaningful social relationships, consolidating and elevating social status, establishing political standing, and ultimately earning an income to have a better lifestyle for themselves (Jameson, 2005). In addition to providing an income for better life circumstances, employment enhances the quality of life of PWDs by providing a meaningful sense of identity, independence, contribution, and belonging and establishing new relationships and interests (Emerson et al., 2011). Consequently, PWDs are often keen to participate in community growth and become financially independent (Waterhouse et al., 2010). However, in Malaysia, PWDs have notably higher unemployment rates compared to people with no disability (Ang, 2017). Various studies have demonstrated barriers to employment for PWDs in general (Ang, 2017; Fraser et al., 2011; Houtenville & Kalargyrou, 2012; Schur et al., 2017; Shier et al., 2009; Sundar et al., 2018; Ta & Leng, 2013). Nevertheless, there is a lack of studies that examine barriers specific to people with Down syndrome (PDS). The existing data often include PDS as part of the larger group of PWDs or people with intellectual disabilities (ID). Therefore, to address this gap, the barriers and opportunities of employment for PDS should be explored from multiple perspectives.

Video-Conference Interviewing as a New Norm

Within the realm of qualitative research, the most common data collection method is interviewing (Braun & Clarke, 2013). Utilising a qualitative investigation perspective, several different forms of interview designs were developed to obtain thick and rich data (Creswell et al., 2007). There are various interviewing methods, including narrative, active, grounded theory, and feminist approaches (Braun & Clarke, 2013). With an interview, we are able to explore things that cannot be readily observed, such as people's intentions, feelings, and behaviour, or how they perceive the world around them (Merriam & Tisdell, 2015). Therefore, interviews offer rich, in-depth information on people's experiences and perceptions of a subject matter (Turner, 2014). With regard to online interviewing of PDS, to our knowledge there is a dearth of research investigating the development of the interview protocol and its operationalisation. Therefore, this chapter hopes to contribute to the qualitative methodology literature by offering reflections on the video-conference interview protocol refinement process involving PDS.

Traditionally, an in-person interview is a gold standard in interviewing, as the interviewer connects and builds rapport with the respondents while observing their environment and non-verbal cues (Irani, 2019). However, as the COVID-19 pandemic ravages the world, it has posed an unprecedented challenge for in-person interviews. Hence, with travel restrictions imposed to stop the spread of the virus, the authors adopted video-conference interviews for data collection in this study. Researchers had to redesign their methodology to accommodate safe data collection and shift to online interviews instead.

Video-conference simulates an in-person experience while the participants are geographically separate (Krouwel et al., 2019). This internet-based service provides a synchronous (communicating at the same time) experience of communicating audio-visually with the other person, thus permitting current online interviews to be as effective as a face-to-face interviews (Bertrand & Bourdeau, 2010). Since the pandemic started in early 2020, video-conferencing applications such as Zoom, Google Meet, and Microsoft Teams, among others, have flourished on an unprecedented scale (Evans, 2020; Kalia, 2020; Peters, 2020; Thorp-Lancaster, 2020). Zoom reported up to 10 million daily users at the end of December 2020, and had a 20-fold increase to 200 million people daily in March 2021 (Kalia, 2020).

Of crucial significance, video interviewing alleviates the barrier of geography, as participants (and researchers alike) are given the flexibility to engage in the research at their respective locations (Hai-Jew, 2015; Krouwel et al., 2019). Hence, respondents may feel more comfortable participating from their place of choice, as compared to unfamiliar locations for in-person interviews (Hai-Jew, 2015; Krouwel et al., 2019). This ease of logistics is also beneficial for participants who might have reservations or concerns (based on religious restrictions, personal preferences, or safety concerns, among others) over the meeting and being alone with the researcher for the interview session. In addition, the advantage of this protocol over the traditional in-person interview is that it eases the audio-visual recording of the session (Bertrand & Bourdeau, 2010). This may come in handy as the researcher can record crucial non-verbal cues (body language, facial expression) during interviews (Irani, 2019), which may have otherwise been missed. Arguably, this can relieve the researcher from the shackles of multitasking during the interview. Beginner-level researchers, particularly as they focus more on participants' responses, might miss important non-verbal cues. This may prove to be a problem as undocumented or excluded non-verbal cues could lead to drawbacks such as rationalising the data or a researcher's lack of awareness (Begley, 1996).

Despite that, there are limitations to online video interview. The most apparent limitation lies in the technical aspects, such as the availability and suitability of electronic devices, and reliable internet connectivity. For a successful video-conference, both the researcher and the participant would be required to have access to and confidence in using the technology (Mann & Stewart, 2009). Hence, this may effectively exclude a large portion of the population who may not have access to the technology or the knowledge to handle it. Thus, it is of utmost importance that the researchers use this protocol to practice reflectivity in their participant selection. Therefore, as Deakin and Wakefield (2014) described, video-conferencing offers both research versatility and methodological and ethical potential.

Different Types of Interview Methods

The interview method can generally be classified into three groups; (1) *unstructured,* (2) *semi-structured,* and (3) *structured* (Braun & Clarke, 2013). The term 'unstructured interview' is used interchangeably in the literature with terms such as 'in-depth interview', 'informal conversational interview', 'non-standardized interview', or 'ethnographic interview' (Zhang & Wildemuth, 2009). As no research interview completely lacks structure (Braun & Clarke, 2013; Bryman & Burgess, 2002), there have been varied definitions of an unstructured interview (Zhang & Wildemuth, 2009). Minichiello et al. (1990) define them as interviews in which the questions and answers depend on the social interaction between the researcher and the respondent, and they are not predetermined. The researcher enters the interview without a planned set of questions (Sekaran & Bougie, 2016). Hence, the course of this type of interview is heavily participant-led (Braun & Clarke, 2013). Due to this, the unstructured interview is generally preferred in conducting long-term field work that allows self-expression of participants' responses regarding their pace of response and individuality (Corbin & Morse, 2003). In contrast, a structured interview consists of predetermined questions arranged by the researcher before the interview process (Merriam & Tisdell, 2015). The response parameters may also be predetermined (e.g. multiple choice) (Braun & Clarke, 2013), and it can be seen as an oral form of a written survey (Merriam & Tisdell, 2015). Therefore, this interview method finds its purpose in the quantitative study.

A semi-structured interview is a middle ground between the two previous interview methods, and sits on the opposite end of the continuum. A semi-structured interview is 'organized around a set of predetermined open-ended questions, with other questions emerging from the dialogue between interviewer and interviewee/s' (DiCicco-Bloom & Crabtree, 2006, p. 315). In this form of interview, the researcher creates a list of questions, but the participants are allowed to raise matters that are not anticipated (Braun & Clarke, 2013). Typically, specific responses are anticipated from the respondents. However, neither the order of the questions nor the exact wording are prearranged (Merriam & Tisdell, 2015). The open-ended nature of the questions in this type of interview is retained, allowing the participants to contribute rich and in-depth information (Creswell & Creswell, 2018). In contrast, the structure enables probing questions to be asked as a means to clarify the responses and for follow-up (Turner, 2014). Hence, this format allows the researcher to acknowledge the arising worldview of the respondents and any new insights on the subject matter (Merriam & Tisdell, 2015).

The Need for Interview Protocol

In addition to selecting an appropriate interview approach to ensure quality data collection, developing a valid and reliable interview protocol is also important. An interview protocol refers to 'the rules and guidelines for the conduct of the interviews' (Dikko, 2016, p. 532). Typically, it consists of pre- and post-interview procedures with a set of interview questions. For a smooth interview session, an interview protocol should be developed prior to the field testing (Dikko, 2016). An interview protocol may also enhance the efficiency of the interview process by guaranteeing a complete response is gained within the allotted period (Yeong et al., 2018).

With every research design, the data collection instrument must succeed in the validity and reliability tests before it can be regarded as a good measure (Dikko, 2016). A valid and reliable interview protocol may greatly aid novice researchers in successfully conducting the interview sessions to obtain thick and rich data. This is partly because novice researchers tend to stray away from the research objectives due to a lack of experience with the interview process, affecting the consistency and neutrality of the research (Yeong et al., 2018). With these limitations in mind, the authors proposed that the interview protocol undergo a refinement process to ensure its validity and reliability in quality data collection.

Interviewing Person with Down Syndrome

Historically, persons with an ID have been excluded from research (Rosner, 2021). By its nature, qualitative research imposes a power imbalance between the researcher and the respondents (Råheim et al., 2016), and this effect is often amplified in the case of interviewing person with ID, as their participation is influenced by their communicative and cognitive limitations (Emerson, 2004). Down syndrome – the most frequent genetic cause of intellectual disability (Centre for Disease & Prevention, 2019) – is a genetic condition often marked by impaired cognition and communication problems (Rachidi & Lopes, 2010). In terms of cognition, wide individual variation exists; individuals with DS experience mild (IQ 50–75) to severe impairment (IQ 20–35), equivalent to a mental age of 8–9-year-olds (Muhammad Ismail et al., 2019; Mundakel & Lal, 2020; Rachidi & Lopes, 2010). Additionally, it has been well documented that PDS has communicative difficulties with impaired expressive language (Tomaszewski et al., 2018). Therefore, concerns have been raised regarding how people with ID can provide detailed accounts during interview sessions (Corby et al., 2015). Hence, cognitive and communicative impairments may present methodological barriers in interview sessions, impeding the reliability and validity of the data (Hartley & MacLean, 2006).

Therefore, to circumvent the methodological difficulties of interviewing people with ID in general, seeking proxy responses from close family members, caregivers, or professionals is widespread (Cummins, 2002). The use of proxy respondents in research has included commenting on issues associated with a transition plan (Dyke et al., 2013) or challenges of daily needs (Bertoli et al., 2011) to highly subjective matters, such as the quality of life (Hartnett et al., 2008). Nonetheless, the obvious limitation in using proxy responses lies in the possible difficulties for the respondent to separate themselves from their own opinions, hence steering the research away from the PDS and framing the issues from the experience and subjectivity of the proxy instead (Lloyd et al., 2006). Therefore, including people with ID is important to yield valid, rich, and valuable insight into the subject matter. They may have unique perspectives that others might not consider, and should be shown that their opinions and views are respected and valued (Tassé et al., 2005).

The aptitude of the interviewer will influence the extent to which such difficulties will surface. The researchers needs to be capable and well-informed in communicating with people with ID by taking into account the different levels of cognitive impairment and the subject matters under investigation, and should also be able to anticipate potential difficulties that may arise (Tassé et al., 2005). Hence, there is an obligation for the researcher(s) to be adequately equipped and trained before starting the interview session. There is a risk to the validity of the interview sessions should the researcher fail to do the necessary preparation. Thus, there is an urgent need to properly develop an interview protocol and refinement process to address these issues before embarking on the interview process to gain rich, valid, and trustworthy data.

Piloting Interview Protocol

In the field of social research, 'pilot study' is a term used to refer to one of two things (van Teijlingen & Hundley, 2002): (1) a trial run or small-scale study done prior to the major study as a preparation (Polit et al., 2001); (2) a 'try-out' of a particular data collection instrument (Baker, 1994). Although pilot studies may be strongly rooted in the quantitative realm, their usefulness has been expanded into qualitative studies. Over recent years, many qualitative researchers have incorporated pilot testing into their studies (Abd Gani et al., 2020; Dikko, 2016; Kim, 2011; Majid et al., 2017). Its many useful functions include establishing the validity and reliability of the interview prompt, identifying and addressing the potential practical and methodological issues that may arise from the research protocol, familiarising researchers with the interviewing procedures, and exploring the limitations and flaws of the interview design (Abd Gani et al., 2020; Castillo-Montoya, 2016; Dikko, 2016; Kim, 2011; Majid et al., 2017). Thus, the purpose of this pilot exercise is to explore the limitations of the interview protocol developed for a dissertation project on the issues of employment for PDS and ultimately allow the modification of the inter-view prompt and research protocol to address the issues that arose.

Objectives of the Pilot Study

Here, we present critical reflections on the insights gained from the pilot study, where we (1) explore the methodology of the exercise, (2) discuss the practical and methodological issues that arose, and (3) reflect on the lessons learned from the process. It is important to emphasise that findings from the interview research are not explicitly presented in this chapter; rather, we focus on the development and refinement of the online interview protocol and operationalisation of the pilot study, and present the insights gained from it.

Materials and Methods

Study Design

We employed an in-depth semi-structured interview method for data collection for this study, and an interview protocol was developed for this purpose. This section discusses the steps carried out throughout the development and piloting of the interview protocol. For the development, refinement, and pilot testing of the interview protocol we adapted the four-step interview protocol refinement (IPR) Framework by Castillo-Montoya (2016). The IPR framework offers a rigorous systematic method for calibrating the interview protocol and questions (Yeong et al., 2018). Within this framework, the four phases of IPR include (1) 'ensuring interview questions align with research questions', (2) 'constructing an inquiry-based conversation', (3) 'receiving feedback on interview protocols', and (4) 'piloting interview protocol' (Castillo-Montoya, 2016). Staying true to the reiterative process in qualitative inquiry, the authors proposed that the refinement process and piloting do not strictly conform to the order of the IPR framework (Yeong et al., 2018). Hence, this section is presented in seven parts while integrating and adding to the phases of the IPR through further reiteration and refinement of the interview protocol. Figure 12.1 shows the flowchart for the IPR integration process.

Developing the Interview Framework

The aspects of employment, such as hiring decisions and retention, are considered to be formed from the complex interaction between PDS and their environment. This also includes the interaction between PDS and

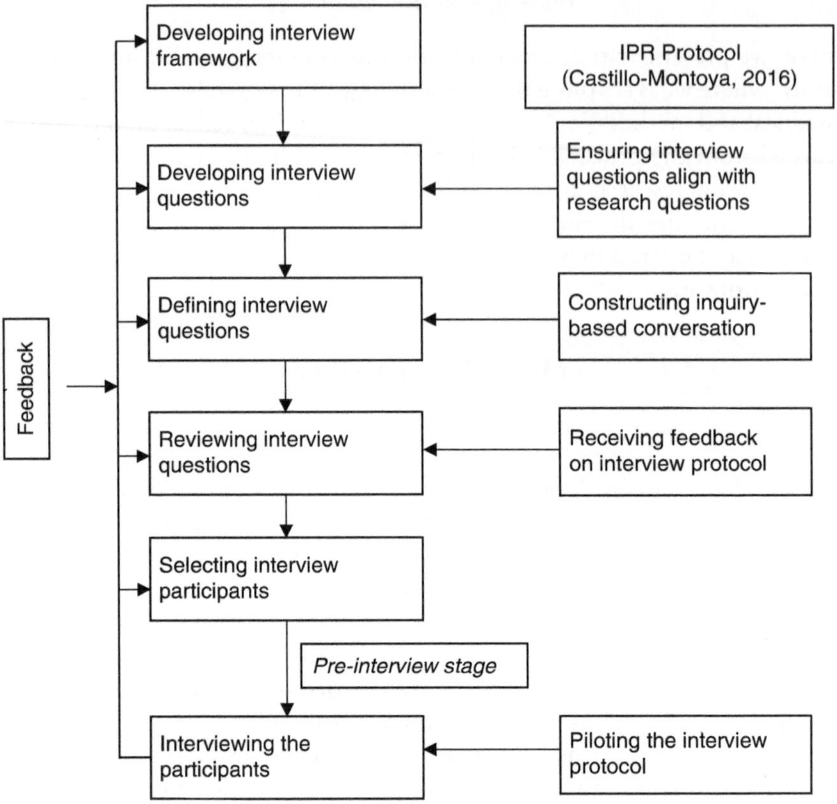

Figure 12.1 Flowchart for the interview protocol refinement process.

others, such as employers, co-workers, and family members. This inter-action can either be an enhancement for or a barrier to a PDS getting hired and retained as an employee. Therefore, the researcher adopted the Social-Ecological Model (SEM) to explore the issues from multiple perspectives.

This model was developed to help understand the multilayered and syner-gistic impacts of the personal and environmental components that influence individual behaviour (Kilanowski, 2017). SEM has been used extensively in health promotion and prevention. It recognises that individual health behav-iour results from numerous influences of family, work, community, and policymaking (Ingram et al., 2021). This model presumes that those multi-level effects are synergistic and reinforcing (Golden & Earp, 2012). Therefore, besides understanding how behaviour develops regarding social-environmental interactions, SEM can also help identify behavioural and organisational leverage points and provide mediators for interventional strategies and policy-making (Centre for Disease Control & Prevention, 2021; Kilanowski, 2017). Hence, with this in mind, we proposed that the issues of barriers to and opportunities for employment for PDS should be viewed through the wide lens of SEM to understand the problem in more depth. Within this model, five hierarchal levels exert influence over behavior: (1) individual, (2) interpersonal, (3) community, (4) organisational, and (5) policy/enabling environment (UNICEF, 2016). Therefore, the authors felt that this model could aid in exploring the issues from multiple perspectives.

Developing Interview Questions

After defining the interview framework, we rigorously discussed and listed all the possible questions for the respondents to elicit a complete picture of the research issues at hand. Next, the questions were properly organised to ensure a logical flow, and were grouped according to their unifying features under a topic list. From there, we identified and constructed the main questions. The initial questions were broad and less probing (Braun & Clarke, 2013). They encompassed the gist of the topic without being too specific and narrow. There were thirteen main questions in total, and these questions were placed under four broad issues: (1) barriers or challenges to employment, (2) benefits and opportunities of employment, (3) knowledge of current laws and policies, and (4) individual's attitude towards and perception of PDS and PWD in general. The remaining questions were then reserved for probing, as they were more specific and more explicitly worded, and hence were deemed to elicit narrow responses from the respondents. Probing questions were developed to explain and clarify the responses, as participants are encouraged to open up, elaborate on their responses, and clarify their answers (Braun & Clarke, 2013).

While developing the protocol, we revisited the research questions to ensure that the interview questions were well-framed. The interview questions for this study included:

(1) What are the challenges faced by a PDS in employment, and what are the potential solutions?
(2) What are the benefits to and enhancers of employment for PDS?
(3) What influences others to hire or support the employment of PDS?
(4) How do the current policies and legislation affect the employment of PDS?
(5) What do others (family members/caregivers, employers, community, policy makers) think about the employment of PDS?

This step runs parallel with the first phase of IPR. It is important as it can enhance the effectiveness of the interview questions and ensures that the interview is able to attain the research objectives (Castillo-Montoya, 2016). For this purpose, an interview protocol matrix was developed to examine the interview questions against the research questions. This permits the researcher to address any information gaps in the interview questions, allowing adjustment and questions (Castillo-Montoya, 2016; Yeong et al., 2018).

Table 12.1 shows the four main topics, the main questions, and their congruence with the research questions. No information gap was found in this phase, and the developed questions addressed the research questions adequately. In addition to developing interview questions that address the subject matter, introductory questions were also developed. These questions aimed to extricate background information such as socio-demographic, company, and organisation profiles. Developing these initial questions is essential to facilitate conversational interaction with the respondents (Yeong et al., 2018) and build rapport.

Defining Interview Questions

In addition to developing the interview questions, an opening remark is also important to build rapport with the respondents. For this purpose, we developed an interview script for opening and closing remarks. The

Table 12.1 *Interview protocol matrix*

Domain	Questions	RQ1	RQ2	RQ3	RQ4	RQ5
Barriers to employment	Q1	x				
	Q2	x	x	x		x
	Q3	x		x		
Benefits of employment	Q1		x			x
Knowledge of current laws and policies	Q1				x	
	Q2				x	
	Q3				x	
	Q4			x	x	x
	Q5			x	x	x
Attitude and perception towards PDS	Q1	x	x	x		x
	Q2	x	x	x		x
	Q3	x	x	x		x
	Q4	x	x	x		x

Q: Question; RQ: Research question.

opening script involves the researcher's introduction as the interviewer, an overview of the study and the research objectives, the respondents' rights to withdraw, and the assurance of confidentiality. Debriefing was made after the end of each session to explain the next step of the research process. Data confidentiality and participants' autonomy were also emphasised during debriefing.

Interview questions need to be refined into inquiry-based conversations (Castillo-Montoya, 2016). The proposed questions were subjected to rephrasing and modification in this phase to suit the daily conversation discourse. We rephrased the language of the interview questions to accommodate the respondent's full understanding of the subject matter. In addition, we also organised the interview questions to ensure the flow of conversation, which maintains social norms (Yeong et al., 2018). The language of the questions should be easily understood by the lay person and should avoid jargon as much as possible. However, when interviewing individuals with vast knowledge and/or experience in the subject matter, using specific terms may enhance rapport and ensure rich data collection (Empson, 2018). Therefore, the iteration of the interview questions should never end here, as it is necessary to constantly reiterate and modify the interview questions to suit individual variations between respondents. After completing this phase, the protocol was then submitted for the reviewing process.

Reviewing the Interview Questions

After the initial questions had been developed, they were shown to the experts for a thorough review. During this phase, two experts were consulted. They were expert researchers in public health and social medicine, with years of experience conducting qualitative studies and supervising such research. For this purpose, a close reading of the protocol was done to ascertain structure, language, length, relevancy, and comprehension (Castillo-Montoya, 2016). The interview question should be devoid of any academic language, succinct, and easy to understand, and should stimulate discussion of the experiences and feelings of the subjects (Brinkmann & Kvale, 2015).

In this phase, there were modifications made to separate the questions into five respective groups, in line with the SEM framework: (1) individuals with PDS, (2) family members or caretakers, (3) employers and co-workers, (4) community members, and (5) policymakers. The gist of the initial main questions and the topic list were preserved. However, the follow-up questions were developed depending on each respective stakeholder group. This was to ensure that the researcher could adapt to the nuances of each group during the interview, as different groups would need different ways of framing the questions. Apart from that, having an anticipated list of follow-up questions specific to each group of stakeholders can ensure a smooth interview process, especially for novice researchers, as they may stumble upon being confronted by unexpected responses from the participants. Some of the questions were rephrased to better suit stakeholders with different background knowledge and experiences. This could ensure a clear picture of the subject matter to enhance understanding. The interview protocol was developed in English and translated into Malay using back-to-back translation. Both the English and Malay versions of the guide were reviewed.

Selecting Interview Participants

A purposeful sampling method was employed to recruit the participants for this study. This involves selecting the research participants according to the study's needs, whereby researchers choose those who can give valuable information suitable to the subject matter (Patton, 2014). For this purpose, all participants should have experience in employing, working with, or taking care of PDS, including those with lived experience (Khayatzadeh-Mahani et al., 2020). Therefore, five groups of stakeholders were identified according to the SEM. Each group would have different backgrounds and levels of interaction with PDS. Different stakeholder groups would provide more depth and offer differing perspectives regarding the employment issues of PDS.

One participant from each stakeholder group was selected for the present pilot test. Inclusion and exclusion criteria were set to ensure the selected participants could give the most detailed and in-depth description of the subject matter. The participant description and the inclusion/exclusion criteria are shown in Table 12.2. The participants' entry source was obtained from the NGOs closely working with marginalised groups, particularly PWDs. The participants were contacted through phone calls, emails, and online flyers for initial recruitment. Once they agreed to participate, a Participant Information Sheet and an Informed Consent Form were sent to their emails. As the COVID-19 pandemic was still ravaging the world and travel restrictions were still in place at the time of data collection, the interviews were conducted via video-conference.

Table 12.2 *Participant's description and selection criteria*

Level	Participants	Inclusion criteria	Exclusion criteria
Individual	• Individuals with Down syndrome	• An adult PDS	
Family	• Parents • Caregivers • Siblings	• Has been involved in taking care of the PDS over a significant period	
Community	• Village headmen • Religious leaders • NGOs • Job coaches	• Has significant experience in dealing with PDS as part of their community	• Unable to give consent • Unable to understand the construct of questions asked
Organisation	• Employers • Co-workers	• Has experience in hiring a PDS • Has experience in working/training a PDS	
Policy level	• Members of Parliament/state legislative council • High officials of ministries in the relevant sectors • Members of state/national representative groups for PWD/PDS	• Has been involved in policy-making for PDS • Has experience in representing PDS or their respective organisations at the state/national level	

Pre-Interview Stage

As the interview session employs video-conferencing, preparations and considerations should be made to ensure a smooth interview process. Following Irani (2019), these are some of the practical considerations that were made before the pilot exercise:

- **Identification of available video-conference tools.** Several video-conference applications were identified, and these features were considered when selecting the apps to be used: (1) any paid subscription needed, (2) audio-visual recording capacity, (3) any time limitation for each video-conference session, (4) device requirements, and (5) security and privacy features. In addition, these additional features are desirable but not essential: (1) automatic transcription features, (2) screen-sharing capacity, (3) multi-platform usability (phone, tablet, desktop computer, etc.). We used the Zoom meeting application as it meets all the stated criteria.
- **Familiarisation with the selected tools.** The researcher must be comfortable in navigating and using the video-conference tools before conducting the interview. Testing the features with colleagues or friends before the interview is important to avoid distraction during the real interview sessions and help the researcher troubleshoot any technical difficulties.
- **Consider participant's level of comfort with the tool.** We gave the participants the autonomy to choose any platform they are comfortable with, which is already available during the recruitment stage. This was to avoid any hassle for the respondents, as they would need to install and learn to navigate a new application.
- **Check the hardware.** We tested the camera, microphone, and other devices to ensure they were working well, thus avoiding any interruption or delays due to hardware failures.
- **Consider an appropriate interview setting.** We conducted the interview session in a place that was free from distraction, well-lit, and private. The participants were given options as to how the interview would be conducted (e.g. time, place, platform). We also took into consideration the quality of internet connectivity in the preferred place to ensure a smooth session.
- **Consider appropriate timing and set up a reminder.** The researcher should accommodate the respondents' requests and availability as much as possible. A reminder, the interview link, and the interview particulars were sent to the participants a day before the interview.

- **Ensure a backup plan is available.** It is wise to have a backup plan readily available should the researcher encounter any problems. In case of technical issues, such as the failure of video-conference applications, the researcher should choose other suitable apps, provided that the respondents are familiar with the tool. However, if the problem persists, the researcher should propose that the interview is postponed to avoid wasting precious time on both ends.

We had obtained verbal consent from the respondents before the interview. The Informed Consent Form and Participant Information Sheet were emailed to each participant during the recruitment phase. A recorded verbal session was undertaken during the interview session after approval was obtained from the respondents. The consent session was recorded separately from the rest of the interview session and was retained for audit purposes. The researcher read the consent form, and the participants stated their agreement at the end. Emphasis was given to the participants' confidentiality and autonomy to withdraw from the study without any consequences.

Interviewing the Participants

We used the Zoom meeting platform for the first, second, third, and fifth interview sessions. The fourth interview session had to be conducted through WhatsApp video call due to poor Wi-Fi connectivity. OBS Studio (a third-party, free, and open-source software for screencasting and online streaming) was used to record the fourth interview session after obtaining consent from the participants. This is because WhatsApp does not support direct audio-visual recording of the video call session. English was used throughout all interview sessions, with infrequent use of the Malay language. For the fourth interview with ET, the Malay language was used, as the respondents were more comfortable conversing in Malay. The discussions were casual between both the researcher and the participants, and throughout the five interviews the body language and facial expressions of all respondents were appropriate and relaxed.

The interview began with the researcher introducing themselves and the research objectives. The researcher also explained the overview of the interview flow to the respondents. Recorded verbal consent was obtained, and the introductory questions were asked to gain each participant's socio-demographic background and further build rapport. The recording then started, and the main questions were asked. The participants guided the direction, flow, and pace of the interview sessions. Therefore, the questions were not asked in any particular order. However, the researcher made an effort to track the questions using the interview guide to ensure all of them were asked. In addition to that, the researcher also made handwritten notes throughout each session to record any interesting and important points. At the end of each session, the participants were allowed to address any other views or concerns they might have, and were invited to reach out to the researchers if they had any further queries.

The first and second interviews (CS, individual, and CH, community) were conducted in tandem, as requested by the participants. CH is currently a job coach for CS since 2019 and this has forged a close relationship between them. During this session, both of them were in the same private room, and the researcher was able to communicate with them via Zoom. The interview session was conducted in two parts; in the first part, CS (individual) was interviewed in the presence of CH (job coach). In the second part of this session, CH was interviewed alone after CS (individual) had concluded. CS was debriefed and then left the room. Both participants had agreed with and were comfortable being interviewed together. In the first part, the questions were posed directly to CS, and she could respond. However, there were a few instances whereby CH offered further clarification as the responses by CS were vague. For the second phase with CH, the same questions were asked, and further opinions on the answers previously given by CS were explored. The responses from each participant were analysed separately.

To embrace the social constructionist paradigm of this research, we adopted a reflexive writing exercise to explore our inner feelings, experiences, and perceptions on the subject matter. Qualitative research fundamentally entails that the researcher has to adopt a reflexive attitude concerning the research situation, the respondents, and the collected data (Birks et al., 2008). Reflexivity eases the researcher's perception of their subjective influences on collecting and interpreting the data, as they are absorbed in the participants' world (Primeau, 2003). Thus, this exercise ensures trustworthiness by providing a mechanism via which the researcher's perspective is recorded for further critical review or confirmation. It is also essential to record the decision-making trail that informs the research, from conception to completion (Birks et al., 2008).

Results

From the exercise, we could gain the insight to clarify and rephrase some interview questions in the guide, refine some practical considerations regarding interviewing the PDS and address a few technical issues that arise during the sessions. The results from the data analysis of the interview sessions are not discussed here, as this chapter focuses on the operationalisation of the protocol refinement process and the findings from the pilot test.

Characteristics of the Participants

The participants in this study comprised four women and a man, all of whom resided in various locations across Malaysia. Each represents a stakeholder group based on the SEM, namely individual, family member, employer, community, and policymaking group. They all have a broad trajectory in involvement with PDS, and a wide range of academic qualifications and occupations. Moreover, they have had a close relationship and involvement with PDS for the past two years. Their age range is 23–70 years old. Table 12.3 summarises their demographic profiles.

Lessons Learned from the Pilot Study

After the interview sessions, the researchers transcribed the recorded sessions verbatim, and the transcripts were emailed to the participants for member checking. The participants were asked to review the transcript for accuracy and resonance with their own experiences (Birt et al., 2016). After they were satisfied with the transcript, the data were analysed according to reflexive thematic analysis (Braun & Clarke, 2013). Atlas Ti. software was used to assist with the data analysis.

Regarding the interview questions, some additional probes and follow-up questions were added to the guide as new insights were gained from each session. One main question was divided into two and rephrased as it was found that the responses were not adequate to cover the entire subject matter. Dividing this question aided in eliciting responses that are more specific to the issue at hand. The use of probes was also found to be beneficial in eliciting a clear response from the participants, as it enhanced understanding of the questions among the participants (see the following example).

[Before pilot]

Q1. From your view, what are the barriers or challenges faced by individuals with Down syndrome in employment?

Table 12.3 *Demographic profiles of participants*

No	Category	Code	Age	Gender	Occupation	Education level	Platform
1	Individual	CS	32	Female	Waitress	Certificate	Zoom meeting
2	Community	CH	48	Female	Job coach for PDS	Bachelor's degree	Zoom meeting
3	Employer	KA	28	Male	Business owner	Bachelor's degree	Zoom meeting
4	Family members	ET	27	Female	Housewife	SPM	WhatsApp video call
5	Policymaking	MM	23	Female	Exco Majlis Belia OKU	Bachelor's degree	Zoom meeting

[After pilot]

Q1. From your view, what are the barriers or challenges faced by individuals with Downs syndrome when they are looking for a job?
Q2. On the other hand, if a person with Down syndrome is already employed, what are the barriers or challenges they face when working?

In addition, revisions were made to rephrase some of the questions to ensure that the interview session was free from terminologies. This was also to ensure that a common casual conversation could be adopted as much as possible. However, if the question needs to use terminologies for a better question frame, the researcher must provide a concise explanation of the terminology. An example from the guide is when the researcher wanted to explore the prospect of employment in the Industrial Revolution 4.0 (IR4.0):

Q1. Currently, we are in the Industrial Revolution 4.0, IR4.0, whereby the use of technology is widespread. For example, in factories, automated machines and robots are used to replace human labour, increasing productivity. Apart from that, the use of the internet to enhance connectivity and productivity has also pushed e-commerce into success. Therefore, regarding the current IR4.0, what are your views on the opportunities and challenges of employment for PDS in the future?

As anticipated, the interview questions asked during the sessions did not follow the order proposed in the protocol. During the sessions, the researcher adjusted the flow based on the participants' responses to encourage a more organic and casual interaction between them. Therefore, it is not mandated to strictly follow the question sequence as long as all questions are covered, and the interview guide can serve as a checklist to ensure this (Yeong et al., 2018).

With regard to interviewing PDS, it was observed from the pilot test that they often gave short answers to the questions. Hence, using probing and follow-up questions helped to explore issues further. For example, when asked about the benefits of employment, probing and follow-up questions helped to clarify this participant's answer:

INTERVIEWER (I): When you are working, what do you think are the benefits of your employment?
CH: Benefit ah . . .
I: What do you gain from your job, from your employment? When you are employed, what are the benefits that you get?
CH: What does benefit mean?
I: Sorry?

CH: What does benefit mean?

I: Benefit means something good that you gain, something beneficial. Something good that you get from working.

CH: Uhm, I'm not sure.

I: Oh, you're not sure?

CH: I think it is the salary.

I: Sorry?

CH: Salary.

I: I see. So, you can get your own salary from working?

CH: Experience.

I: I understand. May I know why do you think salary is beneficial for you? What can you do when you get the salary? Normally, what are the things that you do with your salary?

CH: The salary . . . I have to save in the bank.

I: I see, understand. For future use, is it?

CH: And I do work very well, then I get salary.

I: I understand. So, it's for your saving?

CH: Uh hmm . . . To protection . . . to protect me [chuckled].

I: Sorry, pardon?

CH: To protect me.

I: Protection fee?

CS: Insurance.

I: For your own security, is it?

CH: Uhh, insurance.

I: I see. So, you pay your insurance with the salary. I understand.

We explored further by using probes and follow-up questions to get a clearer picture of the response. The researcher should also anticipate explaining simple terms, such as 'benefit', as per the example above, should the PDS require further clarification. Apart from that, having a proxy present in the interview session can help alleviate some of the communication difficulties encountered. The proxy understands from the example above that 'protection' refers to 'insurance.' Hence, this can aid in the flow of the interview session and help clarify the vague responses (D'Eath et al., 2005). However, the proxy response should always be tested to elicit some supportive evidence (Rodgers, 1999). Probing questions such as 'How do you know?' or 'Why do you think that?' are particularly useful for this purpose.

In this pilot exercise, interview #4 with ET could not proceed via Zoom due to poor Wi-Fi connectivity and had to be conducted via video call through the WhatsApp application using a mobile phone instead. This highlights the importance of having a backup plan if any technical issues arise. Researchers should always be ready to troubleshoot any problems and be flexible regarding other non-conventional platforms to conduct the interview. The researcher should also be open to postponing the session to a later date, or even be prepared for an in-person interview if circumstances permit.

Lastly, this pilot testing provides an opportunity for the researcher to familiarise themselves with the interview process before embarking on the major study phase. It gives novice researchers practical lessons in data collection, management, and analysis. Hence, the researcher is more familiar and confident during the following interview sessions.

Discussion

It is worth noting that a benchmark method for the IPR process does not exist (Yeong et al., 2018), and there is no one-size-fits-all method for video-conference interviewing a person with ID. When constructing an interview protocol, the researcher needs to consider the research objectives, study population, and subject matter to construct an appropriate protocol (Castillo-Montoya, 2016; Yeong et al., 2018). Here, we found that integrating IPR into our refinement process is beneficial, especially in the use of a matrix in Phase I. This guides the development of interview questions that align with the research questions and addresses any existing information gap.

Trustworthiness has varying definitions amongst researchers. It generally refers to the research's quality, authenticity, and truthfulness (Cypress, 2017). Trustworthiness relates to the degree of trust or confidence that the readers had in the findings (Schmidt & Brown, 2015), to appraise the quality of a research design (Yin, 1994), and methods to ensure the correct research process (Guba & Lincoln, 1989). Therefore, refinement and pilot testing of the interview protocol are essential in ensuring the trustworthiness and reliability (Dikko, 2016; Yeong et al., 2018) of the collected data. A standalone procedure is insufficient to ensure the validity of the entire course of the research study. Hence, alternative strategies that enhance trustworthiness should also be exercised throughout the research process (Noble & Smith, 2015). Other qualitative validation techniques include data-source triangulation (by selecting participants across different groups and locations), member checking to ensure the validity of transcripts, reflexive writing, and a thick description of the entire research process for the audit trail. Qualitative researchers should always be aware that regardless of how the data collection is carried out or what technique is involved, the sole research instrument and the principal mode of data collection are always the researchers themselves (Cypress, 2017).

Despite the unique challenges in interview research in a global pandemic, qualitative researchers should always adapt to the demands of exploring other means of data collection. More recently, with advances in technology and the wide availability of the internet, video-conferencing is gaining traction as a substitute for in-person interviews (Irani, 2019). Nonetheless, conducting video-conference interview sessions with PDS has its own challenges. Recent research has shown that some PDS have strong computer skills (Kumin et al., 2012; Lazar et al., 2011), therefore navigating the video-conferencing tools by themselves is possible. There are limited articles available which explore their ability to navigate through online video-conference tools. Thus, this pilot testing provides an opportunity to explore the methods to enhance the online interviewing of PDS.

The use of online platforms as a qualitative data collection method has garnered much attention over recent years (Deakin & Wakefield, 2014; Dodds & Hess, 2020; Irani, 2019; Janghorban et al., 2014; Krouwel et al., 2019; Mann & Stewart, 2009; Roberts et al., 2021). Online platforms are able to tackle some of the limits of in-person interviews (Bertrand & Bourdeau, 2010), create succinct yet more substantial responses (Woodyatt et al., 2016), address geographical limitations and transport issues (Krouwel et al., 2019), enable participants to communicate equally, and offer a more comfortable environment for them to disclose sensitive or private information (Woodyatt et al., 2016). Their limitations, on the flip side, may cause a lack of depth in research data due to challenges in probing and conducting online discussion (Abrams et al., 2015; Bertrand & Bourdeau, 2010; Krouwel et al., 2019), or contribute to less participation due to the physical distance/lack of rappport (Reid & Reid, 2005), and the exclusion of those with limited access to or know-how as regards technology (Lijadi & van Schalkwyk, 2015). Therefore, by choosing online interviewing as our data collection method, we effectively excluded a large section of respondents from our research.

We found that posing close-ended and probing questions helped elicit short responses from PDS regarding the interview questions. In the initial stages, broad, open-ended questions should be asked, and the participant's responses should inform the researcher of the individuals' perceptions (Sekaran & Bougie, 2016). This is also true of our research, as we posed broad questions to the PDS. However, the responses were often short and lacked detail. Therefore, posing follow-up and close-ended questions helps with clarification and elaboration. Yeong et al. (2018) also found a similar issue when interviewing people with no disability regarding the Return-To-Work programme in Malaysia. They argue that these short responses are unrelated to literacy level but are concerned with social norms in local education and family background that eventually lead to shyness in sharing their thoughts (Yeong et al., 2018). Therefore, researchers are responsible for supporting the participants' efforts in figuring out the meaning of the questions by probing for a more detailed response. Additional information increases understanding, aids clarification, and, most importantly, determines what to ask next (Roberts, 2020). Previous research has also demonstrated that the exclusive use of close-ended questioning could be advantageous, especially for less articulate participants (Booth & Booth, 1996; Hollomotz, 2018). While this study did not exclusively depend on this question type, close-ended questions were encouraged for less expressive participants (Hollomotz, 2018). Hence, whilst broad, open-ended questions are preferred in qualitative interviewing, narrow, close-ended questions have their place in eliciting clarification when interviewing PDS. With this in mind, numerous questions in the interview guide have options to be rephrased as close-ended questions.

In addition to that, building rapport is one of the most important aspects of qualitative interviewing (Braun & Clarke, 2013; Creswell, 2014; Creswell & Creswell, 2018; Patterson, 2012; Prior, 2018; Sekaran & Bougie, 2016). Qualitative research is 'the study of the nature of phenomena', which includes their quality and different forms, the context in which they emerge, and the perception of different perspectives (Busetto et al., 2020). Within the social constructionist paradigm, the very nature of reality is grounded within people's experiences, context, and social inter-actions (Cohen & Crabtree, 2006). Therefore, qualitative inquiry aims to explore phenomena in-depth through the lens of others. It is fitting that the researchers build a good relationship between themselves and their participants, especially when they engage in interviews and observation to gain rich data (Guillemin & Heggen, 2009). Researchers are advised to get to know the respondents before the interview to build rapport, especially when involving less articulate participants (Arksey & Knight, 1999). One of the ways to achieve this is by meeting the participants several times before the interview to become acquainted with their daily routine and communication style (Hollomotz, 2018). However, this can pose a problem, especially during the global pandemic as social distancing is imposed to curb the spread of the infection. Hence, in this pilot exercise, we used the proxy interview to help address the limitations that arose.

A proxy is an individual who responds in place of the study participant (Caiels et al., 2019). The proxy interview is usually done with someone who is acquainted with the sampled individual's financial, health, and family situation (Weir et al., 2011) and generally includes close family members, spouses, partners, and others with a close connection to the respondent. In essence, those who are best suited to interpret an individual's behaviour or conduct should be chosen as proxy respondents (Patterson, 2012). Within the context of this exercise, we recruited a job coach who for three years has had a close relationship with an individual with DS as their trainee. Since the research questions are about employment issues, we believe that the job coach is an appropriate proxy respondent in this context. The proxy respondent was employed to help build a rapport between PDS and the researcher. The critical aspect of the 'support participant' is that they can help the individual feel safe, unintimidated, supported, and, in some cases, protected, hence facilitating the interviewing process (Dodds & Hess, 2020).

In addition, when assessing a subjective experience, the principal source of information should always be the person at the centre of the experience (Hollomotz, 2018). However, we should also acknowledge the barriers for some PDS: limited vocabulary, difficulties with verbal expression or comprehension, limited ability with words, and (for a small number of them) no language capabilities (Martin et al., 2009; Tomaszewski et al., 2018). Hence, prohibiting proxy respondents would deny involvement to those who are unable to respond in typical ways or those who may depend on someone close to them to translate their communication into the language (Patterson, 2012). Drawing from the pilot test, we also employed proxy responses to explain some words that we, as the researchers, had difficulty in understanding. Therefore, the pilot test can provide better context and depth to the responses gained when interviewing PDS. Care should be taken when eliciting proxy responses to ensure that the proxy merely interprets and translates the words and behaviour of the individuals into typical communication rather than speaking 'for' them. Strategies to improve the validity of proxy responses include having separate interview sessions with the proxy alone to explore their own experiences, views, and feelings on the subject matter and repeated reminders to the proxy to answer as if they were the PDS (Patterson, 2012). Researchers can also elicit some supportive evidence as to why they gave certain answers on behalf of the PDS (Rodgers, 1999). The proxy response should only be sought when the researcher had difficulties eliciting the desired response from the PDS themselves after their best attempt. Hence, when the PDS can communicate well, researchers should make it their best interest to pose the interview questions directly to the PDS before seeking a proxy response.

With these considerations in mind, strategies to mitigate the weakness of online interviews with PDS can be established to ensure continuous, trustworthy data collection during this trying time. In addition, undertaking the refinement process as part of a qualitative inquiry improves insight into crucial research processes, which include data access, participant recruitment, and data collection (Wray et al., 2017).

Strength and Limitations of the Pilot Study

The major limitation of this study is the exclusion of those with limited access to technology. However, within the context of the pandemic, we believe that ensuring the safety of both the participants and researchers alike is of the utmost importance. Moreover, no face-to-face interview was conducted to compare the difference with online video-conference interview sessions. Therefore, further research should compare online interviews involving individuals with Down syndrome with an in-person interview to fully understand their differences and explore whether online interviewing is an adequate alternative for interviewing PDS. In addition, this study did not objectively quantify the level of severity of Down syndrome or the cognitive capacity of each individual. The researchers only recruited those who were able to understand the construct of the questions rather than looking at their level of cognition. Therefore, it is not known whether the level of cognition or severity of Down syndrome would have an effect on an online video interview.

Conclusions

This chapter has explored the operationalisation of the online IPR process involving PDS and garnered new insights and strategies to enhance the data collection method. Therefore, it adds to the growing literature of qualitative data collection methods during the pandemic. As qualitative research traditions continue to evolve with the current state of flux, there is a greater need for guidelines and tools to support researchers in developing valid and reliable data collection methods. This chapter explores particular practical and methodological issues related to the refinement process of video-conference interviews. We have attempted to explain the lessons learned from interview sessions involving PDS. In offering the insights gained from the refinement process and the pilot exercise, we hope that the course of developing a valid and reliable interview protocol has been illustrated in a way that will help those in the process of data collection. Lastly, it is worth emphasising that this process of review and reiteration is not meant to be a linear, one-way process. Instead, multiple interview questions and techniques were repeated throughout the actual fieldwork as further insights were gained from previous sessions.

Hence, this process is organic, reflective, and reiterative, and should always be done in such a manner.

Funding

This research was funded by the Ministry of Higher Education, Malaysia (Ref: Fundamental Research Grant Scheme, FRGS/1/2020/SS0/UNIMAS/01/2).

Acknowledgements

The authors would like to warmly thank the participants for their willingness to participate in this research despite the challenges faced during the COVID-19 pandemic. We are grateful to the Faculty Ethics Committee for ethics approval of this research (Ref # FME/21/12). The authors would also like to thank the Ministry of Higher Education, Malaysia, for funding this research (Ref #: FRGS/1/2020/SS0/UNIMAS/01/2) and Universiti Malaysia Sarawak for their support in conducting this research.

References

Abd Gani, N. I., Rathakrishnan, M., & Krishnasamy, H. N. (2020). A Pilot Test for Establishing Validity and Reliability of Qualitative Interview in the Blended Learning English Proficiency Course. *Journal of Critical Reviews, 7*(5). https://doi.org/10.31838/jcr.07.05.23.

Abrams, K. M., Wang, Z., Song, Y. J., & Galindo-Gonzalez, S. (2015). Data Richness Trade-Offs Between Face-to-Face, Online Audiovisual, and Online Text-Only Focus Groups. *Social Science Computer Review, 33*(1), 80–96. https://doi.org/10.1177/0894439313519733.

Ang, M. C. H. (2017). The Challenges and Benefits of Employing Persons with Disabilities: The Japanese Multinational Corporations' Perspective. *International Journal of Innovation, Management and Technology*, 359–66. https://doi.org/10.18178/ijimt.2017.8.5.754.

Arksey, H., & Knight, P. (1999). *Interviewing for Social Scientists*. SAGE Publications, Ltd. http://methods.sagepub.com/book/interviewing-for-social-scientists.

Baker, T. L. (1994). *Doing Social Research* (2nd ed.). McGraw-Hill.

Begley, C. M. (1996). Triangulation of Communication Skills in Qualitative Research Instruments. *Journal of Advanced Nursing, 24*(4), 688–93. https://doi.org/10.1046/j.1365-2648.1996.02446.x.

Bertoli, M., Biasini, G., Calignano, M. T., et al. (2011). Needs and Challenges of Daily Life for People with Down Syndrome Residing in the City of Rome, Italy. *Journal of Intellectual Disability Research, 55*(8), 801–20. https://doi.org/10.1111/j.1365-2788.2011.01432.x.

Bertrand, C., & Bourdeau, L. (2010). Research Interviews by Skype: A New Data Collection Method. In J. Esteves (Ed.), *Proceedings from the 9th European Conference on Research Methods* (pp. 70–9). IE Business School.

Birks, M., Chapman, Y., & Francis, K. (2008). Memoing in Qualitative Research: Probing Data and Processes. *Journal of Research in Nursing, 13*(1), 68–75. https://doi.org/10.1177/1744987107081254.

Birt, L., Scott, S., Cavers, D., Campbell, C., & Walter, F. (2016). Member Checking: A Tool to Enhance Trustworthiness or Merely a Nod to Validation? *Qualitative Health Research, 26*(13), 1802–11. https://doi.org/10.1177/1049732316654870.

Booth, T., & Booth, W. (1996). Sounds of Silence: Narrative Research with Inarticulate Subjects. *Disability & Society, 11*(1), 55–70. https://doi.org/10.1080/09687599650023326.

Braun, V., & Clarke, V. (2013). *Successful Qualitative Research: A Practical Guide for Beginners.* SAGE.

Brinkmann, S., & Kvale, S. (2015). *InterViews: Learning the Craft of Qualitative Research Interviewing* (3rd ed.). Sage.

Bryman, A., & Burgess, R. G. (2002). Analyzing qualitative data. www.myilibrary .com?id=32268.

Busetto, L., Wick, W., & Gumbinger, C. (2020). How to Use and Assess Qualitative Research Methods. *Neurological Research and Practice, 2*(1), 14. https://doi.org/10 .1186/s42466-020-00059-z.

Caiels, J., Rand, S., Crowther, T., Collins, G., & Forder, J. (2019). Exploring the Views of being a Proxy from the Perspective of Unpaid Carers and Paid Carers: Developing a Proxy Version of the Adult Social Care Outcomes Toolkit (ASCOT). *BMC Health Services Research, 19*(1), 201. https://doi.org/10.1186/ s12913-019-4025-1.

Castillo-Montoya, M. (2016). Preparing for Interview Research: The Interview Protocol Refinement Framework. *The Qualitative Report.* https://doi.org/10.4 6743/2160-3715/2016.2337.

Centers for Disease Control and Prevention. (2019). Facts about Down syndrome. www.cdc.gov/ncbddd/birthdefects/downsyndrome.html.

Centers for Disease Control and Prevention. (2021). The Social-Ecological Model. Violence Prevention. www.cdc.gov/violenceprevention/about/social-ecological model.html.

Cohen, D., & Crabtree, B. (2006). Qualitative Research Guidelines Project. www .qualres.org/HomeInte-3516.html.

Corbin, J., & Morse, J. M. (2003). The Unstructured Interactive Interview: Issues of Reciprocity and Risks when Dealing with Sensitive Topics. *Qualitative Inquiry, 9*(3), 335–54. https://doi.org/10.1177/1077800403009003001.

Corby, D., Taggart, L., & Cousins, W. (2015). People with Intellectual Disability and Human Science Research: A Systematic Review of Phenomenological Studies using Interviews for Data Collection. *Research in Developmental Disabilities, 47*, 451–65. https://doi.org/10.1016/j.ridd.2015.09.001.

Creswell, J. W. (2014). *Research Design: Qualitative, Quantitative, and Mixed Methods Approaches* (4th ed.). SAGE Publications.

Creswell, J. W., & Creswell, J. D. (2018). *Research Design: Qualitative, Quantitative, and Mixed Methods Approaches* (5th ed.). SAGE Publications.

Creswell, J. W., Hanson, W. E., Clark Plano, V. L., & Morales, A. (2007). Qualitative Research Designs: Selection and Implementation. *The Counseling Psychologist, 35*(2), 236–64. https://doi.org/10.1177/0011000006287390.

Cummins, R. A. (2002). Proxy Responding for Subjective Well-Being: A Review. In *International Review of Research in Mental Retardation* (Vol. 25, pp. 183–207). Elsevier. https://linkinghub.elsevier.com/retrieve/pii/S007477500280009X.

Cypress, B. S. (2017). Rigor or Reliability and Validity in Qualitative Research: Perspectives, Strategies, Reconceptualization, and Recommendations. *Dimensions of Critical Care Nursing, 36*(4), 253–63. https://doi.org/10.1097/DCC.0000000000000253.

D'Eath, M., McCormack, B., Fay, B., et al. (2005). Guidelines for Researchers when Interviewing People with an Intellectual Disability. www.fedvol.ie/_file upload/File/Interviewing%20Guidelines%281%29.pdf.

Deakin, H., & Wakefield, K. (2014). Skype Interviewing: Reflections of Two PhD Researchers. *Qualitative Research, 14*(5), 603–16. https://doi.org/10.1177/1468794113488126.

DiCicco-Bloom, B., & Crabtree, B. F. (2006). The Qualitative Research Interview. *Medical Education, 40*(4), 314–21. https://doi.org/10.1111/j.1365-2929.2006.02418.x.

Dikko, M. (2016). Establishing Construct Validity and Reliability: Pilot Testing of a Qualitative Interview for Research in Takaful (Islamic Insurance). *The Qualitative Report.* https://doi.org/10.46743/2160-3715/2016.2243.

Dodds, S., & Hess, A. C. (2020). Adapting Research Methodology during COVID-19: Lessons for Transformative Service Research. *Journal of Service Management, 32*(2), 203–17. https://doi.org/10.1108/JOSM-05-2020-0153.

Dyke, P., Bourke, J., Llewellyn, G., & Leonard, H. (2013). The Experiences of Mothers of Young Adults with an Intellectual Disability Transitioning from Secondary School to Adult Life. *Journal of Intellectual & Developmental Disability, 38*(2), 149–62. https://doi.org/10.3109/13668250.2013.789099.

Emerson, E. (Ed.). (2004). *The International Handbook of Applied Research in Intellectual Disabilities.* Wiley.

Emerson, E., Madden, R., Graham, H., et al. (2011). The Health of Disabled People and the Social Determinants of Health. *Public Health, 125*(3), 145–7. https://doi.org/10.1016/j.puhe.2010.11.003.

Empson, L. (2018). Elite Interviewing in Professional Organizations. *Journal of Professions and Organization, 5*(1), 58–69. https://doi.org/10.1093/jpo/jox010.

Evans, B. (2020). The Zoom Revolution: 10 Eye-Popping Stats from Tech's New Superstar. *Cloud Wars.* https://cloudwars.co/covid-19/zoom-quarter-10-eye-popping-stats-from-techs-new-superstar/.

Fraser, R., Ajzen, I., Johnson, K., Hebert, J., & Chan, F. (2011). Understanding Employers' Hiring Intention in Relation to Qualified Workers with Disabilities. *Journal of Vocational Rehabilitation, 35*(1), 1–11. https://doi.org/10.3233/JVR-2011-0548.

Golden, S. D., & Earp, J. A. L. (2012). Social Ecological Approaches to Individuals and Their Contexts: Twenty Years of Health Promotion Interventions. *Health Education & Behavior*, *39*(3), 364–72. https://doi.org/10.1177/1090198111418634.

Guba, E. G., & Lincoln, Y. S. (1989). *Fourth Generation Evaluation*. Sage Publications.

Guillemin, M., & Heggen, K. (2009). Rapport and Respect: Negotiating Ethical Relations between Researcher and Participant. *Medicine, Health Care and Philosophy*, *12*(3), 291–9. https://doi.org/10.1007/s11019-008-9165-8.

Hai-Jew, S. (Ed.). (2015). Enhancing Qualitative and Mixed Methods Research with Technology. IGI Global. http://services.igi-global.com/resolvedoi/resolve.aspx?doi=10.4018/978-1-4666-6493-7.

Hartley, S. L., & MacLean, W. E. (2006). A Review of the Reliability and Validity of Likert-Type Scales for People with Intellectual Disability. *Journal of Intellectual Disability Research*, *50*(11), 813–27. https://doi.org/10.1111/j.1365-2788.2006.00844.x.

Hartnett, E., Gallagher, P., Kiernan, G., et al. (2008). Day Service Programmes for People with a Severe Intellectual Disability and Quality of Life: Parent and Staff Perspectives. *Journal of Intellectual Disabilities*, *12*(2), 153–72. https://doi.org/10.1177/1744629508091340.

Hollomotz, A. (2018). Successful Interviews with People with Intellectual Disability. *Qualitative Research*, *18*(2), 153–70. https://doi.org/10.1177/1468794117713810.

Houtenville, A., & Kalargyrou, V. (2012). People with Disabilities: Employers' Perspectives on Recruitment Practices, Strategies, and Challenges in Leisure and Hospitality. *Cornell Hospitality Quarterly*, *53*(1), 40–52. https://doi.org/10.1177/1938965511424151.

Ingram, M., Wolf, A. M. A., López-Gálvez, N. I., Griffin, S. C., & Beamer, P. I. (2021). Proposing a Social Ecological Approach to Address Disparities in Occupational Exposures and Health for Low-Wage and Minority Workers Employed in Small Businesses. *Journal of Exposure Science & Environmental Epidemiology*, *31*(3), 404–11. https://doi.org/10.1038/s41370-021-00317-5.

Irani, E. (2019). The Use of Videoconferencing for Qualitative Interviewing: Opportunities, Challenges, and Considerations. *Clinical Nursing Research*, *28*(1), 3–8. https://doi.org/10.1177/1054773818803170.

Jameson, A. (2005). *Disability and Employment: Review of Literature and Research*. Equal Employment Opportunities Trust.

Janghorban, R., Roudsari, R. L., & Taghipour, A. (2014). Skype Interviewing: The New Generation of Online Synchronous Interview in Qualitative Research. *International Journal of Qualitative Studies on Health and Well-Being*, *9*(1), 24152. https://doi.org/10.3402/qhw.v9.24152.

Kalia, A. (2020). The Zoom Boom: How Video-Calling Became a Blessing – And a Curse. *The Guardian*. www.theguardian.com/technology/2020/may/21/the-zoom-boom-how-video-calling-became-a-blessing-and-a-curse.

Khayatzadeh-Mahani, A., Wittevrongel, K., Nicholas, D. B., & Zwicker, J. D. (2020). Prioritizing Barriers and Solutions to Improve Employment for Persons with Developmental Disabilities. *Disability and Rehabilitation*, *42*(19), 2696–706. https://doi.org/10.1080/09638288.2019.1570356.

Kilanowski, J. F. (2017). Breadth of the Socio-Ecological Model. *Journal of Agromedicine*, *22*(4), 295–7. https://doi.org/10.1080/1059924X.2017.1358971.

Kim, Y. (2011). The Pilot Study in Qualitative Inquiry: Identifying Issues and Learning Lessons for Culturally Competent Research. *Qualitative Social Work*, *10*(2), 190–206. https://doi.org/10.1177/1473325010362001.

Krouwel, M., Jolly, K., & Greenfield, S. (2019). Comparing Skype (Video Calling) and In-Person Qualitative Interview Modes in a Study of People with Irritable Bowel Syndrome: An Exploratory Comparative Analysis. *BMC Medical Research Methodology*, *19*(1), 219. https://doi.org/10.1186/s12874-019-0867-9.

Kumin, L., Lazar, J., Feng, J. H., Wentz, B., & Nnanna, E. (2012). A Usability Evaluation of Workplace-Related Tasks on a Multi-Touch Tablet Computer by Adults with Down Syndrome. *Journal of Usability Studies*, *7*(4), 118–42. https://doi.org/10.5555/2835484.2835485.

Lazar, J., Kumin, L., & Feng, J. H. (2011). Understanding the computer skills of adult expert users with down syndrome: an exploratory study. The proceedings of the 13th international ACM SIGACCESS conference. https://doi.org/10.1145/2049536.2049548.

Lijadi, A. A., & van Schalkwyk, G. J. (2015). Online Facebook Focus Group Research of Hard-to-Reach Participants. *International Journal of Qualitative Methods*, *14*(5), 160940691562138. https://doi.org/10.1177/1609406915621383.

Lloyd, V., Gatherer, A., & Kalsy, S. (2006). Conducting Qualitative Interview Research With People With Expressive Language Difficulties. *Qualitative Health Research*, *16*(10), 1386–404. https://doi.org/10.1177/1049732306293846.

Majid, M. A. A., Othman, M., Mohamad, S. F., Lim, S. A. H., & Yusof, A. (2017). Piloting for Interviews in Qualitative Research: Operationalization and Lessons Learnt. *International Journal of Academic Research in Business and Social Sciences*, *7*(4), 1073–80. https://doi.org/10.6007/IJARBSS/v7-i4/2916.

Mann, C., & Stewart, F. (2009). *Internet Communication and Qualitative Research: A Handbook for Researching Online* (Repr ed.). SAGE Publishing.

Martin, G. E., Klusek, J., Estigarribia, B., & Roberts, J. E. (2009). Language Characteristics of Individuals with Down Syndrome. *Topics in Language Disorders*, *29*(2), 112–32. https://doi.org/10.1097/tld.0b013e3181a71fe1.

Merriam, S. B., & Tisdell, E. J. (2015). *Qualitative Research: A Guide to Design and Implementation* (4th ed.). John Wiley & Sons.

Minichiello, V., Aroni, R., Timewell, E., & Alexander, L. (1990). *In-Depth Interviewing: Researching People* (Reprint ed.). Longman.

Muhammad Ismail, H. I., Mohd Ibrahim, H., Ng, H. P., & Thomas, T. (Eds.). (2019). *Pediatrics Protocol for Malaysian Hospitals* (4th ed.). Ministry of Health, Malaysia.

Mundakel, G. T., & Lal, P. (2020). Down Syndrome. *Medscape*. https://emedicine.medscape.com/article/943216-overview#a3.

Noble, H., & Smith, J. (2015). Issues of validity and reliability in qualitative research. *Evidence Based Nursing*, *18*(2), 34–5. https://doi.org/10.1136/eb-2015-102054

Patterson, R. (2012). Strategies to Incorporate the Voices of People with Significant Disabilities in UCEDD Information Gathering and Operations. www.aucd.org/docs/urc/AUCD_StrategiesReport_Final.pdf.

Patton, M. Q. (2014). *Qualitative Research and Evaluation Methods: Integrating Theory and Practice* (4th ed.). Sage.

Peters, J. (2020). Google's Meet teleconferencing service now adding about 3 million users per day. *The Verge.* www.theverge.com/2020/4/28/21240434/google-meet-three-million-users-per-day-pichai-earnings.

Polit, D. F., Beck, C. T., & Hungler, B. P. (2001). *Essentials of Nursing Research: Methods, Appraisal, and Utilization.* Lippincott-Raven.

Primeau, L. A. (2003). Reflections on Self in Qualitative Research: Stories of Family. *The American Journal of Occupational Therapy, 57*(1), 9–16. https://doi.org/10.5014/ajot.57.1.9.

Prior, M. T. (2018). Accomplishing 'Rapport' in Qualitative Research Interviews: Empathic Moments in Interaction. *Applied Linguistics Review, 9*(4), 487–511. https://doi.org/10.1515/applirev-2017-0029.

Rachidi, M., & Lopes, C. (2010). Molecular and Cellular Mechanisms Elucidating Neurocognitive Basis of Functional Impairments Associated with Intellectual Disability in Down Syndrome. *American Journal on Intellectual and Developmental Disabilities, 115*(2), 83–112. https://doi.org/10.1352/1944-7558-115.2.83.

Råheim, M., Magnussen, L. H., Sekse, R. J. T., et al. (2016). Researcher–Researched Rrelationship in Qualitative Research: Shifts in Positions and Researcher Vulnerability. *International Journal of Qualitative Studies on Health and Well-being, 11*(1), 30996. https://doi.org/10.3402/qhw.v11.30996.

Reid, D. J., & Reid, F. J. M. (2005). Online Focus Groups: An In-depth Comparison of Computer-Mediated and Conventional Focus Group Discussions. *International Journal of Market Research, 47*(2), 131–62. https://doi.org/10.1177/147078530504700204.

Roberts, J. K., Pavlakis, A. E., & Richards, M. P. (2021). It's More Complicated Than It Seems: Virtual Qualitative Research in the COVID-19 Era. *International Journal of Qualitative Methods, 20,* 16094069211002959. https://doi.org/10.1177/16094069211002959.

Roberts, R. (2020). Qualitative Interview Questions: Guidance for Novice Researchers. *The Qualitative Report.* https://doi.org/10.46743/2160-3715/2020.4640.

Rodgers, J. (1999). Trying to Get it Right: Undertaking Research Involving People with Learning Difficulties. *Disability & Society, 14*(4), 421–33. https://doi.org/10.1080/09687599926046.

Rosner, I. D. (2021). From Exclusion to Inclusion: Involving People with Intellectual Disabilities in Research. *Tiltai, 72*(3), 119–28. https://doi.org/10.15181/tbb.v72i3.1170.

Schmidt, N. A., & Brown, J. M. (Eds.). (2015). *Evidence-Based Practice for Nurses: Appraisal and Application of Research* (3rd ed.). Jones & Bartlett Learning.

Schur, L., Han, K., Kim, A., et al. (2017). Disability at Work: A Look Back and Forward. *Journal of Occupational Rehabilitation, 27*(4), 482–97. https://doi.org/10.1007/s10926-017-9739-5.

Sekaran, U., & Bougie, R. (2016). *Research Methods for Business: A Skill-Building Approach* (7th ed.). John Wiley & Sons.

Shier, M., Graham, J. R., & Jones, M. E. (2009). Barriers to Employment as Experienced by Disabled People: A Qualitative Analysis in Calgary and Regina, Canada. *Disability & Society, 24*(1), 63–75. https://doi.org/10.1080/09687590802535485.

Sundar, V., O'Neill, J., Houtenville, A. J., et al. (2018). Striving to Work and Overcoming Barriers: Employment Strategies and Successes of People with Disabilities. *Journal of Vocational Rehabilitation, 48*(1), 93–109. https://doi.org/10.3233/JVR-170918.

Ta, T. L., & Leng, K. S. (2013). Challenges Faced by Malaysians with Disabilities in the World of Employment. *Disability, CBR & Inclusive Development, 24*(1), 6. https://doi.org/10.5463/dcid.v24i1.142.

Tassé, M. J., Schlalock, R., Thompson, J. R., & Wehmeyer, M. L. (2005). Guidelines for interviewing people with disabilities: Supports Intensity Scale. www.aaidd.org/docs/default-source/sis-docs/sisguidelinesforinterviewing.pdf.

The World Bank. (2011). Disability Inclusion. www.worldbank.org/en/topic/disability#:~:text=Results-,One%20billion%20people%2C%20or%2015%25%20of%20the%20world's%20population%2C,million%20people%2C%20experience%20significant%20disabilities.

Thorp-Lancaster, D. (2020). Microsoft Teams hits 75 million daily active users, up from 44 million in March. *Windows Central.* www.windowscentral.com/microsoft-teams-hits-75-million-daily-active-users.

Tomaszewski, B., Fidler, D., Talapatra, D., & Riley, K. (2018). Adaptive Behaviour, Executive Function and Employment in Adults with Down Syndrome: Employment in Adults with Down Syndrome. *Journal of Intellectual Disability Research, 62*(1), 41–52. https://doi.org/10.1111/jir.12450.

Turner, D. (2014). Qualitative Interview Design: A Practical Guide for Novice Investigators. *The Qualitative Report.* https://doi.org/10.46743/2160-3715/2010.1178.

UNICEF. (2016). Module I: Understanding Social Ecological Model (SEM) and Communication for Development (C4D). www.unicef.org/media/47781/file/UNICEF_2017_Report_on_Communication_for_Development_C4D.pdf.

van Teijlingen, E., & Hundley, V. (2002). The Importance of Pilot Studies. *Nursing Standard, 16*(40), 33–6. https://doi.org/10.7748/ns2002.06.16.40.33.c3214.

Waterhouse, P., Kimberley, H., Jonas, P., & Glover, J. (2010). What Would It Take? Employer Perspectives on Employing People with a Disability. A National Vocational Education and Training Research and Evaluation Program Report. https://eric.ed.gov/?id=ED508544.

Weir, D., Faul, J., & Langa, K. (2011). Proxy Interviews and Bias in the Distribution of Cognitive Abilities due to Non-Response in Longitudinal

Studies: A Comparison of HRS and ELSA. *Longitudinal and Life Course Studies*, *2*(2), 170–84. https://doi.org/10.14301/llcs.v2i2.116.

Woodyatt, C. R., Finneran, C. A., & Stephenson, R. (2016). In-Person Versus Online Focus Group Discussions: A Comparative Analysis of Data Quality. *Qualitative Health Research*, *26*(6), 741–9. https://doi.org/10.1177/1049732316631510.

Wray, J., Archibong, U., & Walton, S. (2017). Why Undertake a Pilot in a Qualitative PhD Study? Lessons Learned to Promote Success. *Nurse Researcher*, *24*(3), 31–5. https://doi.org/10.7748/nr.2017.e1416.

Yeong, M. L., Ismail, R., Ismail, N. H., & Hamzah, M. I. (2018). Interview Protocol Refinement: Fine-Tuning Qualitative Research Interview Questions for Multi-Racial Populations in Malaysia. *The Qualitative Report*. https://doi .org/10.46743/2160-3715/2018.3412.

Yin, R. K. (1994). Discovering the Future of the Case Study Method in Evaluation Research. *Evaluation Practice*, *15*(3), 283–90. https://doi.org/10.1016/0886-1633 (94)90023-X.

Zhang, Y., & Wildemuth, B. M. (2009). Unstructured interviews. In B. M. Wildemuth (Ed.), *Applications of social research methods to questions in information and library science* (1st ed., pp. 222–31). Libraries Unlimited.

CHAPTER 13

Technology-Aided Programs to Support Leisure, Communication, and Daily Activities in People with Intellectual and Multiple Disabilities

Giulio E. Lancioni, Nirbhay N. Singh, Mark F. O'Reilly, Jeff Sigafoos, and Gloria Alberti

Introduction

People with mild to moderate or moderate to severe intellectual or multiple disabilities are frequently reported to have problems in managing independent access to leisure events, basic communication with partners not present in their immediate environment, and performance of functional daily activities (Badia et al., 2013; Davies et al., 2018; Desideri et al., 2021; Lancioni et al., 2018, 2020d; Lin et al., 2018). Their difficulties in accessing leisure events seem to be largely related to their inability to properly handle devices typically used for activating those events (e.g., music devices, computers and tablets) (Chan et al., 2013; Lancioni et al., 2018). Their difficulties in managing basic communication exchanges with distant partners seem to be primarily due to their inability to use telephone devices or comparable communication means (e.g., tablets and computers) instrumental to those exchanges (Darcy et al., 2017; Lancioni et al., 2016; Light et al., 2019). Finally, their problems in performing functional daily activities appear to be due to their inadequacy in remembering the steps involved in those activities and/or the sequence in which the steps are to be performed (Cannella-Malone & Schaefer, 2017; Desideri et al., 2021; Goo et al., 2019).

In light of the negative implications of the aforementioned difficulties, there is general consensus that specific intervention programs are needed to help people find ways of alleviating such difficulties (Boot et al., 2018). With regard to those programs, the first point to take into consideration is that they need to be conceived as strategies capable of enabling people to reach independence rather than remaining passive or dependent on staff or caregivers' direct supervision. Intervention programs relying on staff or caregivers' direct supervision would, in fact, (a) perpetuate the person's dependence rather than helping them reach new levels of initiative and self-determination, and (b) prove very expensive in terms of time and resources, thus being unaffordable in many daily contexts (Lancioni et al., 2020a, b; Wehmeyer, 2020; Wehmeyer et al., 2020). The second point is an obvious consequence of the first. That is, the use of technology solutions may be a necessary and practical approach to provide the level of support that people need to achieve their goals independent of staff and caregivers' supervision (Cullen et al., 2017; Desmond et al., 2018; Lancioni et al., 2018; Light et al., 2019).

In line with the aforementioned points, a variety of efforts have been made to develop technology-based programs that encourage independence. Generally, the programs were focused on fostering independence in one of the three main areas mentioned earlier: (a) leisure (Lancioni et al., 2014, 2016; Stasolla et al., 2015; Wang et al., 2011), (b) communication (Kagohara et al., 2013; Ricci et al., 2017; van der Meer et al., 2012, 2017a, 2017b), and (c) performance of functional occupational/vocational activities (Desideri et al., 2021; Mechling et al., 2010; Savage & Taber-Doughty, 2017). The largely positive outcomes of the programs focusing on one specific area were viewed as a basis and an incentive for developing new programs that would target two of the areas or all three of them simultaneously. The reasoning was that programs targeting more areas could be more functional for the people exposed to them and the context running them than programs that targeted a single area. For example, providing people the opportunity to freely shift from one type of engagement (e.g., leisure) to another (e.g., communication) could increase their range of opportunities and thus improve the quality of their engagement and their personal satisfaction. Setting up programs that would allow participants to alternate periods of leisure and communication with periods of functional daily activity would ensure a combination of pleasant and functional/practical engagement that could (a) motivate them to remain positively occupied for relatively long periods of time and (b) have important benefits in terms of their overall level of independence as well as in terms of staff and caregivers' time (Kazdin, 2012; Lancioni et al., 2020c, 2022).

The aim of this chapter is to provide an overview of selected studies that have assessed programs focusing on two or three areas simultaneously so as to explain the development of the programs, the technology solutions used to support them, and their outcomes in terms of participants' independent performance. Eight studies are summarized herein. Six of them reported programs targeting two different areas: leisure and communication or leisure and functional daily activities. The other two studies reported programs targeting all three areas: that is, leisure, communication, and functional daily activities simultaneously. Following the presentation of the programs and their outcomes, a discussion section is provided that concentrates on three main issues: (a) effectiveness of the programs and methodological considerations, (b) accessibility and affordability of the programs, and (c) implications of the programs for professionals working in daily contexts. With regard to the last issue, an effort was made to examine ethical and moral questions that may accompany the possible decisions of professionals to adopt those programs in daily contexts.

Studies Targeting Leisure and Communication or Leisure and Daily Activities

The studies summarized in this section have been reported during the last five years and were aimed at helping adult participants with mild or moderate intellectual disabilities, often combined with sensory and/or motor impairments, to achieve independence in two of the three areas mentioned earlier: leisure and communication with distant partners or leisure and daily activities. The technology solutions adopted for the programs varied mainly on the basis of (a) the devices used to suit the characteristics of the participants (e.g., their different motor abilities and response ranges and their different sensory conditions) and (b) the way in which choice options were presented and the participants' response process was arranged (Federici & Scherer, 2017; Scherer, 2019).

Study I. This study (Lancioni et al., 2017b) assessed a program based on the use of a laptop computer with screen and sound amplifier, a mobile communication modem, and a pressure microswitch with relative interface to help participants access various leisure options (e.g., songs, videos and slide shows) and manage communication exchanges with distant partners (i.e., via telephone calls or text messages). The participants were exposed to the program according to an ABAB design (with A and B representing baseline and intervention phases, respectively) and provided with 10-minute sessions across the different phases of the study. At the start of the sessions, the computer showed visual images of the three or four options available for the participant (e.g., images of singers/music, footballers, movies, and telephone), and illuminated and verbally presented each of them in succession. If the participant selected one of the options by activating the pressure microswitch during the program (or a mouse during the baseline), the computer presented a series of alternatives from which the participant could choose. For example, if the participant selected the singers/music option, the computer would present the titles of several songs and the participant could choose one of them via the microswitch (or the mouse during baseline). If the participant selected the telephone option, the computer would present the pictures and names of various relevant communication partners and the participant could, as mentioned, choose one of them (i.e., the one to call or the one to contact via text message) through the microswitch or mouse response. Choosing a leisure event led the computer to present such an event (e.g., song or video) for about two minutes. Choosing a partner to call led the computer to dial that partner's telephone number and start a call. Choosing a partner to contact via text message led the computer to present various messages available for that partner and to send the message the participant chose immediately after the choice had occurred. The results showed that during the baseline phases (i.e., when the mouse was available for use) the participants were unable to make any choices and thus could not access the leisure or communication options. During the intervention phases, they were successful in using the microswitch in connection with the computer system and were positively engaged in leisure and communication throughout the session.

In addition to the participants' leisure and communication engagement data, the study also reported a social validation of the program (carried out by means of a questionnaire presented to staff personnel) and an assessment of the participants' preferences (carried out by requesting them to choose between the program sessions and other presumably positive forms of engagement). The social validation indicated that staff had highly favorable ratings of the program. Moreover, the participants showed very strong preferences for the program sessions.

Study II. This study (Lancioni et al., 2018) reported the use of (a) a smartphone with an Android operating system, near-field communication, music and video player functions, and MacroDroid application, and (b) cards with radio-frequency identification tags. This technology was used for a program aimed at helping participants access different forms of preferred leisure events and make telephone calls with preferred communication partners. The program was introduced according to a nonconcurrent multiple baseline design across participants, which involved fifteen-minute baseline and intervention sessions. During the baseline sessions, the research assistant (a) invited the participants to use a smartphone (which responded to specific verbal utterances and conventional touch inputs) and (b) pointed out the options accessible through the smartphone (e.g., listening to singers/songs and making telephone calls). During the intervention and postintervention sessions, the participants had cards or miniature objects with radio-frequency identification tags. Those cards or miniature objects, which the participants were able to discriminate, represented leisure options as well as preferred communication partners that could be reached via a telephone call. The participants could access the corresponding leisure events or start calls with their preferred partners by holding the cards/objects onto the back of the smartphone. The smartphone recognized the tags of those cards/objects through the MacroDroid application. Therefore, if the participant held a card/object representing a specific leisure event, the smartphone would deliver such an event. Similarly, if the participant held the card/object representing a specific communication partner, the smartphone would automatically set up a telephone call with that partner. During the baseline (without the support of the program), the participants were unable to request/access leisure events or start telephone calls independently. With the use of the program, they succeeded in doing both and spent most of their session time engaging in leisure and communication.

Study III. This study (Lancioni et al., 2020a) assessed a new technology-aided program to support independent leisure and communication engagement, which relied on the use of a tablet with an Android operating system, a NANO SIM card, and the WhatsApp Messenger and MacroDroid applications. The participants were presented with (a) preferred leisure options and the possibility of communication with preferred partners via text messages, and, depending on the alternative they selected, (b) various steps they could take to access leisure events or send messages. Every program session lasted ten minutes and started with the tablet sequentially scanning (illuminating for about five seconds) each of the two pictures representing the two choice areas (i.e., leisure and communication), and verbalizing each area while illuminating it. Some participants could select either area by approaching the proximity sensor of the tablet with their hand while that area was illuminated. Other participants (who did not possess such a motor response) were provided with a smartphone fixed to the headrest of their wheelchair for their selections. In practice, they could select the area they wanted by turning their head toward the smartphone (thus activating the smartphone's proximity sensor) when that area was illuminated. Following the selection of the area, the tablet presented the various alternatives available in that area (e.g., leisure alternatives such as music and videos or various communication partners to whom a message could be sent). Again, the participants were to use one of the aforementioned response strategies to select a leisure alternative or a communication partner. Based on this new selection, the tablet presented various options related to the leisure alternative selected (e.g., different singers or comedians) or listed various messages that could be sent to the partner selected. Selecting a leisure option (e.g., a singer) led the tablet to deliver an event related to it (e.g., a song) that the participants could enjoy. Selecting a message led the tablet to send it out. Incoming messages were automatically read by the tablet. Data showed that the participants were successful in using the technology-aided program and achieved high levels of independent leisure and communication engagement. A social valid-ation of the program carried out by interviewing staff about the program's effective support of the participants (friendliness toward them) and applic-ability in daily contexts provided very positive results (i.e., staff rated the program highly on each of these aspects).

Study IV. This study (Lancioni et al., 2020b) introduced a new tech-nology solution that was seen as advantageous in terms of response require-ment and/or choice process compared to the solutions used before. For example, the response required for making choices was relatively simple in relation to that required for using cards or miniature objects (see Study II). Moreover, the participants were no longer exposed to the successive scanning of the different options and events with the need to wait until the desired option/event was being scanned to make their choice (i.e., as occurred in Studies I and III). The technology used to achieve such an objective was the same as that reported for Study III (i.e., a tablet with Android operating system, a NANO SIM card, and the WhatsApp Messenger and MacroDroid applications). Yet, the program was set up in a different manner so that it would (a) present participants with the choice elements in groups of three, and (b) allow participants to choose the first, second or third element of the group/sequence by touching or covering the tablet's proximity sensor once, twice or three times.

Every intervention or postintervention session (i.e., every session with the support of the technology-aided program) started with the tablet verbally and visually presenting three options (i.e., "music," "films," and "video calls"). The participant could choose the first, second or third option of the sequence by touching/covering the tablet's proximity sensor once, twice or three times. If the participant chose music (i.e., covered the tablet's proximity sensor once), the tablet presented three music alterna-tives (i.e., three different singers). The participant could choose the first, second or third singer using the same response strategy as before (i.e., touching/covering the tablet's sensor once, twice or three times). If the participant refrained from choosing any of the singers, the tablet presented three additional singers. Once a singer had been chosen, the tablet presented three songs by that singer and the participant could choose one of them and listen to it. The same approach was also followed for the films option as well as the communication (video calls) option. If the participant chose video calls, the tablet presented three preferred communication partners that could be called. If the participant chose one of these partners, the tablet set up a video call with that partner through WhatsApp Messenger. If the participant abstained from choosing any of the three partners, the tablet presented three additional partners from which the participant could choose. Data showed that the program was highly effective in helping the participants remain positively engaged in leisure and communication throughout the ten-minute intervention and postintervention sessions.

Study V. In line with the studies summarized earlier, Study V (Lancioni et al., 2020c) focused on the evaluation of technology solutions for providing participants with the opportunity to access leisure events and manage communication exchanges with preferred partners not present in the immediate context. The technology system investigated in this study was designed to require fairly simple responses for its activation and thus to suit individuals with relatively serious developmental disabilities (which could also include blindness) and/or high levels of anxiety with fear of failure. The system allowed participants to make requests for leisure events or communication opportunities through simple hand-pressure responses. Those responses activated mini voice recording devices, each of which contained a recorded voice message/request. The messages/requests recorded in the devices (and activated by the participants' hand-pressure responses) served to trigger the Google Assistant of a smartphone and hence to lead the smartphone to deliver what the messages/requests indicated. Eight devices were used during the intervention and postintervention sessions. The requests of four of those devices concerned preferred leisure options, such as songs and comedy sketches. The requests of the other four devices concerned calls or text messages to specific (preferred) communication partners. Pictures or mini objects indicating those leisure options and partners were attached to the devices to make them easily discernible to the participants. The system was set up in such a way that if a communication partner was unreachable (i.e., could not respond to a call), the smartphone played a pre-recorded response from that partner. Incoming messages would be automatically read by the smartphone. The results underlined the effectiveness of the program. In fact, the participants were not able to access leisure or communication without the full support of the system (i.e., during the preliminary baseline sessions). Following the introduction of the system, however, they were able to successfully engage in leisure and communication with consistency throughout the ten-minute sessions.

The results of a social validation of the program conducted by interviewing staff personnel familiar with these education/rehabilitation issues were quite encouraging. Indeed, the staff interviewed rated the program (i.e., the technology system on which the program relied) as highly effective, enjoyable for the participants to use, suitable/functional for the participants' daily context, and worthy of being recommended.

Study VI. The goal of this this study (Lancioni et al., 2020d) was somewhat different from the goal of the studies summarized earlier. Indeed, this study was aimed at targeting leisure and functional daily activities. The technology involved a smartphone used in combination with special cards. The smartphone had an Android operating system and near-field communication (NFC) function, and was fitted with the MacroDroid application. The smartphone was also supplied with (a) audiovisual files concerning a variety of leisure events (e.g., comic sketches, travel adventures, and songs), as well as (b) pictorial images and verbal instructions concerning the activities to be carried out and the related steps. The cards were fitted with radio-frequency identification tags and represented the leisure options (i.e., as in Study II). The tags made the cards recognizable to the smartphone, which then delivered the corresponding leisure events during the intervention and postintervention sessions (see Study II).

At the start of each of these sessions, the participant was sitting at a desk with the smartphone and eight cards representing eight different leisure options. The participant was expected to choose one of the cards and touch it to the back of the smartphone. This led the smartphone to identify the card and play the corresponding leisure event. At the end of the event, the smartphone started to provide pictorial or verbal and pictorial instructions for one of the daily activities the participant was scheduled to carry out. The instructions were presented one at a time, automatically. Once the instructions for all activity steps had been presented, the smartphone invited the participant to go back to the cards and choose one of them. Choosing a card and bringing it to touch the back of the smartphone led the participant to access a leisure event related to that card. At the end of this, the smartphone presented a second activity (following the same process used for the first one). The session continued until the participant had accessed/enjoyed four different leisure events interspersed with three different activities. The results showed that without the support of the program (i.e., during baseline sessions), the participants were unable to access leisure events and carry out daily activities independent of staff supervision. With the support of the program (i.e., during intervention sessions), the participants were able to manage independent choice of (and access to) leisure events and accurate performance of daily activities. In essence, the participants succeeded in alternating their engagement in leisure events with their engagement in daily activities and remained constructively occupied throughout sessions that lasted near to or for more than thirty minutes.

Studies Targeting Leisure, Communication, and Daily Activities

The two studies summarized in this section were aimed at extending the impact of the technology-aided programs examined earlier. In essence, the new studies focused on all three main areas in which people with intellectual and multiple disabilities may need help (i.e., leisure, communication, and functional daily activities). An improvement of people's performance in those areas is considered to be critical for their general perspectives in terms of development, occupational achievement, and social adjustment. By extending the focus of the programs to all three areas, the studies were generally also able to expand the length of time the participants remained positively/constructively engaged in an independent manner.

Study VII. The participants involved in this study (Lancioni et al., 2020e) were already familiar with a program enabling them to access leisure and communication. Indeed, the participants were able to use cards or miniature objects with tags in connection with a smartphone with an Android operating system (as well as a NFC function, WhatsApp Messenger, and MacroDroid) to request leisure events, start telephone calls with preferred partners, or send those partners text messages. The purpose of the study was to extend the program with the introduction of activity periods similar to those available in Study VI. Sessions started with a period of about three minutes, during which the participants sat at a desk and could make leisure and communication choices. Once the three-minute period had elapsed and any leisure or communication event started within that period was completed, the smartphone presented the verbal instructions for the first activity. The instructions were presented one at a time, automatically, in support of the single steps of the activity so that the participants could perform those steps in the correct sequence.

Following the last activity instruction, the smartphone informed the participants that they could start new leisure and communication choices. They were allowed a new three-minute period to make choices, as for the one described earlier. The end of this second leisure and communication choice period was followed by the instructions for a second activity. The instructions were presented as for the first activity. The results showed that the participants were highly successful in integrating their leisure and communication engagement with the performance of daily activities during intervention and postintervention sessions, which lasted near to or above thirty minutes.

A social validation assessment via staff interviews showed that a program such as the one carried out obtained significantly higher ratings than a program focusing on leisure and communication (i.e., such as those reported in Studies I–V). Higher ratings were provided on items concerning range and variation of occupational opportunities, independent constructive occupation time, and contribution to the participants' rehabilitation process.

Study VIII. This study (Lancioni et al., 2022) assessed the impact of a program relying on the use of a technology package comparable to that used in Study V – that is, a package including (a) a smartphone with an Android operating system, SIM card, Internet connection, Google account, and MacroDroid application, and (b) mini voice recording devices. The participants were to use the voice recording devices to request leisure events and activate telephone calls (i.e., as reported in Study V). The program was set up to alternate periods in which the participants could access leisure and carry out telephone calls (through the use of the aforementioned voice recording devices, each of which had a recorded verbal message capable of activating the smartphone's Google Assistant) with periods in which daily activities were to be carried out. During the latter periods, the participants received instructions vi the smartphone for the single activity steps. Data showed that the program was effective in enabling the participants to independently manage leisure, communication, and daily activities, and to remain successfully engaged for sessions whose mean length varied between approximately thirty to forty minutes.

Effectiveness of the Programs and Methodological Considerations

With regard to the effectiveness of the programs, the data reported by the studies seem to be highly encouraging. The participants' steady leisure and communication engagement or the successful alternation of leisure and communication engagement with accurate performance of daily activities throughout the sessions in which the technology support was available may have a number of simple explanations. First, engaging in preferred leisure activities and communicating with preferred partners are most likely to represent highly motivating forms of engagement, and this may largely account for the participants' positive data reported by the different studies in those areas (Kazdin, 2012; Lancioni et al., 2017b, 2019). It may also be the case that the possibility of switching between the two forms of engagement (i.e., between leisure and communication) could have played a positive role, by allowing the participants engagement variation. Indeed, the participants (a) were free to focus on what was more relevant for them at any particular time (King et al., 2014; Stasolla et al., 2015) and (b) could avoid any protracted use of the same form of engagement with possible declines in their interest levels. Second, the technology solutions employed in the various studies were adapted to the participants' characteristics and abilities, and thus were user-friendly and allowed them to achieve their goals in a fairly successful manner (i.e., avoiding failures and frustration). Third, the participants' successful performance of the scheduled activities was probably due by the fact that (a) the participants possessed the skills to carry out the steps of those activities, (b) the instructions provided were adequate to support the performance of those steps and ensure their correct sequencing, and (c) the participants were comfortable with the activity (instruction) situation and thus experienced a positive quality of engagement and avoided anxiety throughout their activity engagement time.

While the results of the studies underline the effectiveness of the programs, some considerations may be needed regarding the research methodology applied by the studies in order to determine the strength of those results. Regarding this point, it may be noted that the studies were carried out according to single-subject research designs (i.e., ABAB or nonconcurrent multiple baseline across participants). While the ABAB is considered a strong design, the nonconcurrent multiple baseline across participants may be viewed as a weaker design (i.e., a design providing less obvious evidence of the effects of the intervention; Krotochwill et al., 2013; Lobo et al., 2017). In spite of this apparent weakness, there are reasons to believe that the results obtained by the studies using such a design can be considered valid (Lancioni et al., 2021). First, during baseline the participants showed zero or near zero levels of performance in the areas targeted, in contrast to the high levels they reached immediately after the introduction of the programs. Second, history or general environmental variables could not have accounted for those performance changes observed across participants over relatively short periods of time (Lancioni et al., 2021). In fact, those changes were not due to the acquisition of new language or motor skills, but were related to the use of technology that substituted for those skills, which remained absent.

Another point that should be taken into consideration in judging the results of the studies and their possible implications for daily contexts is that all the studies summarized herein were conducted by the same research group. This type of situation certainly limits the possibility of making general/conclusive statements about the evidence and could only be amended through the occurrence of replication studies carried out by different research groups (Kazdin, 2011; Locey, 2020; Travers et al., 2016). One such replication study has just been carried out by a different research group with adolescents emerging from a minimally conscious state (Stasolla et al., 2022). This study pursued independent leisure, communication, and occupation through a technology-aided program similar to those described in this chapter, and reported largely positive results, which strongly corroborate the evidence summarized here. In addition to receiving confirmation from this systematic replication study, the noted evidence is also supported by positive data from many simpler studies that successfully used technology-aided programs. Those studies were typically aimed at helping participants gain independence in one of the three areas addressed in this chapter: leisure (Lancioni et al., 2016; Stasolla et al., 2014; Wang et al., 2011), communication (Kagohara et al. 2013; Lancioni et al., 2014; Ricci et al., 2017; van der Meer et al. 2012, 2017a, 2017b), and functional daily activities (Cullen et al., 2017; Lancioni et al., 2017a; Mechling et al., 2010).

Accessibility and Affordability of the Programs

With regard to the issue of accessibility, the first question is whether the technology used for the programs can be directly obtained/purchased by different communities not connected with the research group that carried out the studies summarized herein (Boot et al., 2018; Borg et al., 2019, de Witte et al., 2018; Federici & Scherer, 2017). Another question is whether the technology can be put into use in a straightforward manner within daily contexts. The answer to the first question is that all the technology employed in the studies can be directly purchased without any restrictions or the need for connections with the research group responsible for its development and assessment. In fact, all components of the technology packages used within the programs are commercially available and thus directly accessible. The answer to the second question is not as simple. While the technology components are commercially available, those components need to be arranged and programmed according to the objectives pursued for the participants. In essence, the technology packages are not ready-made (off-the-shelf) tools that one can directly use in the everyday context, but rather tools that one has to set up based on the scope of the intervention and characteristics of the participants. This operation, albeit not too complex, may be beyond the skills of some staff and caregivers; thus, assistance with the process may be necessary.

With regard to the issue of affordability, the basic question concerns the cost of the packages reported by the studies summarized here. Given the differences among packages, the cost for their acquisition also varies. For example, packages including a smartphone in combination with cards or miniature objects fitted with radio-frequency identification tags are by far the cheapest and most easily affordable (Borg, 2019; Lancioni, 2020d). In fact, a smartphone adequate for the task can be acquired for about US$200, while the MicroDroid application, tags, cards, and miniature objects have negligible costs and thus hardly any impact on affordability. The cost of the packages will obviously increase when a tablet or a combination of a tablet and a smartphone are used within the same program (Study III).

Implications of the Programs for Professionals Working in Daily Contexts (Social and Ethical/Moral Considerations on Program Adoption)

The positive results of the studies summarized and the aforementioned discussion on the issues of program effectiveness, research methodology, program accessibility, and program affordability would seem to make a case in favor of the adoption and use of those programs in daily contexts. Obviously, those contexts may need extra evidence (e.g., may want to see or be involved in replication studies conducted by new research groups) before one commits to implementing such programs as regular rehabilitation tools (Campbell et al., 2014; Campos et al., 2019; Locey, 2020). That commitment may depend on the outcome of the aforementioned replication studies and on the answers to a number of questions that may constitute a social and ethical/moral framework within which a decision on those programs eventually needs to be taken. At least five immediate questions could be envisaged as part of such a framework.

1. Do staff, caregivers, or other service providers and stakeholders consider those programs effective and relevant for the participants' rehabilitation progress and the achievement of better life conditions (i.e., for enhancing the participants' well-being)?
2. Do participants show interest and enjoyment during these programs?
3. Could the participants reach the same objectives without the use of these programs?
4. What would be the most likely alternatives to the programs within daily contexts?
5. Are there social and ethical/moral duties that service providers (e.g., rehabilitation and research personnel) should consider as binding for their decisions following new research (replication studies) and clarifying answers to the aforementioned questions?

While waiting for new/independent replication studies, a number of preliminary, plausible answers might be provided in relation to each of the questions listed herein. Regarding the first question (i.e., staff, caregivers, or other service providers and stakeholders' view of the programs), some evidence is already available. In four of the studies summarized earlier (i.e., Studies I, III, V, and VII) and in the study by Stasolla et al. (2022), social validations of the programs were reported. In those social validations, staff and other relevant rehabilitation and care personnel were interviewed about the impact of the programs in supporting participants' performance and progress as well as about the applicability of the programs. The personnel's ratings relative to all those aspects were quite favorable, suggesting that they had a positive view about the programs' potential and usability.

Regarding the second question (i.e., participants' interest for and enjoyment of the programs), the literature has provided some specific evidence/data as well as anecdotal reports. Indeed, Lancioni et al. (2017b) carried out preference checks in which the participants could choose whether to be involved in a program session or in another form of activity considered to be positive/pleasant for them. Their data showed that the participants preferred to be involved in the program sessions almost consistently. Similarly, Lancioni et al. (2020b, 2020c) and Stasolla et al. (2022) provided anecdotal reports about the participants showing signs of pleasure and satisfaction during the program sessions. One more point that might support the notion of participants' interest for and enjoyment of the program sessions is the high and consistent level of engagement that they displayed throughout the typically extended program assessment periods reported by the studies summarized in this chapter, as well as by other studies (e.g., Lancioni et al., 2019, 2020f; Stasolla et al., 2022).

Regarding the third question (i.e., participants' chances of pursuing the goals of independent leisure, communication, and daily activities without the use of those programs), no direct answer exists. Nonetheless, three points may be put forward which suggest that such an achievement could hardly be obtained independent of the programs. First, all the participants involved in the studies summarized herein were adults and had been attending rehabilitation and care facilities without reaching independent leisure and communication or leisure, communication, and daily activities. Second, given the participants' general conditions, it is most unlikely that they would (or could) have developed the motor and memory skills necessary to achieve the results reported through typical rehabilitation practices or conventional technology (Lancioni et al., 2019, 2021). Third, the programs allowed the participants to bypass their difficulties/weaknesses by bridging the gap between their real skills and the skill level requested of them to achieve independence in the targeted areas.

Regarding the fourth question (i.e., possible/likely alternatives to the programs that one could use within daily contexts), no specific data or answers are available. The most reasonable assumption (also in light of the history of the participants included in the studies summarized herein) is that the participants would be provided with some form of assistance by staff or caregivers so as to allow them to reach at least in part the objectives achievable through the technology-aided programs. Obviously, the use of staff and caregiver support would have two disadvantages: it would perpetrate a level of participants' dependence, and it would have clear costs in terms of staff and caregivers' time and effort (Stasolla et al., 2022; Wehmeyer, 2020).

Regarding the fifth question (i.e., social and ethical/moral duties of staff, service providers, and rehabilitation and research personnel), the best response one can give is that the decisions and practices of all these professionals should be in line with (a) the data currently available, the results of new, independent replication studies, as well as the answers provided to the questions examined earlier, and (b) their commitment to offer the participants the most effective and satisfactory form of support possible (Adams & Boyd, 2010; Man & Kangas, 2020; McDonald et al., 2015). Accepting that the evidence and answers provided herein suggest that the programs can have a good chance of contributing positively to improve the participants' situation would have social and ethical/moral implications for professionals in the area. That is, those professionals would be required to consider the notion (and probably feel the social and ethical/moral duty) of working toward adapting and accommodating the programs for use within their organizations.

Conclusions

This chapter summarizes some recent studies evaluating technology-aided programs to support participants with intellectual and other disabilities to independently manage leisure and communication or combinations of leisure, communication, and daily activities. The encouraging results reported by the studies, and the relative accessibility and affordability of the technology solutions adopted to support the programs, have prompted a discussion concerning the strength of the evidence (and the possibility to generalize such evidence to daily contexts). In debating this point, considerations were made about (a) methodological issues that may raise some caution against drawing direct, strong conclusions from the evidence provided by the studies summarized, and (b) the large amount of data on technology-aided programs that justifies an attitude quite favorable toward such an approach and hopeful as to its beneficial impact for a growing number of persons in need. The final points analyzed were concerned with social and ethical considerations that staff, caregivers, and other service providers can hardly avoid. Those considerations may provide a new impetus toward preparing daily contexts to adopt and sustain technology-aided programs aimed at promoting participants' independence in leisure, communication, and daily activities.

References

Adams, Z. W., & Boyd, S. E. (2010). Ethical challenges in the treatment of individuals with intellectual disabilities. *Ethics & Behavior, 20*(6), 407–418.

Badia, M., Orgaz, M. B., Verdugo, M. A., & Ullán, A. M. (2013). Patterns and determinants of leisure participation of youth and adults with developmental disabilities. *Journal of Intellectual Disability Research, 57*(4), 319–332.

Boot, F. H., Owuor, J., Dinsmore, J., & MacLachlan, M. (2018). Access to assistive technology for people with intellectual disabilities: A systematic review to identify barriers and facilitators. *Journal of Intellectual Disability Research, 62* (10), 900–921.

Borg, J. (2019). Commentary on selection of assistive technology in a context with limited resources. *Disability and Rehabilitation: Assistive Technology, 14*(8), 753–754.

Campbell, M., Robertson, A., & Jahoda, A. (2014). Psychological therapies for people with intellectual disabilities: Comments on a Matrix of evidence for interventions in challenging behaviour. *Journal of Intellectual Disability Research*, *58*(2), 172–188.

Campos, R. C., Holden, R. R., & Lambert, C. E. (2019). Avoidance of psychological pain and suicidal ideation in community samples: Replication across two countries and two languages. *Journal of Clinical Psychology*, *75*(12), 2160–2168.

Cannella-Malone, H. I., & Schaefer, J. M. (2017). A review of research on teaching people with significant disabilities vocational skills. *Career Development and Transition for Exceptional Individuals*, *40*(2), 67–78.

Chan, J. M., Lambdin, L., Van Laarhoven, T., & Johnson, J. W. (2013). Teaching leisure skills to an adult with developmental disabilities using a video prompting intervention package. *Education and Training in Autism and Developmental Disabilities*, *48*(3), 412–420.

Cullen, J. M., Alber-Morgan, S. R., Simmons-Reed, E. A., & Izzo, M. V. 2017. Effects of self-directed video prompting using iPads on the vocational task completion of young adults with intellectual and developmental disabilities. *Journal of Vocational Rehabilitation*, *46*, 361–375.

Darcy, S., Green, J., & Maxwell, H. (2017). I've got a mobile phone too! Hard and soft assistive technology customization and supportive call centres for people with disability. *Disability and Rehabilitation Assistive Technology*, *12*(4), 341–351.

Davies, D. K., Stock, S. E., Herold, R. G., & Wehmeyer, M. L. (2018). GeoTalk: A GPS-enabled portable speech output device for people with intellectual disability. *Advances in Neurodevelopmental Disorders*, *2*(3), 253–261.

Desideri, L., Lancioni, G., Malavasi, M., Gherardini, A., & Cesario, L. (2021). Step instruction technology to help people with intellectual and other disabilities perform multistep tasks: A literature review. *Journal of Developmental and Physical Disabilities*, *33*(6), 857–886.

Desmond, D., Layton, N., Bentley, J., et al. (2018). Assistive technology and people: A position paper from the first global research, innovation and education on assistive technology (GREAT) summit. *Disability and Rehabilitation: Assistive Technology*, *13*(5), 437–444.

De Witte, L., Steel, E., Gupta, S., Delgado Ramos, V., & Roentgen, U. (2018). Assistive technology provision: Towards an international framework for assuring availability and accessibility of affordable high-quality assistive technology. *Disability and Rehabilitation: Assistive Technology*, *13*(5), 467–472.

Federici, S., & Scherer, M. J. (Eds.) (2017). *Assistive technology assessment handbook* (2nd ed.). London: CRC Press.

Goo, M., Maurer, A. L., & Wehmeyer, M. L. (2019). Systematic review of using portable smart devices to teach functional skills to students with intellectual disability. *Education and Training in Autism and Developmental Disabilities*, *54*(1), 57–68.

Kagohara, D. M., van der Meer, L., Ramdoss, S., et al. (2013). Using iPods and iPads in teaching programs for individuals with developmental disabilities: A systematic review. *Research in Developmental Disabilities*, *34*(1), 147–156.

Kazdin, A. E. (2011). *Single-case research designs: Methods for clinical and applied settings* (2th ed.). New York: Oxford University Press.

Kazdin, A. E. (2012). *Behavior modification in applied settings* (7th ed.). New York: Waveland Press.

King, G., Gibson, B. E., Mistry, B., et al. (2014). An integrated methods study of the experiences of youth with severe disabilities in leisure activity settings: The importance of belonging, fun, and control and choice. *Disability and Rehabilitation, 36*(19), 1626–1635.

Kratochwill, T. R., Hitchcock, J. H., Horner, R. H., et al. (2013). Single case intervention research design standards. *Remedial and Special Education, 34*(1), 26–38.

Lancioni, G. E., Desideri, L., Singh, N. N., Sigafoos, J., & O'Reilly, M. F. (2021). A commentary on standards for single-case experimental studies. *International Journal of Developmental Disabilities, 8*(68), 781–783. doi.org/10.1080/20473869.2020.1870420.

Lancioni, G. E., O'Reilly, M., Singh, N., et al. (2016). Technology to support positive occupational engagement and communication in persons with multiple disabilities. *International Journal on Disabilities and Human Development, 15*(1), 111–116.

Lancioni, G. E., Singh, N. N., O'Reilly, M. F., et al. (2017a). Using smartphones to help people with intellectual and sensory disabilities perform daily activities. *Frontiers in Public Health, 5*, 282. https://doi.org/10.3389/fpubh.2017.00282.

Lancioni, G. E., Singh, N. N., O'Reilly, M. F., et al. (2017b). Persons with multiple disabilities manage positive leisure and communication engagement through a technology-aided program. *International Journal of Developmental Disabilities, 63*(3), 148–157.

Lancioni, G. E., Singh, N. N., O'Reilly, M. F., et al. (2018). An upgraded smartphone-based program for leisure and communication of people with intellectual and other disabilities. *Frontiers in Public Health, 6*, 234. https://doi.org/10.3389/fpubh.2018.00234.

Lancioni, G. E., Singh, N. N., O'Reilly, M. F., et al. (2019). A program based on common technology to support communication exchanges and leisure in people with intellectual and other disabilities. *Behavior Modification, 43*(6), 879–897.

Lancioni, G. E., Singh, N. N., O'Reilly, M. F., et al. (2020a). Case series of technology-aided interventions to support leisure and communication in extensive disabilities. *International Journal of Developmental Disabilities, 66*(3), 180–189.

Lancioni, G. E., Singh, N. N., O'Reilly, M. F., et al. (2020b). A new tablet-based program to support leisure and video calls in people with intellectual and motor disabilities. *Technology and Disability, 32*(2), 111–121.

Lancioni, G. E., Singh, N. N., O'Reilly, M. F., et al. (2020c). People with intellectual and visual disabilities access basic leisure and communication using a smartphone's Google Assistant and voice recording devices.

Disability and Rehabilitation: Assistive Technology. https://doi.org/10.1080/17483107.2020.1836047.

Lancioni, G. E., Singh, N. N., O'Reilly, M. F., et al. (2020d). Everyday technology to support leisure and daily activities in people with intellectual and other disabilities. *Developmental Neurorehabilitation, 23*(7), 431–438.

Lancioni, G. E., Singh, N. N., O'Reilly, M. F., et al. (2020e). Extended smartphone-aided program to sustain daily activities, communication and leisure in individuals with intellectual and sensory-motor disabilities. *Research in Developmental Disabilities, 105*, 103722. doi.org/10.1016/j.ridd.2020.103722.

Lancioni, G. E., Singh, N. N., O'Reilly, M. F., et al. (2020f). A tablet-based program to enable people with intellectual and other disabilities to access leisure activities and video calls. *Disability and Rehabilitation: Assistive Technology, 15* (1), 14–20.

Lancioni, G. E., Singh, N. N., O'Reilly, M. F., et al. (2022). A smartphone-based program enabling people with intellectual and other disabilities to access leisure, communication, and functional activities. *Universal Access in the Information Society, 22*, 581–590. doi.org/10.1007/s10209-021-00858-4.

Lancioni, G. E., Singh, N., O'Reilly, M., et al. (2014). Case studies of technology for adults with multiple disabilities to make telephone calls independently. *Perceptual and Motor Skills, 119*(1), 320–331.

Light, J., McNaughton, D., & Caron, J. (2019). New and emerging AAC technology supports for children with complex communication needs and their communication partners: State of the science and future research directions. *Augmentative and Alternative Communication, 35*(1), 26–41.

Lin, M. L., Chiang, M. S., Shih, C. H., & Li, M. F. (2018). Improving the occupational skills of students with intellectual disability by applying video prompting combined with dance pads. *Journal of Applied Research in Intellectual Disabilities, 31*(1), 114–119.

Lobo, M. A., Moeyaert, M., Baraldi Cunha, A., & Babik, I. 2017. Single-case design, analysis, and quality assessment for intervention research. *Journal of Neurologic Physical Therapy, 41*(3), 187–197.

Locey, M. L. (2020). The evolution of behavior analysis: Toward a replication crisis? *Perspectives on Behavior Science, 43*(4), 655–675.

Man, J., & Kangas, M. (2020), Best practice principles when working with individuals with intellectual disability and comorbid mental health concerns. *Qualitative Health Research, 30*(4), 560–571.

McDonald, K. E., Schwartz, N. M., Gibbons, C. M., & Olick, R. S. (2015). "You can't be cold and scientific": Community views on ethical issues in intellectual disability research. *Journal of Empirical Research on Human Research Ethics, 10* (2), 196–208.

Mechling, L. C., Gast, D. L., & Seid, N. H. (2010). Evaluation of a personal digital assistant as a self-prompting device for increasing multi-step task completion by students with moderate intellectual disabilities. *Education and Training in Autism and Developmental Disabilities, 45*(3), 422–439.

Ricci, C., Miglino, O., Alberti, G., Perilli, V., & Lancioni, G. E. (2017). Speech generating technology to support request responses of persons with intellectual and multiple disabilities. *International Journal of Developmental Disabilities, 63* (4), 238–245.

Savage, M. N., & Taber-Doughty, T. (2017). Self-operated auditory prompting systems for individuals with intellectual disability: A meta-analysis of single-subject research. *Journal of Intellectual & Developmental Disability, 42* (3), 249–258.

Scherer, M. J. (2019). Assistive technology selection to outcome assessment: The benefit of having a service delivery protocol. *Disability and Rehabilitation: Assistive Technology, 14*(8), 762–763.

Stasolla, F., Caffò, A. O., Bottiroli, S., & Ciarmoli, D. (2022). An assistive technology program for enabling five adolescents emerging from a minimally conscious state to engage in communication, occupation, and leisure opportunities. *Developmental Neurorehabilitation, 25*(3), 193–204.

Stasolla, F., & De Pace, C. (2014). Assistive technology to promote leisure and constructive engagement by two boys emerged from a minimal conscious state. *NeuroRehabilitation, 35*(2), 253–259.

Stasolla, F., Perilli, V., Di Leone, A., et al. (2015). Technological aids to support choice strategies by three girls with Rett syndrome. *Research in Developmental Disabilities, 36*, 36–44.

Travers, J. C., Cook, B. G., Therrien, W. J., & Coyne, M. D. (2016). Replication research and special education. *Remedial and Special Education, 37*(4), 195–204.

van der Meer, L., Kagohara, D., Achmadi, D., et al. (2012). Speech-generating devices versus manual signing for children with developmental disabilities. *Research in Developmental Disabilities, 33*(5), 1658–1669.

van der Meer, L., Matthews, T., Ogilvie, E., et al. (2017a). Training direct-care staff to provide communication intervention to adults with intellectual disability: A systematic review. *American Journal of Speech-Language Pathology, 26*(4), 1279–1295.

van der Meer, L., Waddington, H., Sigafoos, J., et al. (2017b). Training direct-care staff to implement an iPad®-based communication intervention with adults with developmental disability. International Journal of Developmental Disabilities, *63*(4), 246–255.

Wang, S. H., Chiang, C. S., Su, C. Y., & Wang, C. C. (2011). Effectiveness of virtual reality using Wii gaming technology in children with Down syndrome. *Research in Developmental Disabilities, 32*(1), 312–321.

Wehmeyer, M. L. (2020). The importance of self-determination to the quality of life of people with intellectual disability: A perspective. *International Journal of Environmental Research and Public Health, 17*(19), 7121. https://doi.org/10.3390/ijerph17197121.

Wehmeyer, M. L., Davies, D. K., Stock, S. E., & Tanis, S. (2020). Applied cognitive technologies to support the autonomy of people with intellectual and developmental disabilities. *Advances in Neurodevelopmental Disorders, 4*(4), 389–399.

CHAPTER 14

Virtual Qualitative Data Collection
A South African Autoethnographic Perspective

Shantel Lewis, Charlene Downing, and Christopher M. Hayre

Introduction

COVID-19 has resulted in a rethinking of research processes since contact and travel restrictions limited the traditional face-to-face and in-person interviews used to collect qualitative data (Santana, et al., 2021). A PhD student (author SL) had to rethink her data collection methods for the qualitative phases of a mixed-method study and shared her experience of adapting qualitative data collection through COVID-19. A discussion of the narrative and recommendations ensues thereafter.

An Autoethnographic Account of Virtual Qualitative Data Collection

I (author SL) started my PhD journey in 2019, prior to COVID-19. The research study had three phases of data collection. Data for the first phase was planned to be collected through online questionnaires, and in-person for the second and third phases. However, there was a poor response rate to the online questionnaire, and the period for data collection was extended. Data collection for the study's first phase began in July 2019, and by the end of September 2019, only 94 of the 6,552 diagnostic radiographers in South Africa had responded to the online survey (a 1.4% response rate). A renewed outreach effort through social media platforms and conferences eventuated a final response rate of 6.4% by the end of February 2020. I recall thinking at the time that, thankfully, the subsequent two phases would be in person, and the stress of the poor response would be negated. Little did I know how that would change.

A New Normal on the Horizon

From 26 March 2020, South Africa progressed through various lockdown stages and, in adhering to regulations and COVID-19 protocols, the institution I was enrolled at rescinded ethical clearance of research activities pending review and approval of data collection methods. I submitted a revised data collection plan for phases two and three of the study, indicating that the data would be collected through Skype, Zoom, Microsoft Teams, WhatsApp video, or telephone calls. At that time, I was familiar with only these platforms. The ethical clearance required details of research data and document management. Therefore, the privacy policies of the platforms used to collect data were examined, and all measures to ensure the confidentiality of participants and data were outlined to the ethics committee and were followed throughout the research procedure.

Data was collected for the first phase of the study from 30 July 2019 to 10 February 2020, and 120 respondents provided their contact information to participate in the second phase of the study (Lewis, Downing & Hayre, 2022a). Phase two data collection was premised on the phase one results; therefore, data collection only took place in November 2020, when the analysis of the first phase's results was finalized (Lewis, Downing & Hayre, 2022b).

Participants were emailed at the beginning of November 2020, to introduce the second phase of the study and share the study information letter. The study information letter provided the details of data collection and offered the option of Skype, Zoom, Microsoft Teams, WhatsApp video, and telephone calls. Two weeks after the invitation email was sent, 27 responses of interest were received. I wondered why there were only 27 responses out of the 120 that had been sent. It had been so long since the previous phase of the study; would sending the invitations closer to completing the first phase have made any difference? Some people may not have checked their emails in those two weeks. The most apparent reason was that we were in the midst of a pandemic. At the start of data collection, COVID-19 did not exist, but by November 2020, when the email invitations were sent, the country had gone through the first wave of infections, and we were preparing for the second wave. Considering that the participants were frontline workers who were emotionally, mentally, and physically fatigued, their reticence to participate in the study was understandable.

Thank You, Mr. Bell: Finding the Optimum Digital Platform – Well, Not Quite Digital!

None of the participants opted for Skype, Zoom, Microsoft Teams, or WhatsApp video, but all twenty-seven participants opted for telephone interviews. Participants explained that they preferred using the telephone as it was easiest for them not to worry about downloading apps or the added anxiety of figuring out how to use them. They admitted to feeling slightly anxious before the interview because they did not know how it would go. Some were located in areas where the internet connectivity was intermittent and poor. Some cited data availability, device challenges, and time constraints.

Telephone Interview! I Use the Telephone Every Day. What do I Need to Prepare?

In preparing for the interview calls, I read literature on conducting telephone interviews in qualitative research (Drabble, et al., 2016; Farooq & De Villiers, 2017). Since all participants provided mobile numbers, WhatsApp communications were initiated to arrange the date and time for the interviews and to build rapport. I purchased a large bundle of mobile airtime since the interviews were conducted using a mobile phone. A Dictaphone was procured to record the interviews, and an iPad was used as backup to record the interview. Phone recording applications were expensive and therefore were decided against. I created an interview schedule to guide the telephone conversation, build rapport, and ease my anxiety. I practiced the questions with my family so as to become familiar with them.

Hello, Darkness, my old Friend, Another Night with Candles!

I used a quiet room for each interview, either at home or at work, ensuring that the door was closed. Family members and colleagues were instructed not to disturb me. Participants' details and the interview schedule were printed for each participant. The mobile phone and iPad were fully charged, and new batteries were installed in the Dictaphone. In South Africa, we have load shedding when the electricity supply is stopped, so I had to take all feasible steps to limit my reliance on a continuous electricity supply. The load shedding is usually scheduled; however, unplanned load shedding can occur. I do not have an uninterruptible power supply or backup generator. Therefore, darkness can descend at any time, and candles may be required.

Nailing Biting, Not a Good Idea ...

I was very anxious for the first interview: Would the participants answer? Would everything work? Would I be any good? However, as the interview progressed, my anxiety was alleviated. I did find that I needed to force myself to listen intently and focus on the participant's voice so I could detect any changes or nuances in tone. South Africa is a diverse country with eleven official languages and various accents; thus, I had to listen more intently for some of the interviews. I also had to repeat questions to participants who found it difficult to hear me or understand my accent. The speaker option on the phone helped me to listen closely by limiting distractions. It also allowed easy note taking and enabled audio recordings.

The second interview was much better because the anxiety and stress of everything working and overcoming the "newness" were lessened. The Dictaphone and iPad recordings were clear, and there was minimal background noise. I was happy that I had printed the interview schedule because it allowed me to make notes and easily view all the questions at once. With everything working well, I gained in confidence, and after the second interview I felt completely relaxed with the process. Some interviews went better than others, with some participants being more forthcoming than others who needed more prompting. Reflecting on conducting interviews telephonically, I realized that I was able to obtain substantial accounts even though I could not see the participant or observe their body language. In the end, the telephone interview was not an alien procedure, and participants were happy to have a conversation with me on a device they use daily.

I Got This ... Or Do I?

The third phase of the study was different; two focus group interviews were conducted using Microsoft Teams (Lewis, Downing & Hayre, 2022b). Since the interviews were conducted in groups, I found setting up the dates and times for the focus group interviews much more challenging than the individual telephone interviews. These interviews were conducted in November 2021 and, by then, the participants seemed to have become more accustomed to using online platforms, myself included. Also, participants in this study phase were radiography managers who regularly used

Microsoft Teams for their meetings and administrative tasks. I consulted literature to prepare for the interviews (de Villiers, Farooq & Molinari, 2021; Self, 2021), and meeting links were sent to participants. The interview questions based on appreciative inquiry were included in the meeting description so that participants could prepare. Participants shared that they were happy that they received these questions ahead of the interview so they could think and reflect on their answers.

My Television (Computer) Debut-solo Debut, a Nightmare for an Introvert . . .

On the day of the interviews, I anxiously dressed in my "Sunday best," combed my hair, did a turn in the mirror to check that I could pass as presentable. I tidied the area around me, used the blurred background effect in Microsoft Teams, and checked the camera position and placement of the computer.

Using a fully charged computer, fifteen minutes before the interview I joined Microsoft Teams from a private room with a closed door. I used Wi-Fi for the interviews but bought mobile data in the event of connectivity issues or load shedding. The Microsoft Teams platform's video and sound quality were tested and found to be working well. The interview questions were posted in the chat section so that participants could refer to the questions at any time. Participants did not want to switch on their cameras, either because they were uncomfortable being visible or because their internet connectivity deteriorated with video sharing. I could not force participants to use their cameras, so I had to accept and modify my plans regarding observing participants. In focus group interviews, participants often express agreement or disagreement nonverbally, but I could not observe any of these gestures because the participants' cameras were switched off.

At the start of the interview, I greeted the participants and they introduced themselves. After this, I asked the first question and participants who willingly shared started to answer the questions. No one used the "raised hand" facility to ask to speak; rather, participants waited for the other to finish speaking and then spoke. After the initial dialogue, I asked participants who had not contributed to share their thoughts. That way, all participants were engaged and included in the conversation. In addition, the conversation flowed well, and there was no disruption due to stopping to question a particular participant; this was only done at the end of the free-flowing conversation. When no participants voluntarily responded to a question, individual participants were asked to answer. Technically, the interviews went well: the participants were forthcoming, and substantive accounts were obtained.

Telephone Conversations and TV Debuts Done, Thankfully in the Light or Maybe Grayness as I Reflect

On reflection, the focus group interviews were challenging in terms of the interview method of inquiry. Even though appreciative inquiry focuses on the positive, participants tended to initiate the conversation with negatives. Therefore, much effort was required to steer the conversation; when participants elaborated on the negatives as a group, they generated future possibilities. As a result, the focus group was collaborative, and managers left the sessions with ideas of change. Participants were from different parts of South Africa, and having the interviews virtually improved reach, availability, and recruitment of participants. In-person interviews would have imposed a substantial burden on me, and therefore the virtual interviews alleviated the stress and anxiety of travel and interviews in alien areas.

Is Anybody There?

It was challenging to stare at a blank screen, especially when participants did not answer readily, as I did not know if they were listening or were still there. In addition, I could not tell if there was agreement or disagreement in the group through observation. However, some participants indicated agreement or disagreement in their verbal responses.

All the Questions Racing Through My Mind . . .

I thought about whether having the cameras on or off would have made a difference to the accounts shared, and I am undecided. The data was substantive, but would nonverbal clues add more value? Should I have included that video sharing was required in the information letter so that participants would be prepared for that? Is it ethical to write that in the information letter? Should a specific internet speed and stable internet connectivity be a requirement for virtual qualitative interviews? Should participants be asked to put on their cameras at least to introduce themselves to the focus group participants as a rapport-building gesture? Should I have established set rules of engagement at the beginning of the interview (for example, microphones should be on mute unless you are speaking; you should raise your hand should you wish to speak). I had not done that because I did not want the interview to seem too formal, and participants with experience of using Microsoft Teams had their microphones muted and did not speak over each other at any stage. Maybe these instructions should have been included in the information letter. There is something about speaking to someone in person: the little nuances and gestures that encourage engaging conversations. Did I feel that was missing in these interviews? To a certain extent, yes. I suppose a degree of proximity to the participants was not achieved. Should I have asked participants about their experience of being interviewed via telephone and MS team so that suggestions to improve the experience for the participants could be generated?

In the End

Reflecting on the virtual interviews, I was initially quite anxious, but I became more confident with time and as I became for familiar with the virtual platforms. I learned new skills of engaging with technology and with participants I could not see. I was happy to learn and to adapt. Preparing the area in which the interviews are conducted is vital to limit disruptions. Ensuring devices are charged and functional, and that you have the required mobile airtime, data, or Wi-Fi access, will enable the process of virtual interviewing to proceed smoothly. The interviews did produce rich, engaging dialogue. In the end, one needs to prepare, be flexible, and accept that technology can fail and thus alternatives need to be available. I also appreciated that I did not need to travel throughout South Africa to conduct the interviews, and was thus spared all the planning, preparation, and anxiety this would bring.

In keeping with the pragmatic paradigm adopted in this mixed-method study, I embraced the concept of "what works": a pluralistic, ever-changing, complex, multifaceted worldview in the challenge of COVID-19 restrictions. My experience of the virtual interviews made me think of "planned behaviour" (Ajzen, 1985), the theoretical framework used for the study. Within the theory of planned behavior, a person will succeed in performing an intended behavior if they possess the required information, skills, and abilities, and have the necessary willpower and control over their emotions and compulsions. If both time and opportunity are optimal and people upon whom the behavior depends on act accordingly, then the behavior will be successful. Applying this to the intention and behavior of collecting qualitative data virtually, the required information, skills, and abilities to use digital platforms and technology will facilitate the process. In addition, acknowledging the anxiety of change and finding ways to cope allowed me to gain control over my emotions. Even though I tried to prepare as best as possible for the interviews in terms of my knowledge and skills at the time, I realized that successful data collection was not solely within my control. The success of data collection was also incumbent upon participants' information, skills, abilities, and willingness to participate and the external support of consistent internet and electricity supply.

Discussion

Author SL has shared their experience of conducting qualitative telephone and digital interviews in South Africa. South Africa's classification falls between a developing country (UNCTAD, 2021) and an upper-middle-income country (World Bank, 2022b). South Africa has the third-largest economy in Africa, with the highest persistent inequality rate globally and about 33% of the population living in rural areas (World Bank, 2021, 2022a). South Africans' daily internet use on any device was reported in January 2022 as the highest in the world; 68% of South Africans use the internet, and most access is through computers (Kemp, 2022). High internet and smartphone use were also reported in Malaysia; however, that use was more for internet browsing, networking, and gaming rather than video conferencing. The lack of video conferencing experience meant greater support to enable data collection via this method was needed (Abdul Rashid, Lee, & Jamil, 2021). Similarly, despite South Africans' high use of the internet, SL's narration indicates that participants in the study's second phase opted for telephone interviews over other virtual platforms.

Participants in studies in Lebanon and the United Kingdom also preferred telephone interviews. In Lebanon, scarce internet and connectivity challenges supported telephone interviews (Chen, et al., 2020) and Walker and colleagues (2021) preferred audio calls because this was familiar to their participants. Telephone interviews provide increased anonymity and privacy (Drabble et al., 2016; Farooq & De Villiers, 2017: 4). Drabble et al. (2016) suggest strategies to improve the success of telephone interviews through creating rapport, being responsive, and acknowledging participants. Their study also found that telephone interviews provided rich data.

The narrative reports internet speeds as a reason for participants using only audio even though the video options were available. Similarly, studies in Nepal, Syria, the Democratic Republic of the Congo, Kenya, and

Nigeria reported that intermittent internet connectivity hindered video use (Douedari, et al., 2021; Sah, Singh & Sah, 2020; Turke, et al., 2021). Although video sharing was limited, Douedari et al. (2021) were able to obtain rich data. Sah, Singh and Sah (2020) suggest that internet connectivity and data costs should be considered when conducting research in developing countries. Hunersen and colleagues (2021) suggest that research teams need to determine participants' technological capabilities and preferences, and, in low-income settings, free mobile/internet data should be provided to participants. Deakin and Wakefield's (2014) study interviewed participants using Skype only if they had internet connectivity and possessed the required technical abilities. However, participants in this study still requested not to use video interactions, citing anxiety and uneasiness at sharing their videos. In addition, they experienced increased interruptions when videos were shared (Deakin & Wakefield, 2014).

The narrative detailed the experience of and the multiple questions that arose from using Microsoft Teams. A study conducted by Dodds and Hess (2021) with a vulnerable population collected data face to face prior to COVID-19 and then online during the pandemic. The authors shared that participants felt the online interviews were more comfortable and safe than face-to-face interviews because they were in their home environment supported by their families and the researchers were not in their homes. The researchers reported that it was easier to manage group dynamics and social anxiety during the online interviews. Even though the interviews were shorter than face-to-face interviews, the researchers felt the interviews to be engaging, and that the participants' responses had depth. Researchers and participants indicated familiarity with the online platforms, enabling ease of use. The researchers shared their limitations in not observing some of the participants' body language due to device set-up and positioning. They also found capturing field notes challenging, limiting the context required for that study. The researchers suggest paying attention to the device set-up and the use of a scribe to mitigate the challenges experienced.

Krouwel, Jolly and Greenfield (2019) compared face-to-face or in-person qualitative interviews with virtual interviews and reported that face-to-face interviews were slightly superior to virtual ones. They reported a similar number of words and codes obtained in both interviews; however, face-to-face interviews produced more statements per code than virtual interviews. They reflected that they could build rapport with participants during virtual interviews, found technical challenges an opportunity to bond with participants, and experienced no significant change in the "nature and character" (p. 6) of the interviews. Reñosa and colleagues (2021) reported that rapport building in remote data collection relied on traditional interviewer skills and suggested "unlearning and relearning" from traditional approaches. They found that remote data collection provided meaningful data. However, Deakin and Wakefield (2014) found that building rapport in virtual interviews differed from that of in-person interviews. Abdul Rashid, Lee and Jamil (2021) found online interviews time-consuming. However, Gray and colleagues (2020) found Zoom video conferencing convenient, accessible, and time-saving since travel time is eliminated.

The narrative notes that the author had to plan for "load shedding." Load shedding means the intermittent interruption of electricity supply (Steenkamp et al., 2016). Since 2007/8, South Africa has experienced an energy crisis caused by electricity supply-and-demand deficits (Sewchurran & Davidson, 2021). As a result, load shedding was implemented to redress the supply–demand issue and prevent nationwide blackouts. Electricity interruptions are not uncommon in Sub-Saharan Africa, impacting the economy, health, and education (Farquharson, Jaramillo & Samaras, 2018; Nduhuura, Garschagen & Zerga, 2020). Gray et al. (2020) suggest pre-arranging plans with participants in the event of technical difficulties, disconnecting all devices from the Wi-Fi, and using a fixed-line connection to the internet. Consequently, any activity requiring electricity needs to consider the possible interruption of electricity and plan accordingly. Author SL ensured all electronic devices were fully charged, and data was available for conducting interviews if the Wi-Fi was interrupted.

Recommendations for Conducting Virtual Qualitative Data Collection

Literature provides extensive recommendations for using various online and digital platforms to collect qualitative data (Abdul Rashid, Lee & Jamil, 2021; Chen et al., 2020; de Villiers, Farooq & Molinari, 2021; Deakin & Wakefield, 2014; Dodds & Hess, 2021). The autoethnographic narrative suggests preparing for interviews to consider electricity and internet connectivity, including specific instructions to participants about using video and audio during the interviews. Conversations about the influence of context on the research question will determine the need for participant video sharing. If video sharing is deemed necessary, it is suggested that this is included as a requirement on the information letter to prepare participants and make this explicit for the interview process. In addition, the necessary internet speed to enable optimal video and voice sharing for the number of participants in a focus group should be considered and shared with potential participants. In low-income settings, consider the stability of the internet connectivity and prepare for electricity supply interruptions. Ultimately, experience in interviewing and connecting with the interviewee, whether telephonically or through video, is essential to attain rich data collection in qualitative studies. That being said, the researcher's mental preparation to conduct interviews and overcome "nerves" needs to be part of the dialogue too.

Chapter Summary

The chapter provided an autoethnographic account of collecting qualitative data through telephone interviews and via an online platform in South Africa. The narrative details the impact of intermittent electricity and internet connectivity on data collection.

References

Abdul Rashid, N., Lee, K., & Jamil, N. A. (2021). Conducting qualitative research in the new norms: Are we ready?. *Nursing & Health Sciences, 23*(4), 967–973. https://doi.org/10.1111/nhs.12872.

Ajzen,I. (1985). From intentions to actions: A theory of planned behavior. In J. Kuhl & J. Beckmann (Eds.), *Action control: From cognition to behavior.* New York: Springer-Verlag.

Chen, A., Tossyeh, F., Arnous, M., et al. (2020). Phone-based data collection in a refugee community under COVID-19 lockdown. *The Lancet Psychiatry, 7*(6), e31. https://doi.org/10.1016/S2215-0366(20)30189-9.

De Villiers, C., Farooq, M. & Molinari, M. (2021), Qualitative research interviews using online video technology: Challenges and opportunities. *Meditari Accountancy Research.* https://doi.org/10.1108/MEDAR-03-2021-1252.

Deakin, H. & Wakefield, K. (2014). Skype interviewing: Reflections of two PhD researchers. *Qualitative Research, 14*(5), 603–616. https://doi.org/10.1177/1468794113488126.

Dodds, S., & Hess, A. C. (2021). Adapting research methodology during COVID-19: Lessons for transformative service research. *Journal of Service Management, 32*(2), 203–217. https://doi.org/10.1108/JOSM-05-2020-0153.

Douedari, Y., Alhaffar, M., Duclos, D., et al. (2021). "We need someone to deliver our voices": Reflections from conducting remote qualitative research in Syria. *Conflict and Health, 15*(28). https://doi.org/10.1186/s13031-021-00361-w.

Drabble, L., Trocki, K. F., Salcedo, B., Walker, P. C., & Korcha, R. A. (2016). Conducting qualitative interviews by telephone: Lessons learned from a study of alcohol use among sexual minority and heterosexual women. *Qualitative Social Work: Research and Practice, 15*(1), 118–133. https://doi.org/10.1177/1473325015585613.

Farooq, M. B & De Villiers, C. (2017). Telephonic qualitative research interviews: When to consider them and how to do them. *Meditari Accountancy Research*. https://doi.org/10.1108/MEDAR-10-2016-0083.

Farquharson, D., Jaramillo, P. & Samaras, C. (2018) Sustainability implications of electricity outages in Sub-Saharan Africa. *Nature Sustainability*, 1, 589–597. https://doi.org/10.1038/s41893-018-0151-8.

Gray, L. M., Wong-Wylie, G., Rempel, G. R., & Cook, K. (2020). Expanding qualitative research interviewing strategies: Zoom video communications. *The Qualitative Report*, 25(5), 1292–1301. https://nsuworks.nova.edu/tqr/vol25/iss5/9.

Hunersen, K., Ramaiya, A., Yu, C., et al. (2021). Considerations for remote data collection among adolescents during the COVID-19 pandemic. *The Journal of Adolescent Health*, *68*(3), 439–440. https://doi.org/10.1016/j.jadohealth .2020.11.020.

Kemp, S. (2022). Digital 2022: global overview report. Slide 27. https://datareportal .com/reports/digital-2022-global-overview-report?utm_source=DataReportal& utm_medium=Country_Article_Hyperlink&utm_campaign=Digital_2022& utm_term=South_Africa&utm_content=Global_Promo_Block.

Krouwel, M., Jolly, K., & Greenfield, S. (2019). Comparing Skype (video calling) and in-person qualitative interview modes in a study of people with irritable bowel syndrome: An exploratory comparative analysis. *BMC Medical Research Methodology*, *19*(1), 219. https://doi.org/10.1186/s12874-019-0867-9.

Lewis, S., Downing, C. & Hayre, C. M. (2022a). Using the theory of planned behaviour to determine radiation protection among South African diagnostic radiographers: a cross-sectional survey. *Journal of Medical Radiation Sciences*, *69* (1), 47–55. https://doi.org/10.1002/jmrs.537.

Lewis, S., Downing, C., & Hayre, C.M. (2022c) South African radiography leadership co-constructing radiation protection change ideas. *Journal of Medical Imaging and Radiation Sciences*, 53 (7), 248–255. https://doi.org/10 .1016/j.jmir.2022.03.007.

Lewis, S., Downing, C., & Hayre, C. M. (2022b). South African radiographers' radiation protection practices, a qualitative study. *Radiography*, S1078-8174(21) 00205-4. Advance online publication. https://doi.org/10.1016/j.radi.2021 .12.008.

Lord, R., Bolton, N., Fleming, S. & Anderson, M. (2016). Researching a segmented market: Reflections on telephone interviewing. *Management Research Review*, 39 (7), 786–802. https://dx.doi.org/10.1108/MRR-01-2015-0020.

Nduhuura, P., Garschagen, M., & Zerga, A. (2020). Mapping and spatial analysis of electricity load shedding experiences: A case study of communities in Accra, Ghana. *Energies*, *13*(17). https://doi.org/10.3390/en13174280.

Reñosa, M. D. C., Mwamba, C., Meghani, A., et al. (2021). Selfie consents, remote rapport, and Zoom debriefings: Collecting qualitative data amid a pandemic in four resource-constrained settings. *BMJ Global Health*, 6, e004193. https://doi.org/10.1136/bmjgh-2020-004193.

Sah, L. K., Singh, D. R., & Sah, R. K. (2020). Conducting qualitative interviews using virtual communication tools amid COVID-19 pandemic: A learning opportunity for future research. *Journal of the Nepal Medical Association, 58* (232), 1103–1106. https://doi.org/10.31729/jnma.5738.

Santana, F. N., Wagner, C. H., Rubin, B. N., et al. (2021). A path forward for qualitative research on sustainability in the COVID-19 pandemic. *Sustainability Science, 16*(3), 1061–1067. https://doi.org/10.1007/s11625-020-00894-8.

Self, B. (2021). Conducting interviews during the COVID-19 pandemic and beyond. *Forum Qualitative Sozialforschung/Forum: Qualitative Social Research,* 22(3). https://doi.org/10.17169/fqs-22.3.3741.

Sewchurran, S. & Davidson, I. E. (2021). Technical and financial analysis of large-scale solar-PV in eThekwini Municipality: Residential, business and bulk customers. *Energy Reports, 7,* 4961–4976. https://doi.org/10.1016/j.egyr.2021.07.134.

Steenkamp, H., February, A., September, J., et al. (2016). The influence of load shedding on the productivity of hotel staff in Cape Town, South Africa. *Expert Journal of Business and Management, 4*(2), 69–77.

Turke, S., Nehrling, S., Adebayo, S. O., et al. (2021). Remote interviewer training for COVID-19 data collection: Challenges and lessons learned from 3 countries in Sub-Saharan Africa. *Global Health, Science and Practice, 9*(1), 177–186. https://doi.org/10.9745/GHSP-D-20-00468.

UNCTAD (United Nations Conference on Trade and Development). (2021). Classification Update-March 2021. https://unctadstat.unctad.org/en/Classifica tions/ClassificationsNewsletter_March2021_US_EN.pdf (accessed April 6, 2022) .

Walker, L., Bailey, D., Churchill, R. & Peckham, (2021). Remote data collection during COVID-19 restrictions: An example from a refugee and asylum-seeker participant group in the UK. *Trials* 22, 117 (2021). https://doi.org/10.1186/s130 63-021-05058-2.

World Bank (2021). The World Bank in South Africa. Overview. www.world bank.org/en/country/southafrica/overview#1 (accessed March 10, 2022).

World Bank (2022a). GDP, PPP (current international $). https://data.world bank.org/indicator/NY.GDP.MKTP.PP.CD?view=map (accessed March 10, 2022).

World Bank (2022b). South Africa. Available from: https://data.worldbank.org/country/south-africa?view=chart (accessed March 29, 2022).

Afterword

Paul M. W. Hackett, Christopher M. Hayre, Ava Gordley-Smith,
Marcia Scherer and Dave J. Muller

We have titled this final chapter 'Afterword' as it has been written by us, the editors, and is meant to be the opposite to the preface. To wit, as a complement to the preface, which introduced the content of the book, and rather than summing-up the chapters, this afterword sets forth possibilities: it contains the editors' thoughts about the book's contents. We originally thought of writing a concluding chapter. However, we decided that we were not concluding; rather, we were opening up possibilities in much the same way as a preface or a foreword opens up the possibilities of the text that follows.

To include an afterword in our book is especially appropriate at the present time as the dual events of the Covid-19 pandemic and the war in Ukraine have shaken the world in a way that has not been seen since the two World Wars. Moreover, the pandemic and the war in Ukraine are the first major globally impacting events that have happened since the ubiquity of hand-held digital technologies and mass digital communication of the type that keeps us all informed about what is going on across the world pretty much as it happens. This latter point is especially important as the development of digital technologies, and especially of the mobile smart phone and its myriad apps, has had a significant influence on how we monitor our health as individuals. This is especially true in many areas within the realm of health research, and in terms of the data that is available to the health researcher. Over the last twenty years, digital versions of traditional healthcare research methods (such as focus-groups, digital projective techniques, and in-depth interviews) have been adapted to online formats. Furthermore, new research approaches have also been developed that allow the researcher to conduct research in a uniquely online setting, such as netnography (digital ethnography) and through the use of big-data. With the increasing use of artificial intelligence (AI) applications, research will likely be impacted in many new and varying ways.

In this afterword, when we talk of digital methods we mean both the entirely novel online approaches and those which employ traditional methods which have been adapted to an online context. We also consider the distinctive insights offered by these techniques, along with their associated ethical implications. As we learn to live with Covid-19 there are calls to return to our old ways in many sectors of society, including in healthcare research.[1] However, a return to methods that were unavailable to the health researcher during the pandemic due to fears of spreading the disease (i.e., all forms of in-person data gathering) may, in the future, have to be more thoroughly justified.

With these thoughts in mind about how the health research world may change in a post-Covid world, the editors asked the chapter authors to supply their brief thoughts, comments, and reflections on what it might mean to continue using online digital methods. We are pleased to say that several of the chapter authors decided to share their reflections on the use of digital methods. Here, we present a selection of these comments, which were gathered opportunistically and are not in any way meant to be representative of anything more than ideas that stimulated a consideration of possibilities for future research.

The comments we received from authors were both positive and negative in regard to the adoption of digital methodologies in health research. An example of a negative appraisal came from Colleague 1, who issued caveats in relation to the quality of the information gathered:

> I find that the connections I form with people online are more artificial and less deep. (Colleague 1)

A major component of the qualitative research process, whether this is in a health domain or elsewhere, is the establishment of rapport between the participant and the researcher. This is essential to put participants at ease and to enable them to proffer candid and honest expressions. Therefore, any problem a researcher may experience in connecting with their participants has the potential to derail a research project through a reduction in the quality of the information gathered through online approaches. However, this barrier to researcher–participant communications is not always seen as being a characteristic of online health research, as we will see later in this afterword.

---

[1] At the time of writing, we are unfortunately having to learn to live with the war in Ukraine and its associated death and destruction. However, adapting as societies and individuals to the effects of Covid-19 and the war in Ukraine appear to be very different and the consequences of the former event have a more readily discernible impact in terms of the subject matter of this book.

The same author also noted that the technology used in online research can at times be a barrier to the gathering of information:

> Technology can also be a problem. When doing research with people who don't have technology or who aren't comfortable with technology, it can be very difficult. (Colleague 1)

This point is one that the editors agree with, as this has been part of their own experience whilst conducting online research. The use of computers and smart phones to get online has become much easier and more rapid over the last few years. However, this technology is complicated and may 'break' at any point. Researchers are rarely IT professionals, and when a problem does arise they may not be able to fix it. In these cases, data sets may be incomplete and the participant and researcher may end up spending more time and effort on communication issues than on delving deeply into the subject of the research.

Another technological problem is that fast, robust, and stable access to the internet remains a somewhat scarce entity, particularly in some geographic areas and for those with lower resources, and thus is not equitably distributed throughout societies and across the globe. The unevenness of internet access may lead to wealthier and more privileged populations being over-represented in digital health research and, thus, to yet another health-based advantage being offered to more affluent individuals from countries that have greater degrees of reliable connectivity. The authors of this chapter have indeed found such discrepancies in their research. For example, they have found it very difficult to establish stable connections when communicating digitally with individuals in Africa, India, and other areas that fall under the umbrella of the so-called developing world. They have also experienced similar difficulties in reaching individuals of lower social-economic groups from their own countries. This discrepancy of access may also be true of the many communication apps, email facilities, and the internet in general. The speed of such connections, if established, along with the time zone differences between the universities of the Western world and these regions, also present problems in conducting online health research.

However, this negative mote about the possible barriers that may come between the online researcher and participant is in contrast to the positive comments that we also received. For instance, it was observed that online approaches offered the potential to reveal insights from respondents:

> To my surprise there was much openness despite online data gathering. (Colleague 2)

This comment is echoed by the editors, who have found openness to be a common characteristic in the case of their own online research. Indeed, we have discovered that the online context affords a degree of impersonality and comfort for the participant that can be facilitative of openness and the offering of frank and apparently honest comments. Prior to using online research methods, a researcher may suspect that using online approaches may mean that the data they obtained might be shallow and that engaging with participants may be difficult. This may be the case in some research situations; however, one of our authors summed-up some of the many benefits of using online approaches:

> Online ethnography for my PhD research was found to be more immersive and accessible for me than traditional ethnography. This was because accessing a data collection site would have had to be done a few hours per week over the course of many months and it was difficult to balance this with being physically at work each day. (Colleague 1)

This author's comment clearly acknowledges that some researchers, in some research situations, may benefit from using an online approach.

In the preceding chapters we have also seen that online health research is flexible and adaptable and may involve the use of different types of research procedures. The breadth of such approaches was emphasised in the following comment:

> I've been able to administer a number of online surveys that included both quantitative and qualitative focused questions. (Colleague 3)

We spoke earlier in this chapter about the inequity of access to fast/reliable internet connections and the technology needed to conduct or be a participant in digital health research. The counterbalance to this is that digital access, whilst not being equitably distributed, may allow a researcher to access respondents that are located at a distance from them, or in situations that are problematic for access for many reasons. Indeed, online access may sometimes be the only means to conduct research within a limited budget or timeframe.

Another highly beneficial feature of online research is that, as one of our authors commented:

> The online data collection meant that I could interact with participants every day and 'dip in and out' – this fitted around work and personal responsibilities much more cohesively. (Colleague 1)

In online research it may not be necessary for the researchers and participants to be in the same physical location and the potential flexibility that this implies is echoed in the above statement. The following comment also emphasised that online approaches allowed access to respondents who would not be available using traditional in-person research approaches:

> I've been able to reach nationwide populations that I would have not been able to conduct research with if I relied on an in-person approach. Examples include national samples of adjunct faculty, international graduate students, and representatives from a national disability organization. (Colleague 3)

Another comment also supported the idea that online research provides opportunities for the researcher and the participant to meet in a cooperative manner and for the researcher to access information about individuals:

> Seeing inside people's private spaces (e.g. their bedrooms) and having them see inside yours. (Colleague 3)

However, the same person qualified the opportunity to access individuals by saying that being allowed into a person's private space creates potential difficulties and tensions:

> It is an invasion of privacy that some people might not feel comfortable with; although this does enable a greater degree of immersion in some respects. (Colleague 3)

Notwithstanding this, and regardless of whether an author viewed the move to the digitisation of health research in a positive or negative light, there was an expressed need to consider the ethical implications, and participant protection, in online health research:

> There should be specific considerations for ensuring participant confidentiality by using encrypted technology and overall using an approach that ensures the participant's rights for privacy are honoured. (Colleague 2)

This statement emphasises the point that, as with all forms of health research, the protection of participants must be the primary concern of all researchers. The ethics of conducting online health research are intricate and challenging. Online approaches that allow us to interact with, and gather information from, participants are constantly evolving and being actively developed by those researching in health areas and elsewhere. As these approaches are used in real-world contexts the ethics surrounding their use will similarly evolve. These include addressing issues such as participant confidentiality, data quality and storage, the equitable distribution of research costs and benefits, data ownership, and many other concerns. We do not have any definitive concluding statements in regard to ethics. However, we do emphasise the need to actively engage in considering the rights and the protection of participants, researchers, and society as a whole when we design and use these approaches.

Conclusions

It is now the Spring of 2023 and, on reflection, it is evident that in response to the worldwide pandemic that started three years ago, there has been a remarkable acceleration in digital and online forms of health research. This rapid growth has naturally led not only to advantages and opportunities for researchers and participants, but, just as importantly, to disadvantages and dangers. It is interesting to note that the negative and positive aspects of digital research are similar in that they are both often concerned with the provision of access to the internet and digital connectivity. The new and challenging questions that surround the holding and use of private data by companies such as Google and Meta is a much-discussed topic at present. We are at presently facing many ethical questions. An example of these includes questions in regard to the conflicts of different rights – for instance, between allowing personal privacy through end-to-end email encryption versus allowing access to email content in order to attempt to disrupt groups committing illegal and anti-social actions. These dilemmas also exist in relation to online health research and when using personal digital data in health research. The answers to these questions are still being wrestled with.

Another unresolved question is in regard to how much the imposition of having to conduct research remotely from participants using digital approaches will remain now that such restrictions are largely part of our past. Will digital health grow in its use and scope? Will we embrace these new approaches, or will we clamber back to our old research ways? At the very least, it would appear that the abstemious use of digital approaches to health care research is here to stay. As an editorial team we have not necessarily and unequivocally swooned over digital methods, but we do look forward to digital methods being accepted in health care with some degree of alacrity. We believe that the contents of this book have demonstrated the enormous benefits of digital research methods that are becoming ever more relevant to the way we live our lives in the third decade of the twentieth century.

One thing that we, as an editorial team, have been especially impressed by, is the manner in which members of the health research community responded to the Covid-19 pandemic. The pandemic required a change in lifestyles and practices by communities across the globe. Qualitative researchers responded to the challenges presented by the pandemic with enthusiasm, flexibility, and imagination. New methods were devised and developed, and old ones were reformulated so they could be used in situations in which face-to-face contact was not possible. Many of the digital approaches that emerged out of the pandemic are robust and exciting ways of gathering information about peoples' health, and these are likely to become staples of the health researcher's tool kit. This is important as health crises and pandemics occur with some frequency. The editorial team for this book, as a group of qualitative researchers, recognise both positive and negative aspects of adopting online health research. In both this afterword and in the book overall, we have attempted to present some of the new alternative and supplementary online approaches that the health researcher now has at their disposal. It is our hope that we have also illustrated both the benefits and the drawbacks of these approaches.

Index